The Philosophical Foundations of Marxism

THE PHILOSOPHICAL

FOUNDATIONS OF MARXISM

LOUIS DUPRÉ
Georgetown University

Harcourt, Brace & World, Inc.
New York / Chicago / San Francisco / Atlanta

Library of Congress Catalog Card Number: 66–17348

Printed in the United States of America

To My Parents

Preface

MARX'S IMPACT upon the modern world is not a recent phenomenon; it began during his own lifetime. But until forty years ago his reputation was due mainly to his organization of the international workers' movement and to his social-economic studies. The rediscovery of Marx's "philosophy" followed the publication of his early philosophical writings by the Marx-Engels Institute in Moscow. Since then, the interest of Western scholars has gradually shifted from Marx the social reformer to Marx the humanistic philosopher. While forty years ago *The Communist Manifesto* and *Capital* held all the attention, today *The German Ideology* and the *Economic and Philosophic Manuscripts* of 1844 are in the spotlight.

Where does Marx's philosophy end and his positive, social-economic science begin? The reader will find out for himself why it is impossible to separate the two entirely. Nevertheless, a distinction undoubtedly exists. I have solved the problem in a practical way by limiting my discussion to Marx's early works—up to and including *The Communist Manifesto* (1848). The later works have been excluded because they are not *primarily* philosophical. By the same token, the early works are discussed only to the extent that they are relevant to philosophical theory. With *The German Ideology* (1845), Marx's philosophy turns into a theory of action based upon scientific—sociological, economic, and historical—data. In *The Poverty of Philosophy* (1847) and *The Communist Manifesto* the new theory is first applied. For this reason I have included these two works, as well as some basic quotations from *The Class Struggles in France* and *The Eighteenth Brumaire of Louis Bonaparte.* These four works represent the practical test of Marx's philosophical theory.

The material in Marx's early writings has revolutionized the interpretation of Marx's entire thought. It is now becoming evident that Marx's own *Weltanschauung* differs considerably from what "dialectical materialists," particularly in Communist countries, have traditionally presented as Marxist doctrine. The "scientific" materialism of the Communist party line is in fact the result of an evolution which started with Engels and was continued by Lenin and Stalin. This does not mean, as Sartre claims, that Communism has deviated completely from Marx's thought, for Marx's thought itself is ambiguous and contains the germ of scientific materialism. Yet the fact remains that Marx himself was not a materialist. While today's dialectical materialism may be dismissed as a shallow and simplistic theory of man and the universe, Marx's own dialectical philosophy remains an important contribution to Western thinking. That man creates himself in a dialectical relation to nature and that he is a dynamic rather than a static being are important truths which had never been clearly formulated before Marx and which one can fully appreciate without subscribing to the political and economic principles of the Marxist movement. It is the significance of Marx's early philosophy, rather than its later evolution as "Marxism," which inspired the present study.

Our study, however, does not deal with Marx alone. The first two chapters of the book are devoted to Hegel's thought, from his earliest theological writings to the *Philosophy of Right.* Such an introduction is crucial in a work which analyzes the philosophical *foundations* of Marxism. At first sight nothing would seem to be further from the "scientific" socialism of *The Communist Manifesto* than the theological manuscripts of the young Hegel. But a closer look reveals how Hegel's romantic idea of man as a dynamic being, realizing himself in ethical striving within the community, led quite naturally to

Marx's concept of man as a social-economic being, dialectically related to nature and society. Marx's scientific socialism is the "realistic" solution to Hegel's romantic problem. An analysis of Marx's philosophy without reference to Hegel would be like a dialogue in which one hears only one interlocutor. Marx's early works represent one long struggle to detach Hegel's dialectical method from his idealistic system; without a solid knowledge of both, Marx cannot be understood.

Marx's philosophy and its relation to Hegel's thought have been investigated in several interpretive works. Among the best of these are Sidney Hook's detailed work on the sources of Marxist philosophy (*From Hegel to Marx*), Herbert Marcuse's study of Marxism within the framework of German philosophy (*Reason and Revolution*), and Robert Tucker's synthesis of Marx's thought (*Philosophy and Myth in Karl Marx*), as well as translations of the classics by Auguste Cornu (*Karl Marx et Friedrich Engels*) and Jean-Paul Sartre (*Critique de la raison dialectique*). I feel, however, that a book is still needed to introduce the reader directly to the original texts of the major works of Hegel and Marx. I have found that students are often unable to cope with these original materials even after having read some excellent literature on the subject. This study is intended to explain the texts, and therefore its approach is primarily analytical, rather than synthetic or historical. I hope that by avoiding interpretive structures this approach will expose the reader to the intricate and highly technical method of thinking predominant in nineteenth-century German philosophy.

Each chapter begins by sketching the historical context of the works to be discussed; each chapter ends with critical observations on the works discussed or with comparisons to earlier works. The final chapter presents a critique of the method and main theses of Marx's historical materialism. But historical and critical discussions are confined to these specific sections, so as not to interfere with the main goal of the book: to present the ideas of Hegel and Marx with as few structural barriers as possible.

For Marx's works until 1848 I have referred exclusively to the *Karl Marx–Friedrich Engels Historisch-Kritische Gesamtausgabe, Werke, Schriften, Briefe,* commissioned by the Marx-Engels Institute, Moscow (ed. by D. Rjazanov, Frankfurt am Main, 1927); this edition will be referred to as *MEGA.* For Engels and the later works of Marx, we have used the more recent edition, Karl Marx–Friedrich Engels, *Werke,* commissioned by the Institute for Marxism and Leninism (Dietz Verlag, Berlin, 1961–62); this edition is referred to as *Werke.*

I wish to express my thanks to my former students, Messrs. Thomas Anderson, Thomas Wolfe, and Michael McDermott, for their many suggestions and constant help regarding the language and general style of writing; also to Miss Elizabeth Nicholson for her invaluable assistance in many ways, not least of which was the typing of the manuscript.

Louis Dupré

Georgetown University

Contents

The Philosophical Foundations of Marxism

1

The Development of Hegel's Social Theory

CONTEMPORARY STUDY of Hegel's early work has helped greatly to provide a proper background for the understanding of his system. The logical construction of his mature philosophy all too often obscures the richness of its content. But a study of Hegel's spiritual development takes us back to the original intuition of which the later system is the more technical expression. Such a study is particularly useful for Hegel's controversial political theories, which have been so violently attacked during the last several decades. The *Philosophy of Right* can be understood only as the logical conclusion of an intellectual evolution which originated in the Romantic movement and in its idealized view of the Greek city-State.

Hegel's Early Writings

Like his fellow students in Tübingen's theological seminary, Schelling and Hölderlin, the young Hegel was carried away by the Neoclassical movement. Romanticism had reawakened the consciousness of the eternal conflict between man's infinite potential and his actual, finite achievements. Their harmonious reunification remained Hegel's basic problem. His later system is a gigantic attempt to give rational expression to the process by which an infinity posits itself as finite, in order to become absolute. This process is only an idealistic-philosophical transposition of what Christianity apprehends in an intuitive and symbolic way in the mystery of Christ's incarnation: God becomes man in order that man may become God.

The Ideal of the Polis

Yet, it was not in Christianity but in Classical Antiquity that romantic philosophy first saw the realization of its ideal of a finite infinity. Ancient man lived in such intimate harmony with the universe that he could consider himself a part of the divine totality (*ein Teil des göttlichen Ganzen*). The source from which the ancient harmony of life proceeded was the city-State—the *polis*. As creator of religion, art, and wisdom, the *polis* satisfied all the aspirations of the human mind. It was both finite and infinite, real and ideal. Through the city the individual became integrated in the divine totality of the Spirit.

Hegel shared this *polis* ideal with his friends Schelling and Hölderlin, but from the very beginning there was a difference in their spiritual orientations. For Hölderlin, the ancient State was a dream world in the past, in which he tried to forget the bitter reality of the present. Schelling, on the contrary, was firmly determined to reform the world, but he did not expect much aid from politics. In fact, he did not have even the superficial interest of Hölderlin in the political reform of Germany.[1] He saw the Greek State as merely an ideal of beauty and harmony which reconciles the finite with the infinite.

For Hegel, the ancient *polis* is mainly an ideal of moral perfection. The absolute, according to him, is not reached through aesthetic intuition, but in freedom, which can be realized only when private and public life are in perfect harmony, as in the Greek city-State. In this ethical Classicism we feel the influence of Herder, who believed that the individual in Antiquity had reached an unusually high degree of spiritual freedom through

[1] Th. Haering, *Hegel, sein Wollen und sein Werk* (Leipzig-Berlin, 1924), I, 39.

his solidarity with the community. To Hegel, as to Herder, the *polis* is primarily a cultural structure which shapes a communal spirit (the *Volksgeist*). Antiquity achieved moral greatness through a strong community feeling.⌉

The Individualism of Christian Morality

√ Christian morality, on the other hand, focuses exclusively on the person: the good life is to be attained by the individual, not by the community. Also, the morality of the Gospel is primarily interior: it is more concerned with purity of heart than with external acts. Kant attempted to give this interior morality philosophical expression. In his system, only the *intention* had moral significance. The external acts belong to a physical world, ruled by physical laws, for which man can never take full responsibility. They are subject to the compulsion of external laws, rather than to the moral law of conscience.

Despite his admiration for the Ancient State, Hegel, from the very beginning, saw the sublimity of the Christian ideal of interiority. However, he thought that it was one-sided and incomplete. He therefore attempted to find a new synthesis of Greek ethics and Christian morality.[2] This was no easy task, for Ancient ethics consisted of active participation by the individual in the life of the community, while Christian morality, as he saw it, was strictly individual.⌊Christian religion, then, was private. Ancient religion was public: it embodied the spirit of the community. "The morality of individuals is made by a private religion, by parents, personal design, and circumstances—but the spirit of a people is formed partly by the folk religion and partly by political relations."[3]⌉

[2] In his terminology the distinction between ethics and morality is not yet fixed at this point. But the distinction itself is clearly present: one is social, the other strictly individual.

[3] *Hegels theologische Jugendschriften* (ed. by Herman Nohl, Tübingen, 1907), p. 27. Henceforth this book will be referred to as "Nohl." A partial translation was made by T. M. Knox, *Early Theological Writings* (Chicago,

Hegel's aim, then, was to work toward a political unification of Germany in order to make a true national spirit possible and to explore Christianity's potential as a folk religion. While still a theology student in Tübingen, Hegel set himself to work on this program. In 1793, he wrote the fragments which in Nohl's edition of the theological works are arranged under the title *Folk Religion and Christianity (Volks-Religion und Christentum)*. Hegel here proves that ethics always needs the support of religion. Understanding alone is unable to move man to moral action. "The understanding is a courtier who is always ready for the caprices of his lord . . . it is a perfect servant of self-love." [4] Understanding usually rationalizes the inclination to follow one's impulse and instinct. But even if it remains objective, its abstract principles cannot provide practical guidance for action. For the same reason, a purely rational religion would be insufficient. Even if such a religion did satisfy a few, it could never move the community as a whole. What is needed is a religion deeply rooted in the cultural tradition of the people, a folk religion. "Folk religion is distinguished from private religion mainly because it strongly affects heart and imagination and thus inspires the soul with the force, the enthusiasm, and the spirit that are indispensable for high virtue." [5]

In spite of these romantic expressions, Hegel's writings at this point still show many traces of the Enlightenment. Even the text just quoted reveals a typical eighteenth-century moralism: religion is more important for its impact upon morality than for its intrinsic value. But, more important, Hegel's religion remains within the boundaries of reason: it is *Vernunftreligion*. "Dogmas, even when they are based on divine revelation, ought to be such that they can lay claim to the authority of universal human reason and that every man can realize their obligatory character." [6]

1948). Copyright 1948, by the University of Chicago. Reprinted by permission. We will refer to it as "Knox."
[4] Nohl, p. 12.   [5] Nohl, p. 19.   [6] Nohl, p. 21.

Kant's Concept of Moral Autonomy

This influence of the Enlightenment grew even stronger as Hegel, who at that time was a private teacher in Bern, read Schelling's first publications: *On the Possibility of a Form of Philosophy in General* (*Über die Möglichkeit einer Form der Philosophie überhaupt*, 1794) and *On the Ego as the Principle of Philosophy* (*Vom Ich als Prinzip der Philosophie*, 1795). These readings converted Hegel into a fervent adherent of Kant's philosophy. In one of his enthusiastic letters written to Schelling during his Bern period, he says: "From Kant's system I expect a revolution in Germany. It will start from principles which are always present and which only have to be worked out and applied to what already is known." [7]

What attracted Hegel most in Kant's philosophy was the principle of moral *autonomy*. This principle declares the will to be its own law and rejects any extrinsic determination, any *heteronomy*, as conflicting with the nature of the will and therefore immoral. However inspiring the Ancient *polis* ideal may be, the principle of autonomy marks an important step forward in man's moral development. For it radically regards man's rational nature as the ultimate moral norm and thus eliminates all determinations which do not originate in the moral subject itself.

But Kant's principle of autonomy was hard to reconcile with the requirements of a folk religion. How could a religion, based upon tradition and authority rather than reason, be justified at all from a purely rational point of view? And if the principle of autonomy was absolutely valid, should religion not be restricted to the purely rational?

To answer this question Hegel undertook a serious study of Kant's *Religion within the Limits of Reason Alone* (*Religion innerhalb der Grenzen der blossen Vernunft*, 1793), in which

---

[7] Hegel, *Briefe*, in *Sämtliche Werke* (ed. by G. Lasson and J. Hoffmeister, Hamburg, 1952), XXVII, 23–24.

Kant applies his principle of autonomy to the Christian religion. An initial result of these reflections was a fragment of the *Life of Jesus* (*Das Leben Jesu*, 1795), which in true Kantian fashion presents Jesus as an ideal of moral autonomy. It is obvious that this view is irreconcilable with Hegel's previous theory of religion as well as with his Ancient ideal of ethics. But the *Life of Jesus* fragment should be considered as a reflection on Kant's thoughts rather than as an expression of Hegel's own ideas.

More original is *The Positivity of the Christian Religion* (*Die Positivität der christlichen Religion*), written in the same year. Jesus here is no longer presented merely as a moral ideal but also as the teacher of a positive religion, that is, of "a system of religious axioms which must be true because it is offered to us by a higher authority to which we cannot refuse to subject our faith." [8] It has become clear to Hegel that "while the [Christian] religion, of course, contains principles of virtue, it also contains positive prescriptions for acquiring God's favor by exercises, feelings, and actions, rather than by morality." [9] Positive and moral elements are in perfect harmony with each other in Jesus' teaching, for although the bases of this teaching are the positive principles of faith in Christ and obedience to the will of God, it emphasizes an interior moral attitude over ritual practice and positive doctrine.[10] Jesus places the fundamental condition for God's favor in the following of the moral law, prescribed by each man's conscience.[11] After Jesus' death, however, his followers attributed the imperative character of their master's doctrine to his authority rather than to its intrinsic content, thus changing Christianity into a merely positive religion. "The religion of Jesus became a *positive* doctrine about *virtue*." [12] The freedom of the Gospel is replaced again by the servitude of the law. Hegel rejects this pure positivity, even

8 Nohl, p. 233.
9 Nohl, p. 155; Knox, p. 71.
10 Nohl, p. 158; Knox, p. 75.
11 Nohl, p. 158; Knox, p. 75.
12 Nohl, p. 166; Knox, p. 86.

though he maintains that some positive elements are essential to religion.[13]

The Law of Love: Synthesis of Positive Religion and Moral Autonomy

During the next period (1796–1800) in Frankfurt, Hegel, under the influence of religious and romantic authors (the Fourth Gospel, Hölderlin, Schiller), decisively transcended Kant's rational religion. In *The Spirit of Christianity and Its Fate* (*Der Geist des Christentums und sein Schicksal,* 1798–99), he introduces the notion of fate as a basic component of religion, which cannot be reduced to moral categories. Thus it was the special destiny of the Jews to live in complete isolation from the surrounding world. Abraham, who was called away from Chaldea, is the prototype of this "self-maintenance in strict opposition to everything." Wandering over the world, he is alone with himself, merely *for himself* (*für sich*). By accepting this isolation as their religious destiny, the Jews overcame the legalism which would have resulted from the strongly positive character of their religion.

As Judaism transcended religious legalism by *accepting* its destiny, so Christianity transcends mere morality by making man *love* his destiny. The moral obligation as such cannot be the highest expression of human freedom, for it still opposes the moral subject to his conscience. To be sure, conscience does not command from without as a positive law does, but its orders nonetheless retain the form of laws. The Sermon on the Mount, however, goes beyond all law by teaching love as the supreme moral principle and thus abolishes the commands as such.

[13] Jean Hyppolite implies that Hegel at this point had already made a clear distinction between a "good" and a "bad" positivity, but all the texts he quotes are from the first part of the manuscript, which was written in 1800 after a long evolution. See his *Introduction à la Philosophie de l'Histoire de Hegel* (Paris, 1948), pp. 34–39.

In the Sermon on the Mount, Jesus strips the law of its legal form. "The Sermon does not teach reverence for the laws; on the contrary, it exhibits that which fulfills the law but annuls it as law and so is something higher than obedience to law and makes law superfluous." [14] Thus the new doctrine annuls the law *qua* law, the moral as well as the positive; but at the same time it is the fulfillment, the *pleroma* of the law, inasmuch as the synthesis of love also includes the content of the law. The Gospel does not abolish the law, but it transforms its commands into works of love. "[Whereas] the commands of duty presuppose a cleavage [between reason and inclination] and . . . the domination of the concept declares itself in a 'thou shalt,' that which is raised above this cleavage is by contrast an 'is,' a modification of life." [15]

By identifying religion with love, Christianity has reconciled positivity with moral autonomy, the two basic elements of religion which previously seemed to exclude each other. But, according to Hegel, Christianity also had its tragic fate. After Jesus' departure, the affection of his followers retained no other objective basis than the memory of his words and deeds. As a result, their love assumed "the form of a datum" imposed from without, and Christianity turned into a positive, historical religion.[16]

While desiring to keep herself undefiled and separated from this sinful and loveless world, the Christian Church, by her faithfulness to the historical aspect of her Founder, lost the very essence of His message—all-inclusive, universal love. A new dichotomy thus arose between the pure, infinite universe to which the Christian aspires and the profane, finite world in

[14] Nohl, p. 266; Knox, p. 212.
[15] Nohl, p. 266; Knox, p. 212. The distinction between the perfect ethics of *what is* and the imperfect morality of *what ought to be* is a reaction against Fichte and will increasingly dominate Hegel's practical philosophy. The *ought* has its ultimate reality in what *is*.
[16] Lukacs calls attention to the fact that Hegel's concept of positivity becomes more dynamic than in the previous period: an institution becomes *positive* when the spirit has fled from it. Gyorgy Lukacs, *Der junge Hegel und die Probleme der kapitalistischen Gesellschaft* (Berlin, 1954), p. 168.

which he lives. Hegel concludes that the final reconciliation between the finite and the infinite can no longer be provided by Christianity alone, however important its contribution to this reconciliation will be. In spite of its superior spiritual character, Christianity lacks the ethical possibilities which the more closed Ancient folk religion possessed.

Hegel then turned all his attention to the other point on his ethical program, the political unity which would lead to the development of a national spirit. While still in Tübingen, Hegel had written that the formation of a national spirit does not depend on folk religion alone but on political conditions as well. With the French Revolution, he was more than ever convinced of the importance of a realistic policy for the attainment of his ethical ideal.

Hegel's Early Political Writings

In Bern, Hegel had started to read Benjamin Constant. The inadequacy of the old-fashioned aristocratic government of the Swiss city made him all the more receptive to liberal ideas. His first essay in political science had been a translation, with very sharp personal comments, of a French pamphlet on the Bern government, to make Switzerland aware of its backward political situation in the middle of a changing world.[17]

In Frankfurt, Hegel's political interest increased, as is illustrated by various shorter writings from 1796 to 1797 and especially by the important criticism of the political constitution of his home state, Württemberg, entitled *On the Latest Internal Situation of Württemberg, Especially Concerning the Defects of the State Constitution* (*Über die neuesten innern Verhältnisse Württembergs, besonders über die Gebrechen der Magistratsverfassung,* 1798). Inspired by the French Revolution, this work affirms that a juridical order which ignores the natural rights of

---

[17] E. Vermeil, "La Pensée politique de Hegel," *Revue de métaphysique de morale,* XXXVIII (1931), 444.

man, or whose positive institutions no longer correspond to actual needs, must be replaced without delay. "How blind are
those who believe that institutions, constitutions, laws which no
longer agree with the mores, needs, ideas of the people, and
from which the spirit has fled, are still alive; that forms which
no longer correspond to intellect and experience are strong
enough to keep a people united." [18]

Hegel himself here anticipated the dynamic concept of right
which Marx was to use later against the conservatism of the
Philosophy of Right. The attack on royal absolutism also evokes
a parallelism with Marx. Yet, Hegel's theories are not revolutionary; they are inspired by a conservative desire to preserve
the good elements in the Württemberg constitution, and to
prevent "a much more violent eruption in which desire for re-
venge would accompany the need of reform." [19]

Remarkable in Hegel's early political writings are a sober objectivity and a practical sense which are entirely missing in the
writings of his contemporaries. Hence some critics have con-
cluded the existence of a dichotomy between Hegel's political
writings and his speculative philosophy. [20] According to them, the
political life of his day presented such a sad picture that it
could not possibly be reconciled with the high ideals of German
Romanticism. Consequently, along with his political philosophy,
Hegel would have embraced some practical principles which
anticipated Bismark's infamous *Realpolitik.*

We believe that this interpretation is not correct. Hegel certainly realized that political life in Germany at the end of the
eighteenth century was far behind that in France and other

[18] *Schriften zur Politik und Rechtsphilosophie* (henceforth referred to as
SPR), in *Sämtliche Werke* (ed. by G. Lasson, Leipzig, 1913), VII, 151. Only
five pages of the aforementioned work remain.
[19] *SPR*, p. 151. During his Frankfurt period, Hegel also wrote a critical
commentary on Stewart's *Political Economy.* We have no other source of
information on this essay than Rosenkranz's biography of Hegel. Cf. Haering, I, 592.
[20] See, for example, Vermeil, pp. 474–84. This probably started with Franz
Rosenzweig, *Hegel und der Staat* (München-Berlin, 1920), I, 51, for whom
Hegel anticipates Bismarck's political principles.

European countries, and, inspired by the Enlightenment and the French Revolution, he was, from the very outset, opposed to the existing state of affairs. It is also true that, until the advent of Napoleon, Hegel did not discern any area of public life in his own country where he could begin to apply his political ideas. He therefore wanted first an elementary political reorganization. However, it seems exaggerated to conclude that his writings on political science contradict his speculative works, for first of all, Hegel had no speculative theory on the State. Until 1798 his speculative writings were mainly theological and contained only vague references to the Greek *polis* and Herder's *Volksgeist*. Furthermore, the difference between the method of speculative philosophy and that of a positive political science offers a sufficient explanation for the apparent dichotomy.

Hegel's Philosophical Development

In 1801 Hegel was appointed professor at the University of Jena. As we know from the *Fragment of a System (Systemfragment)*, written just before his departure from Frankfurt, Hegel now had definitely abandoned the Enlightenment and had placed himself more than ever under the influence of Schelling.

Hegel's Critique of Fichte's Ethical Theory

The first result of this renewed contact was the opusculum *On the Difference between Fichte's and Schelling's Systems (Über die Differenz des Fichteschen und Schellingschen Systems,* 1801). In it, Hegel unreservedly adopts Schelling's philosophy in hopes of finding at last the absolute reconciliation of subject and object, of finite and infinite. In fact, Hegel's ideas already deviate considerably from Schelling's. The absolute for him is the Spirit, and not Schelling's "point of indifference," which comprehends both nature and Spirit. But Hegel is not conscious yet of this fundamental split: considering himself an orthodox disciple of Schelling, he uses the latter's terminology for the development of his own ideas.[21]

Fichte's philosophy may be seen as a search for the unconditioned condition of all experience, the absolute foundation of consciousness which itself lies beyond consciousness. This ultimate he found in Kant's transcendental subject, the unity of apperception. As all idealists, Fichte assumed that the ultimate must be *one,* and since he had defined it as a transcendental subject, he was obliged to reduce all objectivity ultimately to this pure self. But according to Hegel, experience implies both an object and a subject, and no pure subject can ever be the foundation of a subject-object relation. Fichte's first principle, then, is too subjective to account for any objective reality.[22] Instead of eliminating the opposition between object and subject, Fichte in fact simply eliminates the object, while the original opposition remains.

Fichte's political theories reveal a similar opposition, which is also abolished by suppressing one of the two opposite terms. The State for him is the highest expression of the pure impulse of the *Spirit* which moves man into the realm of freedom. Yet, the impulse of the Spirit is so fundamentally opposed to the impulse of nature, which is just as real in man's appetitive life, that harmony can be obtained only by the death of either one of the antagonists. What Fichte calls "freedom," therefore, marks, in Hegel's words, the triumph of reason over life. "Because of the absolute opposition between the pure impulse and the impulse of nature, natural right becomes a product of concrete domination by reason and suppression of life." [23] Far from

21 Haering, I, 607–08.
22 Hegel, *Erste Drückschriften,* in *Sämtliche Werke* (ed. by Lasson), I, 3.
23 *Drückschriften,* p. 69.

being the supreme expression of human freedom, Fichte's State sacrifices true freedom.[24]

Fichte's ethical system also opposes nature to reason. But here the compulsion of right is replaced by that of rational duty. "In the State right will rule, in the realm of ethics duty will have power, only inasmuch as they are acknowledged as law by in-dividual reason. . . . There is one difference. The relation be-tween freedom and nature becomes more unnatural when, as in ethics, a subjective master-and-slave relationship suppresses one's own nature; whereas in natural right the imperative-and-authoritative appears as something that stands outside the living individual." [25]

Everywhere in Fichte we meet the same opposition between the *is* of nature and the *ought* of reason. Hegel, on the contrary, following Schelling's lead, proposes a concept of freedom that includes the impulse of nature (*Naturtrieb*) as well as reason, and which is at once the highest ethical ideal and the ultimate principle of law. He thus eliminates the opposition between na-ture and reason (*Vernunft*), as well as the one between the good of society (which represents the universal law of reason) and the private strivings of the individual (which stem from the impulse of nature).

During 1801 Hegel also wrote the major part of *The German Constitution* (*Die Verfassung Deutschlands*), which he was never to publish. The very fact that political science still in-terested him in these years of intensive philosophical reflection indicates a strong continuity of purpose. As in his opusculum on the Württemberg Constitution, his aim was to awaken the Germans from their dreams and to make them face the sad politi-cal reality of their country. "In their concepts of right and duty they assume a necessity, but in fact nothing happens according to this necessity." [26] Hegel hoped that once the Germans under-stood the origin and historical background of their political

[24] *Drückschriften*, p. 64.   [25] *Drückschriften*, p. 70.
[26] *SPR*, p. 6. On this work, see also Herbert Marcuse, *Reason and Revolu-tion: Hegel and the Rise of Social Theory* (Boston, 1960), pp. 49–56.

situation, they would realize how outdated it was. The German people's desire for freedom, which had always opposed a central authority, was the cause of Germany's political fragmentation. In the past this desire had protected Germany against tyranny; at the present, however, political division blocked the way to progress. The same love of freedom which formerly had divided the Germans should now reunite them. National consciousness alone was insufficient to create a German State. What was most needed was a strong political force. "To form a State, a mass must fashion a common defense and political authority." [27]

Here again, Hegel remains far from a *Realpolitik,* but he does realize that "plans and theories, although only realistic inasmuch as they can be executed, are equally valuable whether they exist in reality or not, whereas a political theory can be called a State and a Constitution only when it is real." [28]

Hegel's Critique of Natural Law Theories

For the fall semester in 1802, Hegel announced a course in natural right, the main ideas of which are set down in his *System of Ethics.*[29] This is the first elaboration on a problem that had occupied him for a long time. During the same year he published in the *Kritische Journal der Philosophie,* which he edited with Schelling, a complementary critical study: "On the Scientific Treatments of Natural Law" ("Über die Wissenschaftlichen Behandlungsarten des Naturrechts") .[30] There is an intimate connection between these two writings. We will first discuss the article, which is logically prior.

Hegel introduces his treatise about natural law with a discussion on method. In the footsteps of Schelling, who reintegrated empirical sciences such as physics and mechanics into philosophy, he attempts a new synthesis of the empirical and the *a priori* in the moral sciences. Empirical knowledge has developed

27 *SPR,* p. 18.   29 *SPR,* pp. 419–503.
28 *SPR,* p. 18.   30 *SPR,* pp. 329–416.

into an autonomous science independent of the philosophical *a priori;* but until this new science is subsumed under the *a priori* of philosophy, it remains unaware of its own limitations. Critical philosophy, on the other hand, has banned as "non-objective" all empirical science from the realm of philosophy; but its restrictive attitude has resulted in empty formalism.[31]

The opposition between empirical sciences and philosophy has been particularly disastrous in the field of natural law. Because of the normative character of this science, both empirical science and critical idealism, contrary to their basic principles, have intruded into each other's domain. Empirical science has lifted certain data out of context and, on the basis of these excerpts, has tried to explain all the others without respecting the organic structure of the whole. It thereby assumes that to discover the essence of human society, one must eliminate all contingent and accidental elements so that the absolutely necessary may become apparent.[32] But Hegel wonders where empiricism gets its criterion for distinguishing the necessary from the accidental. Furthermore, by presupposing an initial asocial "state of nature," the empiricists made the social state of right into an arbitrary structure, subjecting the individual to a merely external order in which he has to give up some "natural" rights in order to receive the social protection of law.

Hegel's criticism of natural law is not leveled at juridical systems of the sixteenth and seventeenth centuries, which accepted the lawless state of nature and the social contract only as an unproven assumption, a working hypothesis, that had no real impact on the development of their purely juridical theories.[33] He rather has in mind the "philosophical" theories of the eighteenth century, in which this working hypothesis had become an unshakable dogma with philosophical pretensions. From the Archimedian point of a lawless state of nature these philosophers claimed to explain the entire juridical order, despite the fact

---

[31] *SPR*, p. 33. [32] *SPR*, p. 338.
[33] H. Cunow, *Die Marxsche Geschichts-, Gesellschafts- und Staatstheorie* (Berlin, 1923), I, 59.

that the very notion of lawlessness itself presupposes a state of law.[34] The definition of this artificial state of nature was left entirely to subjective insights and feelings about human nature. Vague intuitions and rationalistic schemas thus became the ultimate philosophical norm of right.

Hegel considered it greatly to the credit of Kant and Rousseau to have made a clean sweep of those arbitrary and mostly sentimental conceptions of human nature. Rousseau founded life in society on the spiritual principle of the general will (*la volonté générale*) and thus placed the social in the sphere of the rational and the necessary. He rejected both the asocial state of the natural law theorists and the "social feelings" of the English sentimentalists. Hegel felt, however, that Rousseau never drew the ultimate conclusions from his rational concept of society and still adhered to an individualist notion of freedom in maintaining that the individual *abdicates* certain natural rights in order to receive protection from society. This position still implies that life in society is irreconcilable with *full* individual freedom.

Empiricist prejudices prevented Rousseau from seeing in the State a reality as authentic as the individual. On an empirical basis he admitted that all men are social, but he failed to see that *man as such,* by his very nature, must be social. As a result, says Hegel, he committed the classic empiricist error of trying to establish a universal and necessary principle on a purely empirical basis. Another result is that Rousseau had to retain the social contract theory, for it was the only way to bring together elements which by themselves were insufficient to establish society as an *essential* human necessity.

[34] *SPR*, p. 344.

Hegel's Critique of Kant and Fichte on Right and Morals

Kant's theory of right offered a more philosophical explanation of society. Right has its foundation in the *universal*, rational *nature* of man, and the "social contract" is to be understood as man's universal and, therefore, social nature, rather than as a formal agreement between individuals. By making man's rational nature into the basis of right, Kant went beyond Rousseau, whose *volonté générale* never reached full universality. With him natural right now became rational right (*Vernunftrecht*).

In spite of these great qualities, Kant's theory retained some of the inherent defects of contractualism. Society is still considered a restriction of individual freedom which man accepts in order to make a better use of what is left. In this respect, the State in Kant is not basically different from what it was in previous political theories. One can only agree with Gentile's statement: "Until Hegel, the State has always been conceived as something negative, as limiting the actuation of the Spirit, which is represented by the individual, who alone is conscious and therefore alone represents the reality of the Spirit. And whoever says 'limit,' also says 'negation.' "[35]

Hegel ultimately attributed Kant's failure to integrate right and society in freedom to the fact that his concept of reason—which he correctly made into the foundation of right and ethics—remained divorced from the world of empirical experience. Kant's philosophy of right and his ethical system suffered from the same dualism as his epistemology: an unsurmountable separation between consciousness and reality. By confining law and society to the external world of compulsion and excluding them from the realm of freedom proper, Kant lost most of the benefits which the rational foundation of the juridical and social

---

[35] Giovanni Gentile, "Il concetto dello Stato in Hegel," in *Verhandlungen des 2. Hegelkongresses* (Haarlem, 1932), p. 121.

order yielded. His notion of freedom remained restricted to the interior universe of the moral intention.

Even from a purely moral point of view, Kant's position raised some serious questions. For what is to determine the intention itself? How can the rational will be its own purpose and motive of action unless it specifies itself? And how can it specify itself into a concrete moral norm without integrating the external aspect of the act? According to Kant, the rational character of the will provides a sufficient criterion of action, for it implies that one must act in such a way that one's course of action can be universally accepted.

Any action, therefore, which conflicts with the imperative of reason becomes self-contradictory as soon as it is made into a universal norm. If someone does not return money which he received in deposit, he destroys the very idea of property, since his attitude, if generalized, would lead to the contradiction that property is not property. But Hegel questions whether such a violation of property would be a contradiction. What in human nature makes property into an absolute and inescapable necessity, so that even he who does not respect it implicitly must admit its necessity in the very act which denies it? As long as this point has not been clarified, the theoretical formulation of theft is rather: "No property is no property," which is not contradictory. In fact, no action can be excluded by pure reason alone, for any action, no matter how criminal, can be made into a principle of universal law without becoming an intrinsic contradition.[36] Kant has extended the unconditional character of the form of the moral imperative to its content. "Surreptitiously Kant has superimposed an absolute form over an unreal, conditional content." But this has a disastrous effect on moral philosophy, for it allows one to justify any possible behavior in the name of an absolute morality.

Hegel's critique applies even more to Fichte.[37] Fichte's will

[36] *SPR*, pp. 354–55.
[37] Hegel's best criticism of Fichte is found in another article in the *Kritischer Journal der Philosophie*, "Belief and Knowledge" ("Glauben und Wissen"),

can remain pure only as long as it is empty of any content. But to make his criterion of morality, duty for duty's sake, into a concrete rule of action, Fichte must give it some content from without, and at that point morality becomes arbitrary. For even the most immoral action has some aspects which could be considered to be part of one's duty, just as the most virtuous one has aspects which, taken separately, conflict with duty. Consequently, whatever course of action one chooses, it can always be rationalized by an empty, formal notion of duty.

Nor is Fichte's theory of law basically different from Kant's. For although he accepts that freedom extends its effects to the outside world, the essence of freedom for him is just as purely interior as it is for Kant. The law or, for that matter, any social institution remains excluded from the inner core of freedom. They are expressions of inner freedom, but are in no way part of it.

Hegel summarizes his critique of Kant and Fichte as follows:

> A primary aspect of the philosophy of Kant and Fichte is the identity of right and duty with the essence of the thinking and willing subject. . . . It is its best side. But it has not remained faithful to this identity, for it posits the separation of unity of the spirit and multiplicity of the empirical world as *just as absolute* and equivalent with the other.[38]

No identification of the ideal and the real seems possible in the systems of Kant and Fichte. On the other hand, since the whole ethical order is *per se* normative and, therefore, must subsume the real multiplicity of the empirical order under the ideal unity of the spirit, the entire philosophical construction collapses and is replaced by empirical law and custom. Thus, transcendental idealism ultimately turns into some sort of moral empiricism.

---

of which the third part is entirely devoted to Fichte. Since the article was published in the same year, 1802, I also refer to Hegel's discussion in it of Fichte's ethical system.
[38] *SPR,* p. 361.

The Identity of the Ideal and the Real
in Hegel's Ethical Theory

To this empty formalism and unphilosophical empiricism, Hegel opposes his own ethical theory, in which the basis of morality and right is no longer an abstract concept, but an ideal entity with a real content: man's universal nature realizes itself in the concrete, spiritual, and ethical totality of the nation. Individual morality is only part of a more comprehensive ethical whole which culminates in the State. In such an ethical theory there can be no opposition between the ideal and the real, between what *ought* to be and what *is,* for the State, as reality of the ethical ideal, reconciles the *ought* and the *is.* Kant's opposition between an internal order of morality and an external order of law, one of which is pure freedom and the other pure compulsion, is also eliminated: the individual can be fully free and ethical only as a member of a society, which always requires some external juridical organization. Hegel does not deny that there is a distinction between external right and internal morality, but to the two distinct spheres he adds a third one, the ethical totality (*Sittlichkeit*), which unites both in a higher synthesis.

For Hegel, a nation and, even more, a national State are organic beings. As such, their juridical systems are the product of an organic process rooted in a people's cultural past, rather than the result of a deduction from abstract principles.

> That is why Montesquieu has founded his immortal work on the individual character of the various peoples. True enough, he has not been able to raise himself up to the fully living Idea, but at least he has interpreted particular laws and institutions on the basis of the whole and its individuality . . . rather than deducing them from "reason" or abstracting them from experience and raising them later to a certain universality.[39]

[39] *SPR,* p. 411.

To preserve a state's individuality and consolidate it, war is a necessity, for never more than in wartime does a State affirm its own unique identity. Moreover, it is only in war that the individual's devotion to his ethical ideal is put to the test. Hegel therefore rejects Kant's "perpetual peace" and the Enlightenment's vague ideas of universal brotherhood.

Hegel's System of Ethics

The *System of Ethics* (*System der Sittlichkeit,* 1802) is the positive counterpart of the "Scientific Treatments of Natural Law." Hegel here attempts to give a description of the phenomena of the ethical consciousness. But he fails, mainly because of his involved and inconsistent use of Schelling's terminology, which no longer fits his own ideas and makes this work almost unintelligible.

The *System of Ethics* describes the evolution from the lowest "natural" to the highest "absolute" ethics. In its primitive, natural form of sensuous striving (*Trieb*), the ethical consciousness is hardly recognizable as ethical. At this stage its goal is merely sensuous pleasure. When sensuous striving reaches satisfaction, the moral subject becomes empty again and ready to pursue a new object on a higher level. A more detached and spiritual form of possession is attained through labor. By using tools man is able to produce beyond his needs and to possess without consuming. This marks the origin of property and, as commercial and economic relations develop, of a juridical order. At first this order is limited to the abstract right of a person to possess property.

After some considerations about the family—which, more than the juridical order, unites universal goals with individual objectives—Hegel proceeds to a discussion of his "absolute ethics." Here the individual reaches a full, conscious identification with the universal. In the organic unity of the people the individual consciousness concretely unites itself with the community as with its *own* universality. Absolute ethics, then, completely transcends the opposition between right and morality, between the external and the internal. "We have eliminated the prevailing distinction between legality and morality . . . not by confusing both principles but by sublating [40] them and constituting an absolute ethical identity." [41] Hegel here anticipates his later triad, right-morality-ethics.

Individual morality is not treated as an independent sphere in Hegel's *System of Ethics*. It is merely discussed as a negative part of absolute ethics. The reason for this is probably that the moral order, insofar as it is purely interior and opposed to the external order of right, can express its principles only in a negative form.[42] Hegel's positive theory of morals is to be found in his "absolute ethics," which, in the nation or the State, synthesizes internal disposition with external law. Following Plato's example in the *Republic*, he bases the State's organic structure on the division of the population into classes. Each class represents a particular virtue, and together they constitute the complete ethical reality. A perfect life is possible only when the individual is organically integrated into the ethical totality. The basis of ethics is the group ethos, and, in this first period, Hegel believed the class to be the significant group. Later, impressed by the centralized Prussian State, he was to regard the State as the basic social unit.

It is interesting to notice that at this point Hegel did not feel

---

40 The word "sublate" will be explained more fully in Chapter 2. Its basic meaning is to elevate two mutually exclusive stages to a higher level where they can be synthesized.

41 *SPR*, p. 397.

42 That is precisely why Kant and Fichte, who adhere to an individualistic philosophy of morals, never transcend a negative concept of freedom. Jean Hyppolite rightly remarks: "By limiting themselves to the separate individual, those philosophies remain in the stage of morality; this explains the merely negative character of their freedom, which, while expressing the necessity to transcend this moment, obliges this necessity to remain forever without consequences." (Hegel, *Principes de la Philosophie du Droit* [tr. by A. Kaan, Paris, 1949], Preface, p. 15.)

the need to place the spiritual values of art, religion, and science beyond the sphere of the State. The reason for this is that in the *System of Ethics* Hegel still remained basically faithful to the Greek ideal according to which these values are obtained exclusively through the State.

Hegel's Mature Thought

Hegel's *Realphilosophie*, written in 1805–06, is of interest only insofar as it anticipates some of the views which Hegel was to express fifteen years later in the *Philosophy of Right*. Two are particularly noteworthy:

1. His faith in the Ancient ideal had given way to a more modern conception of the State, of which Napoleon was the herald. The French Revolution, with its Ancient ideals, had degenerated into a reign of terror, thus proving that history knows no return. The State can no longer fulfill the function which it had in Antiquity, because the Christian notion of the *person* as an absolute end partly transcends all ethical structures. Hegel, therefore, tops his philosophy of the State with a philosophy of the *Absolute Spirit*. He does not abandon the Ancient ideal altogether—the State remains the highest realization of ethical life—but art, religion, and philosophy belong to a domain to which ethical life itself is subordinated. The ambiguity of this solution is obvious. Even in his final *Philosophy of Right* Hegel will not overcome it.

2. Another definitive category developed here for the first time is the sphere of economic life, in the *Philosophy of Right* referred to as the *civil society* (*bürgerliche Gemeinschaft*.) [43]

---

[43] During his Frankfurt period, Hegel had already dealt seriously with the problems of the civil society, but, as Lukacs points out, merely from a subjective point of view: the individual's relations with civil society. In Jena, for the first time, he was to make a study of its *objective* essence. See Lukacs, p. 130. For a discussion of the *Realphilosophie* in general, see Marcuse, pp. 73–90.

Already in his *System of Ethics,* Hegel showed much understanding of the relative independence of the economic sphere of life. The reading of Adam Smith's *Wealth of Nations* (1776) enabled him to give this sphere its definitive place. His description of the development of economic life is profoundly pessimistic and anticipates the views of Marx: the rich accumulate wealth while the poor sink more and more into distress.

The Phenomenology of Consciousness

In the *Phenomenology of Mind* (*Phänomenologie des Geistes,* 1807) Hegel brings all his previous insights together in a vast synthesis. He calls his work a description of the stages of consciousness. But consciousness is taken on three different levels: the *Phenomenology* is at once an analysis of the elements of human experience, of the historical evolution of consciousness, and of the ideologies which resulted from this evolution.[44] It is this complexity which makes the *Phenomenology* one of the most difficult works ever written. Here we are primarily interested in its vision of history and of man's social relations.

Consciousness is not a passive screen on which a static reality casts its reflection. It is involved in a life-and-death struggle with reality, during which each antagonist conquers the other's position. Reality usually designates that which rests in itself and is therefore self-identical. This static self-possession is expressed by the term "substance." Consciousness, on the other hand, is that which must actively strive to attain the end of self-possession. It never *is* fully self-identical, but is always in the process of becoming it. Philosophical tradition calls this active and reflective form of being "subject." Now, at the end of the dialectical struggle of consciousness with reality, reality is no longer mere substance, nor is the mind a mere subject, for the substance has become subject, and the subject substance. The mov-

---

[44] Jaap Kruithof, *Het Uitgangspunt van Hegel's Ontologie* (Bruges, 1959), p. 95.

ing force of this identification process is the *Spirit,* in which subject and substance coincide. In the Introduction to the *Phenomenology* Hegel writes:

> That substance is essentially subject, is expressed in the idea which represents the Absolute as Spirit *(Geist)* —the grandest conception of all, and one which is due to modern times and its religion [i.e. Christianity and, more particularly, Protestantism with its strong emphasis on the personal and spiritual nature of God].[45]

Yet, the Spirit has no existence prior to and independent of the process by which it becomes itself. The evolutionary process itself by which consciousness develops from an initial *opposition* between consciousness and reality to an absolute consciousness, in which the ideal world of consciousness coincides with the real, is called "dialectic." The dialectic, then, is not just one philosophical method among others: it is the self-development of thought, and of reality.[46]

That thought develops in a dialectical way follows from the very nature of consciousness. For consciousness is reflection, and reflection always marks a return of a subject into itself. This presupposes that the subject first goes out of itself until an obstacle checks its outward movement and forces it to return to itself. In this movement of return (which constitutes consciousness) the subject refers this obstacle to itself and denies that it possesses its own universality. Reflection, then, is primarily a negative movement: the subject becomes aware of what it is only after discovering what it is not. In the negation of the *other's* universality, it becomes conscious of its own and makes the other into a determinate object. The entire meaning of the dialectic is that the Spirit must oppose itself to itself in order to be able to return to itself and become conscious.

[45] Hegel, *Phänomenologie des Geistes* in *Sämtliche Werke* (ed. by Hermann Glockner, Stuttgart, 1951), II, 27; *The Phenomenology of Mind* (tr. by J. B. Baillie, George Allen & Unwin Ltd., New York, 1949), pp. 85–86. By permission of the publisher.
[46] The dialectical method will be explained more fully in Chapter 2.

As subject it is pure and simple negativity, and just on
that account a process of splitting up what is simple and
undifferentiated, a process of duplicating and setting factors in opposition. . . . True reality is merely this process
of reinstating self-identity, of reflecting into its own self in
and from its other, and is not an original and primal
unity as such, not an immediate unity as such. It is the
process of its own becoming, the circle which presupposes
its end as its purpose, and has its end for its beginning: it
becomes concrete and actual only by being carried out,
and by the end it involves.[47]

The negative power of consciousness is manifest even on
the elementary level of sense perception. A bare sensation
(which can never exist as such) would consist in the mere acceptance of a *this,* here and now. But as soon as reflection attempts to make conscious this immediately given datum, the
this of the sensation becomes entirely meaningless and contradictory. Indeed, when I turn my back to the object, the *here*
becomes something entirely different. The same happens to the
now: what was true five minutes ago is no longer true at the
present. Only a return of the subject into itself, which annuls
the immediacy of the given datum, can convey a positive meaning to sensation. *This* becomes meaningful when it is lifted out
of the pure sensation and transferred to the universality of the
mind. It then becomes the abstract quality of *thisness.*

Without the negative movement away from the object and
back to the subject, there would be no consciousness at all. Consciousness needs the opposition of the other than itself, but it
also needs the subsequent negation of this otherness. The otherness is the alienation, the estrangement of the mind, but an
estrangement which belongs to the mind itself. It exists only
for the mind, in order that the mind may become *for itself,* i.e.
consciously return into itself.

[47] *Phänomenologie,* p. 23; *Phenomenology,* pp. 80–81.

The Phenomenology of Self-consciousness

Consciousness develops into "self-consciousness." The more the object is known, the more the subject realizes that all its intelligibility of the object comes from itself. Self-consciousness is consciousness of freedom: [48] the realization that consciousness receives all its determinations *from itself*. More and more, the subject becomes aware that the entire reality of the object of knowledge is to be *for consciousness* and that it has no independent existence. This does not mean that its *otherness* disappears, but only that this otherness becomes integrated as a *moment*, that is, as an intrinsic stage in the process of self-consciousness. "For self-consciousness, then, otherness is a fact, it does exist as a distinct moment; but the unity of itself with this difference is also a fact for self-consciousness and is a second distinct moment." [49]

This newly acquired awareness of the subject's identity with its object is first expressed in *desire*. In desire the subject considers the object as a potential part of itself and actively attempts to absorb it. The object ceases to exist *in itself* (*an sich*), as it did in perception—it now exists for the subject. In his commentary on the *Phenomenology*, Jean Hyppolite paraphrases this as follows:

> The individual object of desire, the fruit which I am going to pick, is no longer an object posited in its independence: one may say that as object of desire, it is and that it is not; it is but soon it will not be any more; its truth is to be consumed, denied, so that self-consciousness through this negation of the other may re-collect itself.[50]

Through the object of its desire the self becomes aware of its identity with itself—it becomes self-consciousness.

A similar reflection by the object corresponds to the reflective

---

[48] The notion of freedom receives its final exposition in the *Philosophy of Right*. We will therefore reserve its explanation for the next chapter.
[49] *Phänomenologie*, p. 141; *Phenomenology*, pp. 219–20.
[50] Jean Hyppolite, *Genèse et structure de la Phénoménologie de l'Esprit de Hegel* (Paris, 1946), I, 154.

movement of the subject upon itself in self-consciousness. Every subject has its own object. Self-consciousness is no longer satisfied with the dead object of perception—it calls for an object which performs an immanent return upon itself (similar to its own) —*life*. Since the ego searches for its own immanence in desire, the object of desire must have an immanence of its own. But precisely because of its *own* immanence, the living object, having an existence of its own, resists any absorption by the subject. Paradoxically enough, this resistance is precisely what enables the subject to return from the other into itself. If the object of desire could be assimilated without resistance, consciousness would never progress beyond perception. The independence of another living being keeps the desire, and thereby also self-consciousness, alive. On the other hand, there can be no self-consciousness unless the independence of the desire's object is annulled. If the dialectic were halted by the resistance of the living object, consciousness would be back at the initial opposition between consciousness and the other-than-consciousness. There is only one way out of this impasse: since consciousness is unable to annul the otherness of the independent object, the object itself must negate its own otherness. This requires that the *other* also be self-conscious, for only self-consciousness can cancel *otherness*. Hegel therefore concludes that self-consciousness is born out of the confrontation of one consciousness with another consciousness. It is a reduplication of consciousness. "This has a double significance. First it [self-consciousness] has lost its own self, since it finds itself as an *other* being; secondly, it has thereby sublated that other, for it does not regard the other as essentially real, but sees its own self in the other." [51]

However, this confrontation of two self-consciousnesses leads to a life-and-death struggle in which each of the two opponents tries to be recognized by the other as what he is *for himself*. Self-consciousness affirms itself in desire, and all desire tends to annihilate its object. On both sides there is the same tendency to destroy the other. The self-conscious being, then, has no choice but to risk his life if he wants recognition of his identity. "The individual who has not staked his life may, no doubt, be recognized as a person; but he has not attained the truth of this recognition as . . . an independent self-consciousness. In the same way each must aim at the death of the other, as [he] risks [his] own life thereby."[52] If the complete destruction of one of the opponents is to be prevented, one of them must recognize the other without himself being recognized. He who does this realizes that consciousness itself depends on life and that death is the negation of consciousness—he therefore wants to save his life rather than risk it for recognition. The other holds his self-affirmation above his life—he wants recognition rather than safety. The latter is pure self-consciousness, the former is consciousness *for another*. One is the Master, the other the Slave. The Master is the pure *for itself*, the negation of life—the Slave is the pure *in itself*, the negation of consciousness. Each moment taken by itself is abstract and depends upon the other for its existence. The Slave preserves his life only through the self-consciousness of the Master. Yet, as we will see, to maintain this self-consciousness the Master needs the *mediation* of the Slave.

At first it may look as if the Master were fully independent and the Slave totally dependent. Indeed, the Slave depends on the Master for his life. Life is the "chain from which he could not in the struggle get away, and for that reason he proved himself to be dependent. . . ."[53] The Master has full control over the Slave's life. As a result, he alone has the immediate satisfaction of his desire: through the work of the Slave he is able to negate all independent objects—he consumes them, uses them for his own enjoyment. The resistance of independent things which *desire* encountered no longer exists for him—it only exists for the Slave through his labor. The Slave receives all the hardship—the Master all the enjoyment. But when the Master has

[52] *Phänomenologie*, pp. 151–52; *Phenomenology*, p. 233.
[53] *Phänomenologie*, pp. 153–54; *Phenomenology*, p. 235.

effectively achieved his lordship, he finds himself strangely enough dependent on the Slave, who guarantees the self-consciousness of the Master. It is the Slave who makes him Master, and his identity consists entirely in the "unessential" consciousness of the Slave. The Master, then, becomes more and more dependent. Furthermore, he is unable to acquire a permanent foothold in this world, for as soon as an object is offered to him, he can only consume it and then start the process all over. He never proceeds beyond his original primitive stage of self-consciousness.

While the Master's situation gradually deteriorates, the Slave's position, on the contrary, is bound to improve. He is forced "to have his independence in the shape of thinghood": [54] he lives in and through material things. But that is his salvation, for it enables him to give his own consciousness, however "unessential" it is, permanent reality in the world. Through his work, then, he reaches a level of self-consciousness which the Master is unable to attain. For the Slave, things retain their own independence—he has to labor upon them. But through his work he imposes his own form and shape on the object: by hard labor he manages to make independent things part of himself and thus to give his consciousness the substance which his Master's lacks. "Thus precisely in labor where there seemed to be merely some outsider's mind and ideas involved, the [Slave] becomes aware, through this rediscovery of himself by himself, of having and being a 'mind of his own.' " [55]

Thus the Slave alone is able to give the *for itself,* which he borrowed from the Master, the permanence of the *in itself.* In the Slave's work the original opposition between life and consciousness disappears. The Slave has reached the stage of *thinking* self-consciousness, that is, consciousness which has no content other than itself. But by becoming object to itself, consciousness becomes autonomous; it now is free consciousness.

---

[54] *Phänomenologie,* p. 154; *Phenomenology,* p. 235.
[55] *Phänomenologie,* p. 157; *Phenomenology,* p. 239.

The Phenomenology of Freedom

At first, this freedom is still empty and abstract. It only maintains itself by withdrawing from the world and concentrating
upon itself. The complexity of life, of which consciousness in
desire and labor was so keenly aware, is simply ignored and replaced by a negative attitude of self-sufficiency. This abstract
freedom found its historical expression in Stoicism. The Stoic is
aware that he possesses his freedom in himself, and he is not concerned about the outer world. The material conditions of his
existence leave him indifferent; whether he is an emperor (as
Marcus Aurelius) or a slave (as Epictetus), he is satisfied with
his interior freedom. The distinction of Master and Slave has
ceased to exist.

However noble the attitude of the Stoic is, it lacks the concrete
filling of life. "It is, therefore, merely the notion of freedom,
not living freedom itself; for it is, to begin with, only thinking
in general that is its essence, the form as such, which has turned
away from the independence of things and gone back into itself." [56] The Stoic thought has no content. To protect his freedom against all intrusion from without, the Stoic refuses to give
it any specific determination. Freedom is thereby condemned
to remain formal: it preserves itself only by not committing
itself.

In the end, the purely negative attitude of the Stoic leads to
scepticism. By concentrating on pure thought and pure freedom,
the Stoic has, in fact, dismissed the complex substance of reality
from his consciousness. But this complexity continues to exist.
The sceptical consciousness will, in self-confident irony, oppose
the intricate determinateness of the world to the independent
thought and freedom of the Stoic. Thought is infinite, unlimited
and undetermined—the world is finite, limited, and determinate.
Both exist together and exclude each other. This state of affairs
cannot last and, soon enough, consciousness realizes its tragic

---

[56] *Phänomenologie*, p. 161; *Phenomenology*, p. 245.

implications. The irony makes place for unhappiness. Consciousness has affirmed itself only by breaking away from life. It now engages in a long and painful search for what it has lost.

In his brilliant analysis of the unhappy consciousness, Hegel returns to some of the situations described in his theological writings. The Frankfurt description of Abraham wandering over the world, alone with himself, separated from life, finds its definitive meaning in this part of the *Phenomenology*. The unhappy consciousness suffers from the same separation of the finite and the infinite which the theological writings attributed to the Jewish mind.

In a first moment the unhappy consciousness tries to reconcile its freedom with the determinateness of life by removing freedom from particular existence and positing it in a transcendent sphere. Old Testament religion offers a typical illustration of this consciousness alienated from itself. To the Jewish mind, the infinite is "the alien external Being which passes sentence on particular existence." [57] God and man are opposed to each other: God is the one who *is*—man is not. Man possesses his freedom only outside himself, in God.

In the next stage, exemplified in Christianity, the universal self-consciousness is reintegrated in a particular existence: God becomes a particular man—the infinite becomes finite. Yet, the reidentification of consciousness is not complete, for, by uniting itself with one particular existence, the universal becomes opposed to other particular existents. The free self-consciousness, therefore, still is estranged from the particularity of existence because it is now *another* particular existence. "That *other* cannot be found where it is sought; for it is meant to be just a *beyond,* that which can *not* be found." [58]

Hegel here evokes the image of the medieval Crusaders, forever wandering over the world to meet Christ and not finding anything but his tomb. Christianity has reunited the universal

---

[57] *Phänomenologie*, p. 169; *Phenomenology*, p. 253.
[58] *Phänomenologie*, p. 173; *Phenomenology*, p. 258.

and infinite with the particular and finite. But the infinite and the finite do not really penetrate each other; they merely co-exist in one particular instance, the historical person of Christ. The infinite has not conquered the essence of the particular in order to make the particular universal, and the universal particular. This positive form of Christianity remains purely historical and contingent—it merely represents consciousness as particular. Unable to find its own universality in this historical particularity, consciousness withdraws into itself. "Consciousness thus abandons itself to a sort of individualism, of self-feeling. I, at least, insofar as I desire and strain myself, I exist, has said the disciple in the presence of the dead Christ." [59]

The unhappy consciousness, then, returns to its former activity: through desire and labor it attempts to assert itself against all external reality. But its heart is no longer in its work; it has lost its inner certainty and nothing can ever restore it. Its toiling in the world only confirms its insecurity. Even the external reality is no longer the same. In Christ's incarnation, the physical world has become sacred, and the finite has become a *symbol* of the infinite. The proud feeling of independence which generated the Stoic consciousness has given way to a feeling of dependence on God: cancellation of divine reality can be achieved only by divine grace. Consciousness no longer takes confidence in itself. It now attempts to unite the particular and the universal through humility and gratitude.

At this stage self-negation is assigned the task of reuniting the particular with the universal, the finite with the infinite. Only humble prayer and asceticism can lead to salvation. The medieval monk gives up all concern about earthly values, all interest in external activity, in order to concentrate solely on self-alienation. Only by sacrificing his independence is he able to realize his union with the infinite. But this unfreedom leads the monk to a higher freedom. Only self-sacrifice can lift consciousness

[59] J. Wahl, *Le Malheur de la conscience dans la philosophie de Hegel* (Paris, 1951), p. 144.

above its finite conditions and transform the particular will into a universal will.

The newly acquired identity of the universal and the particular inaugurates a further stage in the development of consciousness—*reason*. What Christianity initiated is now completed: the particular subject has taken the universal substance as content. Freedom has become real. The sacrifice of all particular attachments has enabled consciousness to move out into the world without losing its independence. A new relation of consciousness with the external world has begun, of which the Slave's activity was only a nonreflective prefiguration. Freedom requires commitment to particular, determinate acts. Yet, at the same time it must transcend all determination, for as *universal* consciousness freedom refuses to identify itself with any limited form of being.

To preserve its universality, freedom withdraws from its work as soon as it is accomplished. The acting consciousness always transcends the particularity of its achievements. Even the greatest artist is aware that he is more than all his works together. "The consciousness which withdraws from its work is in point of fact universal—because it becomes, in this opposition between work and consciousness, absolute negativity, the process of action—and stands over against its work, which is determinate and particular. It thus goes beyond itself *qua* work." [60]

Thus, after a long detour, consciousness rejoins the point from which it started, the negation of all determination. Yet, now the negation has become eminently positive. It negates the limiting determination which the free subject suffers in its work, but it strongly affirms the presence of the free subject in this work. The transcendence of the subject over its work opposes it to any particular work, but, at the same time, implies the necessity of the operation itself, for without this operation the subject would never become aware of its own transcendent freedom. Now, insofar as the operation also includes its own product, the latter

[60] *Phänomenologie,* p. 310; *Phenomenology,* p. 426.

ceases to be a mere *thing;* it becomes both a spiritual object transformed by the self and a part of the self. The original opposition between a pure consciousness of freedom, on the one hand, and a determinate, unfree world, on the other, has completely vanished: through man's work, the world has become part of consciousness. Hegel calls this identity of nature and freedom *the real fact (die Sache selbst)*, as opposed to *the thing (das Ding)* of perception. Henceforth the world is seen as a system of man's making. On its side, consciousness is no longer opposed to reality—it has become reality itself. The *for itself* has permeated the *in itself*. In the process of humanization, freedom has become objective, and nature free.

The *Phenomenology* contains no elaborate philosophy of the State. Yet, the entire work shows that the individual consciousness attains its ultimate truth in becoming Spirit. Since the Spirit is objectified in the State, full self-consciousness can be reached only through the State. The individual takes part in a process of which the State, in a sense, is the ultimate term.[61] In the *Phenomenology* Hegel merely sketches the outlines of a philosophy of the State which he fully develops in the *Philosophy of Right*. We will, therefore, postpone the discussion of his political theory until the next chapter.

In the *Phenomenology*, Hegel's thought reached philosophical maturity. From then on, he only worked out elements already intuitively present in the *Phenomenology*. But he developed them in an original and sometimes startling way. Hegel's later thought gave ontological status to the phenomena of consciousness of the *Phenomenology*. What was originally a description of the development of consciousness later became an ambitious, all-comprehensive explication of being. Whether Hegel's philosophy profited by this ontological trend is a question which we will discuss at the end of the next chapter.

---

[61] We write "in a sense," for in another sense the *Phenomenology* considers philosophy as the final term of the development of the Spirit. The relation between what Hegel will later call the "Absolute Spirit" (art-religion-philosophy) and the "Objective Spirit" will always remain ambiguous.

2

Hegel's Philosophy of Right

The Logical Foundations
of Hegel's Political Philosophy

From Liberalism to Prussianism

WITH THE FRENCH occupation, the Neoclassical mirage of the Revolution and of Napoleon lost much of its glamour in the eyes of the German romantics, and the ideal of freedom gradually turned into a German nationalist movement. Fichte, who had been one of the staunchest defenders of the ideas of the Revolution, was now gaining more and more popularity by his aggressively anti-French *Addresses to the German Nation* (*Reden an die deutsche Nation,* 1808). This change in attitude was typical for many German intellectuals. While formerly the Romantic aspirations went to the French ideal of universal brotherhood, they now concentrated on the liberation of the common fatherland. Of this new national State, Prussia became the nucleus during its war against the French.

Hegel, who along with his sympathies for the French Revolution had always cultivated the Herderian notion of a national spirit, saw his political dream finally come true, and he enthusiastically joined the Prussian nationalist movement. His earlier contempt for Prussia as "the spiritless, military State of the Great Elector" changed into a deep regard for the eminently spiritual vocation of the State that was to shape the new nation. Only in Prussia, he thought, existed the national consciousness necessary for the development of an authentic German culture. In his inaugural address at the University of Berlin, where he was appointed professor in 1818, he said:

> It is especially by its spiritual prestige that this State, which now has received me, has raised itself into the reality of politics and has been able to equal, in power and independence, states which are more affluent. Here culture and flourishing science belong as an essential moment in the State's very life.

The shift from liberalism to Prussianism caused some drastic changes in the political attitude of many German intellectuals. The Restoration had stemmed the democratic tide in Europe. After the Congress of Vienna, the archconservative King Frederick William III was less willing than ever to grant his Prussian subjects a constitution. Most German romantics who felt the need of a strong government in the dynamic State saw no other choice than to accommodate their ideal of democratic freedom to their nationalism, and they became political conservatives. Hegel was one of them. The former defender of the French Revolution now became the official philosopher of Frederick William's absolute monarchy.

It is unfair to explain this evolution, as Karl Popper does, as the result of personal ambition and political opportunism.[1] Hegel never betrayed the ideals of his youth, nor was his philosophy ever a mere rationalization of the King's conservative policy. To an attentive reader the differences between his philosophy of the State and the actually existing State are obvious. If, in spite of these personal differences, he lent the King his full support, it was because he felt that the realization of his political ideals, particularly the creation of a German national spirit, required the cohesive force of the monarchy.

Even before he came to Berlin, Hegel had attempted to systematize his social and political views. But it would take him

[1] Karl Popper, *The Open Society and Its Enemies* (New York, 1962), II, 49–58.

several more years to synthesize the various elements of his thought in a coherent system. The impressive final result of these efforts is the *Philosophy of Right* (*Grundlinien der Philosophie des Rechts*, 1821).

The Identity of Thought and Reality

The Introduction to this work enunciates the logical foundation of Hegel's political philosophy: "What is real is rational, and what is rational is real." As we saw in the *Phenomenology*, Hegel's philosophy assumes that thought and being are related to each other and that this relationship itself is possible only if they ultimately coincide. Every reality must be an object of knowledge in some form or other; it is not fully real before it is brought to its ideal completion. On the other hand, all thought refers to reality. This is true even for error, because the very distinction which the mind makes between truth and error presupposes that reality is ultimately accessible to thought. Otherwise the distinction itself would lose its meaning. Thought becomes objective only by being identical with reality.

This fundamental identity does not imply that reality exists only by the grace of the human mind. It does follow, however, that reality is *fully* real only when it becomes ideal, and, likewise, that thought in its perfection coincides with reality. The *ens rationis*—thought which is not supported by reality—finds no more favor in Hegel's eyes than the *thing in itself*, reality which is unable to become thought.

Philosophy, the highest form of knowledge, constitutes reality in the pure form of thought.[2] For this reason, philosophy is also the final moment of reality, which, in it, reaches its own ideal perfection. But philosophy is only the *final* moment. It therefore must never anticipate reality and show how it ought to de-

---

[2] Hegel, *Encyclopädie der philosophischen Wissenschaften*, in *Sämtliche Werke* (ed. by G. Lasson, Leipzig, 1913), V, 158. In future, this work will be referred to as *Enc.*, followed by the paragraph number.

velop. Philosophy does not deal with what *ought* to be, but with what *is*. Consequently, a sound political philosophy never teaches how the State *ought* to be, but why the existing State is necessarily what it is.]

Philosophy reflects upon reality and can therefore only *follow* the development of a reality which is already fully constituted.

> Only when actuality is mature . . . the ideal . . . appears over against the real. [It is then that the ideal apprehends for itself] this same real world in its substance and builds it up for itself into the shape of an intellectual realm. . . . The owl of Minerva spreads its wings only with the falling of the dusk.[3]

When a philosophical theory goes beyond the present political life, it constructs for itself a world which exists only in "the soft element of opinion." The end of philosophy is to understand *what is*, not in one aspect as science does, but in its totality. Political philosophy, therefore, considers the State as a stage in the development of the Spirit, and shows why it *necessarily* is what it is.

[The philosophical necessity of the State does not mean that every existing political system is perfect, but that, in spite of its imperfections, it always has an ideal aspect which makes it necessary in its historical context. Philosophy's task is to reveal this necessity and thus to justify what *is*.] This justification implies that *what is* has a reason for its existence; it does not imply that any particular State realizes the Idea in all its fullness. To understand Hegel's position on this point, the relation between the ideal and the real must be further clarified:

The identity of thought and reality, by which the real reveals itself in thought and thought realizes itself in reality, is not static: it is a dialectical process which is never completed. In the dialectic, the absolute (that is, the perfect identity) *becomes*

[3] Hegel, *Grundlinien der Philosophie des Rechts*, in *Sämtliche Werke* (ed. by G. Lasson) , VI, Introduction. This work in future will be referred to as *R.*, followed by the paragraph numbers, which are the same in all editions in both languages. Unless otherwise stated, our translation is taken from T. M. Knox, *Hegel's Philosophy of Right* (Oxford, 1945) , by permission of the Clarendon Press, Oxford.

by an ever renewed negation of the opposition between thought and reality. In the previous chapter we learned that dialectic is more than just one philosophical method among others; it is at once the self-development of thought and of reality.

"The dialectic is anything but a method of thinking or an artifice in a philosophical exposition. It is the very structure of concrete reality itself, and it only enters philosophical thought insofar as it describes reality as a whole." [4] The process of thinking is the logical expression of the ontological self-movement of the absolute.⟨Dialectic, therefore, rightly can be called the unfolding of the absolute.⟩Through the dialectic, thought becomes ontological—self-explication of reality; it transcends conceptual abstractions of the *understanding* and becomes concrete *reason*.

An interpretation of reality based upon the categories of understanding results in contradictions. Precisely because it was limited to the understanding, Kant's philosophy was unable to overcome the antinomies of the transcendental "dialectic" and to proceed to a complete, rational explanation of the real. But a philosophy of reason overcomes these oppositions by making them into moments of the dialectic of the Spirit. This process does not eliminate the oppositions, for they reappear within the higher syntheses. But⟨by being constantly overcome, they lose their absolute character. In the antitheses thought manifests its relative opposition to reality, but in the continuous transcendence of these antitheses it identifies itself with reality and becomes absolute.⟩

The absolute identity of thought and reality, brought about by the dialectical method, is the *notion*. The notion, therefore, is logical as well as ontological: it is the reflection of reality and the reality of reflection.[6] It is the fulfillment of reality rather

[4] A. Kojève, "Hegel, Marx, et le Christianisme," *Critique I* (1946), p. 339. We would rather say "explicates" instead of "describes," which still seems to imply a *basic* duality of thought and its content.
[5] S. Marck, *Hegelianismus und Marxismus* (Berlin, 1922), p. 5. Also N. Hartmann, *Die Philosophie des deutschen Idealismus* (Berlin, 1960), II, 181.
[6] *Enc.*, 158.

than an abstraction of the understanding. Far from being an abstract common denominator of individual realities, the notion is particular and individual as well as universal, and it particularizes itself without losing its universality.[7] Unlike abstract univocal forms, it is not *applied* to an indefinite number of individuals, but it *becomes* individual by internal necessity. Rather than a univocal, abstract concept, Hegel's *notion* is a self-developing spiritual organism.

This organism develops in three successive stages. In the first stage the notion simply affirms its identity with itself. Hegel calls it the *universal* moment: it is that aspect of the notion which remains identical throughout all changes. It is indefinite enough to stand for all possible individuals. The notion at this stage is simply what it is: it is immediate or *in itself.* If there were no other aspects, the notion would merely be a static, abstract concept. Yet, it also determines itself to a *particular,* finite form which embodies the universal. Since all determination is a negation, the notion as particular negates its universality. It opposes itself to itself or, as Hegel says, it is alienated from itself. But by thus being away from itself, it creates the possibility of a return upon itself, that is, of reflection. Hegel expresses this by saying that the notion in this second moment becomes *for itself.* Since the opposition between the universal and the particular occurs within the one notion, a higher synthesis will ultimately reconcile the two opposite terms. In this final moment, which is both universal and particular, the notion returns to its own identity. But this identity is no longer immediate: it is both *in itself* and *for itself.* Hegel calls this synthetic moment the *individual.*

Hegel's notion obviously differs from an abstract, static concept. It is as concrete and dynamic as life itself. And yet, in one sense, the notion may be called abstract, insofar as it is still undeveloped in its initial stage.[8] Although real from the very beginning, the notion at first includes its concrete content only

[7] *Enc.,* 163.　　　　[8] *Enc.,* 164.

implicitly. In order to reach full concreteness, it must be explicated in the various branches of philosophy. Developed into all
its determinations, the notion is called "Idea." The Idea, therefore, is the explicated notion, the synthesis of the real and the
ideal, the identity of truth and reality.[9]

If, properly speaking, there is only one notion, it is obvious
that, likewise, there can be only one Idea. Yet this Idea, although
fully concrete from the beginning, reveals itself in various
stages. Thus the State for Hegel is the Idea, and, as such, the absolute; but at this level the absolute does not yet reveal itself as
absolute, for then it would be as much subjective as objective,
which the objective institution of the State is obviously not. In
another respect, however, the State is absolute insofar as it concretely synthesizes an ideal universal with a finite historical
reality. If the Idea were merely universal and infinite, it would
be opposed to and limited by the finite. But the absolute is both
infinite and finite. From this absolute character of the State it
also follows that the State must always be more than merely
finite and historical. The finite, historical aspect of the State is
only the empirical *appearance* of the infinite, rational Idea. It
is this ideal aspect which gives meaning and reality to the historical appearance of the State. On the other hand, the notion
itself would be a mere abstract concept if it had no finite appearance. To become concrete, the infinite has to go through the
mediation of the finite.

The State: Supreme Synthesis
of the Objective Spirit

Hegel never simply identified Spirit with consciousness. In
the dialectical development of the Spirit, the individual consciousness, by its spiritual character, transcends its own con-

[9] *Enc.*, 213.

tingent particularity and universalizes itself in an Objective Spirit. By this conception, Hegel avoided enclosing himself within a Cartesian philosophy of consciousness and became the first to construct a truly universal concept of the State. For him the State is not based upon individual and subjective decision; it is a moment in the necessary evolution of individual freedom to a trans-individual and objective Spirit. In the State the Spirit becomes objective: subjective thinking becomes "objective thought," and subjective willing, "substantial will."

. After having posited itself as a purely universal and ideal *notion,* the Spirit negates its ideal universality in the finite reality of a material *nature,* in order to return to itself in the various moments of *consciousness.* At first this consciousness is merely individual and subjective: it is thinking rather than objective thought, and willing rather than objective will.

In the subjective stage of the Spirit, consciousness is split in a basic opposition between subject and object. Consciousness' tendency to overcome this opposition in the identity of the Spirit leads to a twofold activity: a thinking process which objectifies, that is, constitutes reality for the subject, and a willing process which subjectifies, that is, attributes value to an objective reality. While cognition creates the object, volition creates the value of the object. Consequently, volition can have no other content than the object of cognition. But since the will is nothing more than the Spirit's drive to realize itself, it follows that freedom actualizes its full spiritual potentiality only when it has the *in and for itself* rational as object. The highest freedom—that is, self-possession of the Spirit—therefore will be realized when the will gives itself a universal, rational content. At this point, the will becomes *substantial will,* and the Spirit *Objective Spirit.*[10]

---

[10] Hegel frequently uses "substantial" and "universal" interchangeably to indicate the one permanent element to which the transitory and—taken by themselves—contingent elements are related as to an end which, through them, realizes itself necessarily.

As Objective Spirit, freedom is no longer an empty universality (as was the Stoic consciousness in the *Phenomenology*), nor is it determined by particular, finite objects in which it loses its own self-consciousness. Instead, the will determines itself in the self-created institutions of law, society, and State. The objective will has itself as "content, object, and aim" [11] and thus identifies universal freedom with particular determination. But to become *concrete* the Objective Spirit must pass through the three stages of freedom: *in itself* (abstract right), *for itself* (morality), and *in and for itself* (ethics). The first stage in the evolution is the sphere of abstract right, in which freedom is merely *in itself*.

The Sphere of Abstract Right

Hegel describes right as "the existence of the free will." [12] Far from being a limitation of freedom, as it is for Kant, right is the first realization of concrete freedom. Yet, although the obligations of the law are determinations which freedom has given itself, the individual consciousness mostly experiences them as a restriction of its freedom. In the sphere of right, the universal appears in the form of an external law imposing certain duties which are acceptable only because they guarantee an equal number of rights. Right and duty coincide in the static identity of positive laws which are the same for everyone. "In those abstract spheres, what is one man's right ought also to be another's, and what is one man's duty ought also to be another's." [13]

The relation between the individual person and the substantial universality of his freedom has not yet reached the interior unity which it will attain in morality. Right originates from extrinsic social-economic relations. The satisfaction of material needs creates some form of property which can be maintained only by universal recognition and punishment of violations.

[11] *R.*, 7.   [12] *R.*, 29.   [13] *R.*, 261.

This assurance is exactly what right provides.[14] Yet, within the compulsion of abstract right, the freedom of the Spirit is at work. Ultimately the will here determines itself, rather than being determined by external factors. The basic precept of abstract right, "Be a person and respect others as persons," [15] already implies the freedom of the Spirit. Indeed, the concept of person "implies that . . . in finitude I know myself as something infinite, universal, and free." [16]

But this being-a-person as yet is merely abstract. "Be a person" means, in the sphere of abstract right, "behave as somebody who has duties in regard to other individuals"; "respect others as persons" means "treat others as individuals who have right." There is no concrete identity between the individual and the universal: the universal is accepted only because of each person's particular interest in maintaining his own rights, not because of itself. It thus remains a mere means for the attainment of particular goals. The *concrete* identity of individual and universal freedom is reserved for the ethical order. But before reaching this final synthesis, freedom still has to pass through the stage of *morality,* in which the abstract identity of particular and universal, which was achieved on the level of right, is

14 Vogel, who devoted a thorough study to the social-economic aspects in Hegel's philosophy, rightly concludes: "Economy and right are two inseparable parts of one whole social life. . . . Economy is the empirical-concrete content, right the empirical-concrete form of life in society." These considerations seem to come very close to Marx's conception of right. However, one must not forget that for Hegel the driving force of right and economic life is the Spirit; whereas for Marx a system of right is primarily determined by man's relation to nature. Vogel also reacts against a materialistic determinism.

> By need, necessity, and struggle for life alone Hegel cannot explain the origin of right. He is convinced, rather, that all juridical bonds of social life would collapse and would never build the artistic structure of society if they were not necessary expressions of the Spirit, which, through them, frees itself from the crushing bondage of nature and clears itself a way to self-determination.

(P. Vogel, *Hegels Gesellschaftsbegriff und seine geschichtliche Fortbildung durch Lorenz Stein, Marx, Engels, und Lassalle* [Berlin, 1925], p. 103.)
15 *R.,* 36.   16 *R.,* 35.

broken up again. This new opposition of the particular and universal is the result of an interiorization of freedom.

The Sphere of Morality

While Hegel calls abstract right "the external existence of freedom" (*Äusseres Dasein der Freiheit*), morality is defined as its "internal existence" (*Inneres Dasein*). The universal law here is no longer experienced as an external compulsion, but as the law of one's own conscience. Yet, even though man finds the universal within himself, it remains separated from his own particular existence. The subjective conscience *obeys* it as one obeys a higher authority. "It is the Idea in its separation." However, this separation does not destroy the basic self-identity of freedom. For it is precisely through the interiorization process of the moral stage—in which freedom reveals itself as autonomous and opposed to all extrinsic determinations—that man becomes aware of an opposition within his own autonomous will. Although both are aspects of the one rational will, the *good* of the moral obligation remains forever separated from the subjective aspect of conscience. Conscience is that which *ought* to be good, but which never fully is. Man's particular will is related to the universal objectives of reason; it is never *identical* with them. The good remains forever an ideal, separated from reality, since no particular will can fully actualize it. In the sphere of ethics, however, the ideal of the good becomes real in actually existing institutions: the family and the economic community, which are called by Hegel the civil society and the State.

The Sphere of Ethics

The concrete identity of the particular and the universal will is brought about in the sphere of ethics. The identity, being *concrete*, still contains a particular and a universal aspect, but

the two no longer exclude each other. Only in the ethical sphere
are the particular and the universal identical with each other
while, at the same time, they preserve their proper character, as
right and duty always do. It is this identity in opposition which
allows us to define the ethical universal as duty, and the particular as right. In the sphere of abstract *right,* right and duty in
the full sense did not exist, for they could not be distinguished:
a juridical right is, at the same time and in the same respect, a
juridical duty. In ethics, on the contrary, the two terms have
fully developed their proper character and, at first, they may
look quite distinct: one is universal, the other particular. But, on
the ethical level, the universal always evokes the particular and
the particular the universal. "Duty is primarily a relation to
something which from my point of view is . . . absolutely universal." [17] But this universality would be purely extrinsic and
destroy the very basis of ethics, the identity of the particular and
the universal, if the relation to the universal were not paralleled
by a relation in which the universal is "embodied" in a particular way. And this is the ethical right which, in Hegel's terminology, "enshrines my particular freedom." For each relation of
duty, then, there is a relation of right, but one is by no means
the same as the other, as was the case in abstract right.

Nor does the correlation of right and duty exclude the possibility that one may be more emphasized than the other. In the
first moment of ethics, the *family,* the accent is on duty. Ethics
here is present in the form of *natural* love of the members of the
family for each other—not as conscious striving for the ends of
reason. When the individual has grown up and the family no
longer takes care of him, he is received into *civil society.* More
than the family, where each one is mindful primarily of his
duty, society emphasizes the relation of *right.* Finally, in the
State, the synthetic moment of ethics, the accent will be on the
identity of both right and duty.

[17] *R.,* 261.

"In the State, as something ethical, as the interpenetration of the substantive and the particular, my obligation to what is substantive is at the same time the embodiment of my particular freedom. This means that in the State duty and right are united in one and the same relation." [18]

In the *Philosophy of Right,* Hegel defines the State as *the reality of the ethical Idea.*[19] This definition was foreshadowed in the *System of Ethics* by his description of absolute ethics as the particular consciousness which in the people elevates itself to universality. In the State, freedom reaches its full concreteness and the particular will becomes universal. As we saw earlier, Hegel often expresses the same idea by saying that in the State the will becomes *substantial will.* Substance is that which has its foundation in itself and which is, therefore, self-sufficient. With respect to the will, it refers to an end, the realization of which is not contingent upon a free choice, but which, because of its rational character, *imposes itself* on a rational will. Once it has realized this end, and thereby actualized the potential of it own rational nature, the will may be called *substantial* or fully rational. The term *substantial* is often equated with *universal* in this part of Hegel's philosophy, because universality is the first (but not the only) characteristic of the rational.[20] "The State, as the actuality of the substantial *will*—an actuality which it has through the particular self-consciousness when elevated onto a universal level—is that which is in and for itself *rational.*" [21] Only in the State can man be fully free.

Family and civil society are preparatory moments in a development which has not yet reached completion. Full spiritual freedom can exist only in the State, where the universal and particular ends are identified. Still, this freedom is already un-

---

[18] *R.,* 261.   [19] *R.,* 257.
[20] For the meaning of "substance" in the *Philosophy of Right,* see Franz Grégoire, *Etudes hégéliennes* (Louvain, 1958), pp. 228–38.
[21] *R.,* 258; tr. by J. M. Sterrett in *The Philosophy of Hegel* (ed. by Carl J. Friedrich, New York, 1954), p. 281. "In and for itself rational" means fully, concretely rational in both its substantial (in itself) and its subjective (for itself) aspects.

consciously at work in the lower spheres. In the family it is hidden under instinctive love, in the civil society under particular needs.

It is precisely from the ethical totality by which they are connected with the State that these spheres receive their proper meaning. This implies that their true reality can be understood only from within the State, but it also implies that the State, as completion of the ethical totality, depends on the preceding moments for the achievement of its own spiritual goals.

Undoubtedly, the subordination of the lower spheres to the State is sometimes experienced as a compulsory subjection to nonindividual and, therefore, "foreign" aims. Yet, this aspect of opposition is secondary, for both family and civil society have their immanent, ultimate end in the State. They exist only as moments of the Idea which is fulfilled in the concrete universality of the State. Their subordination is their very existence. All the strength of the State "lies in the unity of its own universal end and aim with the particular interest of individuals." [22]

To realize its universal end on a level where man has eyes only for his particular interests, the Idea uses a trick (*List der Vernunft*). The universal presents itself in such a way that family and civil society see in it merely a protection of their particular interests. To assure his own profits, the individual has recourse to a community which transcends his particular interests. Thus, in pursuing his particular ends, the individual is unconsciously brought to the ends of the Idea. However, in this reliance on the State institutions, man realizes the universal only through its particular aspect: the satisfaction of his needs. Even if he devotes himself to some occupation directed to the common good, he nevertheless uses it primarily as a means for his personal subsistence.

Only when the individual becomes aware of his substantial being-a-person, that is of the universal spiritual will, does he reach the pure ethical consciousness.

[22] *R.*, 261.

"This substantial unity is an absolute, unchanging end-in-itself (*Selbstzweck*) in which freedom gains its supreme right." [23] Such freedom, therefore, is not a hypothetical goal of the individual, but his own spiritual essence. "It is the absolute end of reason that freedom be real." [24] As long as the individual has not identified himself with the concrete universality of his spiritual nature as it is realized in the State, he has not become a *person* in the full sense of the word. The State, therefore, is not a mere means that one takes or leaves; as concrete freedom, it is the end of the individual who, as spiritual being, is to develop himself universally and to become free.

Irreconcilable with this conception is the standpoint of the natural right school, which subordinates the State to the needs of individuals. Such a theory mistakes the limited goals of the individual for the highest realization of human freedom. But, far from culminating in the arbitrariness of the individual, true freedom is absolute necessity. The State, therefore, is not a *means* allowing the individual (or the greatest possible number of individuals) to pursue his private goals—it is the highest *end* of the individual as such. It is not the individual, but the person, who is the ultimate end of freedom, and the latter is realized only in the State.

The subordination of the individual to the State does not mean that man is simply a means to serve the purposes of a superhuman organization. No human value is sacrificed to the State. In numerous passages, Hegel defines religion and philosophy as absolute ends to which politics in all its aspects is subordinate.[25] What the individual sacrifices to the State is merely arbitrariness; what he gains is humanity. The State is an *end* for the *individual,* but a means for man. Professor Franz Grégoire therefore concludes that State and individual are both end and means for each other.

[23] *R.,* 258; Sterrett, p. 281.
[24] *R.,* 258; Sterrett, pp. 282–83.
[25] Cf. Grégoire, "L'Etat et la vie spirituelle de l'homme," *Tijdschrift voor Philosophie* (1947), pp. 637–60.

State and individual are partial ends for each other in different domains or in different parts of the same domain. . . . As Hegel himself points out several times, he conceives the various storeys of his dialectical architecture as elements of an organism. But Hegel takes over Kant's idea of organism; a whole of which the parts are for each other at once means and ends.[26]

One could summarize Hegel's concept by saying that in his contingency the individual is a means for the State. With respect to his personality, however, which finds its fulfillment in art, religion, and philosophy, the State is a means for the individual. The State exists for the person—not the opposite. Hegel explicitly states in his *Philosophy of Right:* "Even the State, laws, and duties are in their actuality something determinate which refers to a higher sphere as to its foundation." [27] But one must not forget thereby that even the highest realizations of the Spirit have an external aspect, by which they belong to the juridical order and fall under the State's authority. The State, then, gives access to the highest personal values without being itself the highest personal value.

The Structure of the State

The spiritual freedom of the State is no longer determined by the *extrinsic* laws of economic needs but exclusively by the *inner* self-development of the Idea.[28] It is precisely this organic-spiritual conception which makes Hegel's State different from that of his predecessors in political philosophy, for whom the State was merely static. The only philosopher to admit evolution as a vital element in political institutions was Montesquieu. But even his theory lacked the idea of an organic unit develop-

26 Grégoire, "Hegel et la divinité de l'Etat," in *Actes du IIIe Congrès des Sociétés de Philosophie de Langue française* (Louvain, 1947), pp. 250–56.
27 R., 270 (my translation). See also *Enc.,* 453.
28 R., 267.

ing *in and through itself,* for the evolution was determined entirely by external factors.

The organic structure of the State is manifest in its external organization. Because of the spiritual nature of the political organism, "each moment taken by itself is at the same time the totality," contrary to the parts of a material organism where each part excludes all the others.[29] Each new ramification of the political structure modifies the totality.

As we learned in the previous section, Hegel's notion passes through three stages: the *universal* as the identity with itself, the *particular* as the determination, and the *individual* as the reality which is determined and identical with itself.[30] Since the State is Idea, its structure shows the same articulation. The universal moment is represented by the legislative power, the particularization of the universal by the executive power, and the synthesis of both, as individual reality, by the constitutional monarchy.[31] But one must never forget that the three moments are not to be separated from each other.

The democratic (universal), aristocratic (particular), and monarchic (individual) elements of the State, then, always appear together, and each of these moments considered separately also contains the two others. The *individual* decision of the monarch, for instance, presupposes the existence of *universally* approved laws and of *particular* organisms to enforce its execution. But the proper element of the monarchy is the ultimate, individual decision.

Since the State is the supreme synthesis of the Objective Spirit, that is of the substantial *will,* its ultimate moment must be pure self-determination. And since the sovereignty of the State becomes fully concrete only in its individual moment, this self-determination becomes the decision of an individual person. "Hence this absolutely decisive moment of the whole is not individuality in general, but a single individual, the monarch."[32]

29 *Enc.,* 160.
30 *Enc.,* 163.

31 *R.,* 273.
32 *R.,* 279.

Thus, the State-Idea in the final moment of its development becomes a not-further-justifiable *"Sic volo"* (This is my decision) .

Such a purely subjective decision as final synthesis of the Objective Spirit is quite startling. To understand it, one must consider that the State is merely the objective stage of a Spirit which, as absolute, must return to its own subjectivity after it has completed its objective process. Nothing then is more in order than pure subjectivity when the subject has posited itself as object and is ready to reintegrate this entire objectivity into itself. Hegel's description of this final moment as an "abstract and therefore groundless self-determination of the will" does not mean that the end of freedom's development is identical with its abstract and arbitrary beginning.[33] It means that the objective realization of freedom concludes in a moment which, *in its own way,* corresponds to the merely abstract arbitrariness of the beginning—a mere "I will" without any further justification. Between pure arbitrariness and the highest synthesis of ethics lies the whole evolution toward rational freedom. The monarch's decision is the Spirit's subjectivity which, after it has passed through all the moments of objectivity, returns to itself objectified. Precisely because it has absorbed the whole objectivity, this subjective moment is at once itself and the apex of the Objective Spirit. In this sense, Hegel can say: "sovereignty . . . comes into existence only as subjectivity sure of itself." [34]

As highest synthesis of the Objective Spirit, the monarchy is sharply opposed to the civil society. The latter is within the sphere of the understanding, the former within that of reason. They are brought together in the Idea of the State by two intermediate moments, the executive and the legislative powers.

The executive power constitutes a first mediation. Via the civil service, the universal descends to the sphere of particular interests, and penetrates into every branch of civil society, in order to integrate it in the universality of the State.[35]

On the side of the civil society, there is a similar advance toward the State. In following their particular interests, individuals form societies to protect their common interests within the same profession or trade: the corporations. Although founded exclusively on self-interest, these societies pave the way to the universality of the State. To achieve their purpose, they must have recourse to a universal legislation which recognizes and protects them with respect to other communities of interest. Thus the particular interests of the civil society require a universal social order, and through the corporations the citizens first become aware that the interests of the State are their own.[36] The corporations, therefore, constitute a mediation between civil society and State, similar to that of the executive power.

The Legislature

However, the mediating advances of the executive power and the corporations also require an *official* meeting ground. This is provided by the legislature. It is difficult to delineate the function of the legislature sharply from that of the constitution and the executive power. The legislature exists only by grace of a constitution which makes its decisions binding. But the constitution presupposes a legislative power to compose it and to amend it later if this would be necessary. Hegel solves the problem as follows:

> The legislature is concerned (*a*) with the laws as such insofar as they require fresh and extended determination; and (*b*) with the content of home affairs affecting the entire State.
> The legislature is itself a part of the constitution which is presupposed by it and to that extent lies absolutely outside

the sphere directly determined by it; nonetheless, the constitution becomes progressively more mature in the course of the further elaboration of the laws and the advancing character of the universal business of government.[37]

The legislature, then, is the dynamic part of the constitution and thus protects it against stagnation. As to the distinction between the legislative and executive, Hegel says that the former is concerned with the "wholly universal," while the latter deals with "the particular and the mode of execution." [38] The vagueness of this distinction is, in Hegel's opinion, compensated for by the fact that the various powers are not opposed to each other, but are moments of an organic unity in which it is "one single mind which both establishes the universal and also brings it into its determinate actuality and carries it out." [39]

Of primary importance in the legislature is the representation of the Estates, because in them the universality of the State enters into the empirical consciousness of the people. Were it not for the Estates, the State would be universal *in itself,* without being *for itself.* The Estates lead the empirical consciousness of the people beyond the sphere of private interests into the universality of the State.

The Estates mediate between the people—an inorganic conglomeration of particular interests—and the government—representing the universal. They prevent the isolation of the particular interests by elevating them to the sphere of the common good. The Estates must unite the qualities of both extremes and be devoted to the common as well as the particular interests. "Their function requires them to possess a political and administrative sense and temper, no less than a sense for the interests of individuals and particular groups." [40]

Just as the executive power, representing the universal in the particular sphere, mediates between *State* and civil society, the Estates, as representatives of the particular interests *within*

37 *R.,* 298.   39 *R.,* 299.
38 *R.,* 299.   40 *R.,* 302.

the sphere of the universal, mediate between the *civil society* and the State. The particular interests have alrealy organized themselves into social and economic groups within the civil society. The composition of the Estates reflects these organizations on a political level. The groups through which the civil society satisfies its needs and the Estates of the legislature are the *same* reality on two different levels (the German uses the same word, *Stände,* for both) . If the State failed to give the existing social structures political status, it would pose itself as a new reality beside and against civil society, whereas in fact the State *is* the final synthesis of those structures.

Yet, insofar as they represent the multiplicity of civil society on the political level, the Estates remain opposed to the pure unity of the monarchic principle. To bring the two opposite moments together, new mediators are needed from each side. The executive power mediates the monarch's decision with the people. And on the other side, the hereditary class of landowners within the Estates mediates the fluctuating element of the representatives of social-economic groups with the monarchy. Since its members attain their position by birth and are therefore less dependent than other classes on social and economic changes, this class is especially fitted to unite particular and universal interests. The landowner's class in one respect "reflects the moment of the monarchical power and in other respects shares the needs and rights of the other extreme," [41] i.e. of the civil society.

Hegel here introduces property, a category of private right, as a determinant political factor. This raises the problem of the relation between abstract right and State. It is obvious that property could have no political significance whatever if the spheres of private and civil right were entirely separated. Hegel's position rests on the intimate connection which his philosophy makes between the two spheres.

Right is a moment of the Idea. It therefore can never be *exclusively* positive, a mere product of climate, geography, and

[41] *R.,* 307 (my translation) .

economic factors, as the historical school of Herder and Adelung claimed. Nor is right ever *purely* customary, without rational content. "Since it is only animals which have their law as instinct, while it is man alone who has law as custom, even systems of customary law contain the moment of being thoughts and being known." [42] A juridical system becomes more perfect as it becomes more rational. Since only the State can make right universal and rational, "right" which is not founded in the State is *purely positive* and basically incomplete. The rational character of right by no means excludes positivity. The very essence of the juridical order requires that its ultimate determinations be positive and not *a priori* deducible. That is, at a certain point the rational must translate itself in purely positive determinations. This is particularly true in the case of criminal law. No one can determine on purely rational grounds whether a criminal should be sentenced to ten rather than nine years of imprisonment. Yet, this does not make the sentence arbitrary. Positivity becomes arbitrariness only when it *conflicts* with the rational.

A Comparison of Hegel's *Philosophy of Right* with the *Phenomenology*

Hegel's approach to reality in the *Philosophy of Right* differs considerably from that in the *Phenomenology*. Since Marx's early criticism will concentrate mainly on the discrepancy between the dialectical method as it first appears in the *Phenomenology* and its application in the later works, it will be useful to institute a critical comparison between the two.

In the *Phenomenology*, moments are stages in the evolution of consciousness. The *Phenomenology* concludes with the abso-

[42] *R.,* 211.

lute identity of thought and reality. It is with this identity that Hegel's System [43] (of which the *Philosophy of Right* is a part) starts. In it, Hegel *absolutizes* the moments through which consciousness develops itself in the *Phenomenology*. Consciousness here has reached the level of philosophy; it has become the science of the absolute. This absolute science has no object outside itself—it is *thought* which has itself as object and which, therefore, is both subject and object. Philosophy no longer depends on extrinsic data, as phenomenology still did. The final stage of the *Phenomenology* interiorized any relation of thought to a relation *within* thought. Yet, the stages of the *Phenomenology* return in the System, for every phenomenon was an appearance of an ideal reality, and, therefore, of the absolute. Hegel, therefore, reviews once more the moments of the *Phenomenology*. But he now considers from the inside what, thus far, was examined only in its manifestations. The System deals with the reality of what in the phenomenal was present only as appearance.

However, this method raises considerable difficulties, for, although Hegel's System claims to be absolute and thereby beyond any *particular* standpoint, it nevertheless takes its content from the finite consciousness, which is merely on its way to the absolute. True, the preparatory stages of the *Phenomenology* were appearances of the absolute—but not more than appearances, and as such, basically distinct from the absolute itself (otherwise the distinction between the absolute notion and subjective consciousness loses all its meaning). Hegel's logical System, however, tends to identify the subjective consciousness of the absolute with the absolute itself.

In the *Logic*,[44] Hegel does not abandon the starting point of the *Phenomenology*—with its abstract immediacy

---

[43] A term encompassing all Hegel's works after the *Phenomenology*.
[44] Hegel's *Wissenschaft der Logik* was published in 1812–16—see *Sämtliche Werke* (ed. by G. Lasson, Leipzig, 1934), Vols. III–IV. It was translated as *Hegel's Science of Logic* (ed. by W. H. Johnston and L. G. Struthers, London, 1951).

of being—but instead of describing the development of subjective consciousness, he elevates the ideal determination of this consciousness, which still has to raise itself to truth, into metaphysical concepts. He does not sufficiently emphasize the distinction between subjective knowledge and its highest form, the reflection of the absolute notion.[45]

Because of the identity of the ideal and the real, Hegel is confident that reality can be *thought,* even in its most contingent, material elements. Instead of submitting itself to experience, Hegel's philosophy *constitutes* reality in "a formalization of speculative thought." [46] His philosophical deduction is not halted by the contingent: his dialectic deduces with equal confidence the purely empirical as well as the purely spiritual. Material reality is made into a moment of the Spirit, and thereby submitted to the dialectical necessity of the philosophy of the Spirit. The contingent is present in Hegel's philosophy, but it remains contingent only as long as it is not fully *thought* —at the end of the philosophical reflection it becomes merely another form of necessity.

One might object that the empirical appearance does not *coincide* with the necessary, logical notion: it is only its finite manifestation. But this distinction is irrelevant, since Hegel treats the empirical appearance with the same logical necessity as the notion. How else could he claim with such confidence that the notion manifests itself in *this* particular, and no other finite appearance? The evolution of history ultimately coincides with the development of the notion in the *Science of Logic* (*Wissenschaft der Logik,* 1812–16). It is precisely this illegitimate transition from logic to history which will make Hegel's political theory such an easy target for Marx's attacks. As one noted Marxist scholar puts it: "Hegel has attempted to justify juridical, political, and social institutions from a merely rational

[45] G. Lasson, in Hegel, *Encyclopädie der philosophischen Wissenschaften* (ed. by G. Lasson, Leipzig, 1923) , Introduction, p. xliv.
[46] J. Hyppolite, "La Conception hégelienne de l'Etat et sa critique par K. Marx," *Cahiers internationaux de sociologie,* II (1947) , 149.

standpoint, by identifying their empirical existence, the histori-cal evolution of right, with its logical development." [47]

The point of this criticism is not to deny philosophy the right to deal with concrete problems, such as the essence of the State or the meaning of history. As the science of the ultimate princi-ples, philosophy's task is to understand experience. But it never *produces* experience, any more than experience produces its own object. The unique and individual character of the purely em-pirical remains closed to philosophical inquiry. The philosopher is merely deceiving us when he claims to reach the individual as such, through his science. For the individual is open only to experience. Philosophy can make general considerations about the proposition "This is a man." It also can teach us *what* a man is and deduce from it that he must exist as an *in-dividual*, as a *this*. But to *this* particular individual, philosophy has no access. The dialectic of a historical reality, therefore, al-ways has a contingent aspect which escapes the internal necessity of the Idea.

The *Philosophy of Right* makes this illegitimate intrusion into the individual. In paragraph 279, Hegel writes about the monarchy: "This absolutely decisive moment of the whole is not *individuality* in general, but a single individual, the mon-arch." Philosophically he could deduce the individual charac-ter of the decision, but not this individuality as being realized only in one individual. This can no longer be defined in logical-universal categories.

Hegel has tried to get around the difficulty by making the phenomenal an *antithetic* moment in his dialectical notion. But this solution only raises a new difficulty, for the real issue is the necessity of the relation between the first and the second mo-ment. What evidence is there that the empirical description of the antithesis is really a particularization of what the thesis pro-poses in a universal and infinite way? Philosophical deduction and experience do not simply pass across into each other. Be-

[47] Auguste Cornu, *La Jeunesse de Karl Marx* (Paris, 1934), p. 250.

tween logical universality and individual appearance there is a hiatus which philosophy cannot ignore without being untrue both to itself and to experience.

In his philosophy of history, to which in the final analysis his philosophy of the State also belongs, Hegel has closed his eyes to the unexplainable, the irrational, and the merely contingent, of which world history largely consists. The result is not a philosophy of history, but a philosophy of the rational element in history. This would be perfectly legitimate if Hegel had not claimed that his philosophy explains history and historical institutions *in their totality.* But by making *all* of history rational, he has distorted the facts. As one critical commentator remarked: "The succession in time has its own, nonspeculative and nondialectical course: the rhythm of its evolution has nothing in common with the dialectical rhythm." [48]

Even where Hegel's description of the facts is correct, his philosophical method lacks consistency. For his description is presented as a conclusion of pure reflection, whereas in fact it has been obtained by way of empirical experience. "By a strange turn of fate, Hegel has committed the same mistake of which he accuses Schelling in his Introduction to the *Phenomenology.* He has not really *thought* his content but has merely taken it from without, and fitted it in a preformed schema." [49]

Moreover, by this insertion of historical contingent data, Hegel has made his notion intrinsically dependent on those data, and thereby fixed it on a particular historical moment of its dialectical development. This is particularly visible in the philosophy of the State, which seems to culminate in the Prussian State of 1821. In his effort to understand *what is,* Hegel has made the State-Idea dependent upon the empirical reality of his

[48] I. Iljin, *Die Philosophie Hegels als kontemplative Gotteslehre* (Berlin, 1947), pp. 331–38. To use the expression "nothing in common" seems too strong, for Iljin himself admits prior to the above quotation that Hegel's dialectic presents "the rationality of the rational in history."
[49] Hyppolite, II, 149.

day. [Instead of synthesizing the historical and the universal, Hegel's philosophy ends up being a strange mixture of both.] *Failed to achieve a true synthesis*

This criticism is not directed against the *Phenomenology*, which makes more allowances for the irrational element in his-tory. But with the passage of time, rational *logic* replaced the vital dialectic of Hegel's early work. *Life* stagnated in a logical *Idea*. With the vitality also disappeared the revolutionary element. Whereas the *Phenomenology* stresses the dialectical *struggle* of the Spirit, the later works emphasize the dialectical *reconciliation* of thought and reality. This evolution has been characterized as a transition from pantragism to panlogism. Such a description may be too simplistic, for the basis of this panlogistic conception—the identity of the ideal and the real—is already present in the earlier works, and the tragic current persists throughout his later System. It is precisely after the *Phenomenology* that Hegel will apply the dialectical schema more consistently, as somebody who knows that identity can arise *only* out of opposition. Nevertheless, the fact remains that the later works are more reconciliatory than the *Phenomenology*. This reconciliatory attitude forced Hegel more and more to subject his thought to existing reality [The Left Hegelians, who considered this a stagnation and a betrayal of the dialectical method, tried to bring Hegelianism back to its original, revolutionary vision. Their dialectic was ultimately a return to the *Phenomenology* and the earlier works.]

Hegel's later works were conservative.
Left Hegelians wanted an on-going dialectic.

3

The Formation of Marx's Philosophy

The Left Hegelians

The Young Hegelians of Berlin

In 1836 MARX entered the University of Berlin as a law student. Hegel had been teaching at the same University from 1818 until 1831, and most of the faculty had been converted to his philosophy by the time of Marx's arrival. The young student was immediately attracted by Kant and Fichte. Strangely enough, Hegel's philosophy, which one would have expected to be more in line with Marx's youthful romanticism, was firmly rejected after a short acquaintance. Nevertheless, he attended the lectures of Hegel's disciple, Gans, on the philosophy of right, and his academic record mentions him as "very industrious" (*ausgezeichnet fleissig*) in this course. Gans's interpretation of Hegel's theory of right was to have a profound influence on Marx's early philosophy. [It was in his classroom that Marx's attention was first drawn to the revolutionary aspect of the Hegelian dialectic—that no historical state of affairs can ever be considered final. Rather than freezing juridical institutions, dialectical philosophy must further their progress by its own dynamic character.]

Another of Marx's teachers, Savigny, held almost diametrically opposed views. According to him, the juridical order must be seen exclusively as the result of a historical process, not of a rational development. Consequently, the only possible progress in law comes from a better understanding of its historical sources in the past. A few years later Marx would take advantage of Savigny's nomination as a minister of Prussia to vent all his dislike for the theories of his school: in a penetrating article, Marx attacked the historical theory of Leo Hugo, the founder of the school. For Hugo, man's conduct seems to be rational only in the asocial state of nature, which he assumes to precede life in society. After the completion of the social contract and the subsequent creation of an artificial juridical order, his behavior to his fellow man is primarily determined by social convention. Juridical institutions, therefore, must be studied as positive historical facts which require no rational justification. According to Marx, such an unquestioning acceptance of the juridical order leads to extreme conservatism. To eliminate all reflection on the rationality of juridical institutions is to close off the path to social progress. "For the historical school, there was no more sense in enacting laws than in legislating the kind of fruit a tree is to bring forth. Like the ripe fruit of a tree, the necessary social measures will drop from the tree of history whenever the proper time will have come." [1] It is mainly because of these practical implications that Marx became violently opposed to the historical interpretation of right.

After only a few months in Berlin, Marx became overworked and went to live on the outskirts of the city. He used this forced vacation to write down his philosophical reflections in a dialogue, *Cleanthes, or the Starting Point and Necessary Progress of Philosophy* (*Kleanthes, oder vom Ausgangspunkt und notwendigen Fortgang der Philosophie,* 1837.) In this particularly confused essay, Marx is struggling with the romantic problem of how to overcome the opposition between *what is* and *what ought to be.* Until then, he had had little sympathy for Hegel, but now his own conclusion turned out to be the very starting point of Hegel's philosophy: "What is rational is real, and what is real is rational." Marx then set himself to the reading of He-

[1] Sidney Hook, *From Hegel to Marx* (Ann Arbor, 1962) , p. 137.

gel's complete works and gradually reached the conviction that the path of all true philosophy leads through Hegel. To discuss his problems, he joined the Berlin club of Young Hegelians.

The Young Hegelian movement had originated in the polemics over David Strauss's *A Critical Study of the Life of Jesus* (*Leben Jesu kritisch bearbeitet*, 1835). This work criticized Hegel's concept of religion on some basic points. For Hegel, the content of religion and philosophy are identical, but where philosophy proposes the truth in the pure form of *reason*, religion expresses it in *sensible representation*. The identification of religion with philosophy favors the theoretical content of religion at the expense of its historical form. Against this thesis, Strauss maintained that religious dogmas are irreducible to philosophical concepts, and that, far from being irrelevant, the Gospel narratives form the main content of the Christian religion. These narratives, like all religious doctrines, must be considered not as symbols of rational thought or as historical reports, but as *myths* expressing the aspirations of the original Christian community. Only a historical study of this community can lead to an understanding of the Christian myths. This implies not that the sacred writings are devoid of truth, but only that their truth is neither historical nor symbolic; it is mythical.

Strauss's work preserved the fundamental Hegelian idea of the validity of religious truth, but it destroyed Hegel's ultimate identification of religion with philosophy, as well as the identity of the logical and the historical evolution of truth. Furthermore, by maintaining that the fundamental truth of Christianity is the identity of divine with human nature and that this is realized not in just one exemplar (Christ), but in humanity as a whole, Strauss not only parted from Hegel but definitely divorced his brand of Hegelianism from Christian orthodoxy.

Among the many writers who attacked Strauss, the most noteworthy was Bruno Bauer, who later was to be converted to an even more radical liberalism, denying that the Gospels contained *any* historical truth. In the controversies around Strauss's *Leben Jesu*, the Hegelian school became divided into a right wing which considered the unity of God and man to be realized in a unique and historical way, and a left wing led by Strauss which denied the historical and unique value of the Gospel narratives. Strauss's supporters in Berlin organized themselves in the Young Hegelian movement.

For the Young Hegelians, Hegel's dialectic was the clue to the understanding of reality, but Hegel himself, because of his political and religious conservatism, had refused to accept its revolutionary implications. His philosophy had become an instrument for the preservation of the Prussian monarchy and the established Lutheran Church. The Young Hegelians' attempt to restore the dynamic force to the dialectic soon gave their movement an anti-Christian and antimonarchic character.

In the first chapter of *Ludwig Feuerbach and the End of Classical German Philosophy* (*Ludwig Feuerbach und der Ausgang der klassischen deutschen Philosophie,* 1888), Engels makes a thorough analysis of this development to the left. According to him, the primary cause of the post-Hegelian evolution is the opposition between Hegel's method and system. It is essential to the dialectical method to develop infinitely and not to halt at any particular moment. But Hegel used this method for the construction of a self-contained, complete system.

> In accordance with traditional requirements, a system of philosophy must conclude with some sort of absolute truth. Therefore, however much Hegel, especially in his *Logic,* emphasized that this eternal truth is nothing but the logical, that is the historical process itself, he nevertheless finds himself compelled to supply this process with an end, just because he has to bring his system to a termination [at] some point or other.[2]

Conscious of this opposition between method and system, the Young Hegelians tried to free the dialectical method from the

[2] *Werke,* XXI, 268, translated in Marx and Engels, *Selected Works* (Moscow, 1950), II, 329. *Werke* will appear frequently as a reference; for the facts of publication, see Introduction.

system and thus restore to philosophy its original revolutionary force. They insisted that no dialectical synthesis can ever be final, and that negation is the dynamic force of the dialectical movement. Philosophy, therefore, must be critical rather than conservative. Under the ultraconservative and more-than-orthodox regime of Frederick William IV, religion and politics were bound to be the main targets of this critical philosophy. But because of the increasingly severe censorship, most of the Young Hegelian publications left the political regime untouched and, instead criticized religion. Besides, the religious issue was, from the Young Hegelians' idealistic point of view, the more important: political reforms would necessarily follow the spiritual revolution. This religious critique brought the group in contact with English-French materialism, at that time the only existing form of belligerent atheism. Yet their idealism was somewhat embarrassed by these materialistic affiliations.

The Hallische Jahrbücher *and Ludwig Feuerbach*

New events were to put a political stamp on Young Hegelianism. In 1838 two Young Hegelians of the University of Halle, Arnold Ruge and Theodor Echtermeyer, started a critical review for arts and sciences, the *Hallische Jahrbücher für Wissenschaft und Kunst.* Originally the new journal had a purely literary character. But a contribution by Ludwig Feuerbach gave it a more practical and controversial tinge. In an article entitled "Toward a Critique of Hegel's Philosophy" ("Zur Kritik der Hegelschen Philosophie," 1839), Feuerbach showed that besides the contradiction between system and method, Hegel's philosophy suffers from another evil which affects the dialectical method itself.

Hegel simply assumes that ideality and reality are identical. Instead of being proven at the end of the system, as Hegel promises us in the beginning, this initial assumption remains the sole basis of the very system which is supposed to prove its validity.]Moreover, the assumption is biased in favor of thought, so that the identification of the ideal and the real simply eliminates reality. Indeed, Hegel's *Logic* pretends to start with a pure being which is without any presuppositions whatever.[But *being* without any determination is not real, for the real is always determinate being.] Pure being is, in fact, pure thought. And yet, Hegel treats this merely ideal being as if it were real. He fails to see that his starting point must be mediated to its true antithesis, reality, if his system is ultimately to effect an identity between the ideal and real. The first antithesis of pure thought is sense perception, by which alone consciousness has access to reality. But rather than contrasting pure being with sense perception, Hegel contrasts it with pure nothingness, which is merely another form of pure thought (and an impossible one at that) [The real opposition is not the one between pure being and pure nothingness; it is the one between being as object of thought and being as object of sensuous intuition. These are the two which must be proven to be identical. Hegel, however, never considers sense experience on its own terms. Instead, he dismisses the opposition between sensation and thought as an opposition *within* thought. Rather than considering sense experience as the other-than-thought, Hegel reduces it to a *thought* of the other-than-thought (which is, obviously, still a form of thought).]

> But precisely because Hegel has not really taken the side of the sense experience and has never thought himself into it, because the only objectivity of sense experience (for him) is to be an object of self-consciousness—of thought, because it is merely the exteriorization of thought *within* its own self-certainty—for these reasons the *Phenomenology* (or the *Logic,* since they amount to the same thing) starts with an immediate presupposition of its own conclusion and, consequently, with an unmediated opposition, with a complete severance from sense experience.[3]

[3] Ludwig Feuerbach, "Zur Kritik der Hegelschen Philosophie," in *Sämtliche Werke* (ed. by W. Bolin and F. Jodl, Stuttgart, 1959), II, 187.

For Feuerbach, philosophy is philosophy of *nature*.

> Philosophy is the science of reality in its truth and totality. But the sum total of reality is *nature* (nature in the most universal sense of the word). The most profound mysteries are hidden in the simplest natural things which the speculative philosopher, always aspiring to the beyond, tramples with his feet. The return to nature is the only source of salvation.[4]

A philosophy of nature must be based on sense experience, in which alone nature and consciousness meet. Man has no access to any mysteries beyond sense experience. Even to assume that there are such mysteries is to overstep the boundaries set to the mind in its pursuit of truth. Consciousness is nothing but man's instrument to communicate with nature. When used for this purpose, man's powers for knowing are unlimited. But when philosophy pretends to have a higher object than man's relation to nature, it becomes sheer illusion.

The publication of Feuerbach's article was a milestone in the development of the Young Hegelian movement. The Young Hegelians had been unable to decide between the two extremes of materialism (which seemed to follow from their atheism) and idealism (which was implied by the dialectical method). A materialism which submits all reality to mechanical laws is incompatible with the dialectical method. Yet, this rejection of mechanistic materialism does not necessarily tie the dialectical method to Hegel's idealism. Feuerbach's approach showed them a way of reconciling these extremes. Dialectical philosophy avoids idealism by starting from human reality rather than from an ideal Spirit; it avoids materialism by taking as its initial principle not the finite material world but the concrete nature of man, which is both spiritual and material, finite and infinite. Man, according to Feuerbach, has all the determinations of Hegel's notion—he is an absolute—but, unlike Hegel's notion, he is a *concrete* absolute.

[4] "Kritik," p. 203.

In Feuerbach's clear and incisive thought Young Hegelianism reached maturity. The editors of the *Jahrbücher* found in it a stimulus for practical action. Ruge, who had dispensed with the collaboration of the more conservative Echtermeyer, took the lead in carrying it out. In an article entitled "Karl Streckfuss and Prussianism" ("Karl Streckfuss und das Preussentum," 1839) he openly attacked the political conservatism of the Prussian State. It is unnecessary for our purposes to discuss Ruge's ideas— he was an erudite but not very original thinker, and he is important more for the political cast he gave to Left Hegelianism than for his philosophical insights.[5]

The Berlin group, in spite of their more orthodox Hegelianism, accepted the progressive ideas of their Hallean colleagues, and started contributing to the *Jahrbücher*. Yet, there would always remain a distinction between the speculative group at Berlin and the more practical collaborators of Ruge. In accord with their belief that the work of philosophy must be completed before the world can be reformed, the Hegelians of Berlin were not overly concerned about concretizing their ideas.

Initially Marx shared these speculative views, but soon Ruge would convince him that the true critique of the established order lies in *action*. Unless philosophy is transformed into action, it will always turn into a conservative system. Speculative criticism necessarily trails behind the facts and thus contradicts the dialectical method. To Ruge, the fact that philosophy must have a practical bearing was obvious from the beginning.

> The academic laziness of the Old Hegelians has come to an end. *Practical action,* which brings everything forcefully to its own truth, which puts itself in the stern service of truth and introduces truth everywhere, constitutes a new system. . . . The more true philosophy is, the more it must oppose itself consciously to the dead spirit of the past.

5 On Ruge, see A. Cornu, *Karl Marx et Friedrich Engels* (Paris, 1955), I, 145–75 (this book is a two-volume revision of the author's doctoral dissertation, *La Jeunesse de Karl Marx* [Paris, 1934]) ; and Hook, pp. 126–64.

Against the past, philosophy always takes sides with the true present.[6]

Marx became so completely converted to Ruge's radicalism that he conceived the plan of founding an even more revolutionary journal. His doctoral dissertation in 1841, *On the Difference between the Democritean and the Epicurean Philosophy of Nature* (*Differenz der Demokritischen und Epikureischen Naturphilosophie*), is clearly in disagreement with the speculations of the Young Hegelians of Berlin. It implies that a theoretical critique of Hegel's conservatism is itself unprogressive. What is needed is for philosophy to *realize* itself and thereby to bring about its own downfall. "It is a psychological law that the free theoretical spirit becomes practical energy. . . . This implies that the philosophization of the world is also a secularization of philosophy, that its realization is at the same time its downfall, that what it fights in the outside world is its own internal deficiency." [7] However, it was to take Marx several more years fully to understand how the realization of philosophy is also its negation. Not until the *Introduction to the Critique of Hegel's Philosophy of Right* will he state clearly that the end of philosophy is *revolution,* and that in the revolution philosophy itself disappears.

Marx and the Rheinische Zeitung

In 1842, Marx took an editorial position on the *Rheinische Zeitung,* a newly founded revolutionary newspaper. This journalistic experience would make him acquainted with the social abuses of his day, and would give his thought a social orienta-

---

[6] Arnold Ruge and Theodor Echtermeyer, "Protestantismus und Romantismus," *Hallische Jahrbücher* (March 2, 1840), pp. 417–18.
[7] *MEGA,* I¹, 64. *MEGA* will appear frequently as a reference; for the facts of publication, see Introduction.

tion. Within a few weeks Marx was able to push the relatively radical Rutenberg into the position of editor in chief then held by the conservative Höfken. Marx's own contributions remained insignificant until May, 1842. At that time he published a series of articles on the freedom of the press, which show the influence of Gans's dynamic concept of law. The law, as a conscious expression of human freedom, must never curtail man's basic right of independence. Legal restrictions are justifiable only when a person by criminal action has shown that he rejects the concept of rational freedom itself.

> When the law is really law, i.e. the concrete existence of freedom, it constitutes the real freedom of man. Laws cannot precede human activity, since they are precisely the internal laws of that activity, the conscious reflections of man's life. Consequently, the law must yield to human life as the life of freedom. Only when a man has shown by concrete action that he no longer hearkens to the natural law of freedom, does it, as State law, force him to be free.[8]

In October, 1842, Marx became editor in chief of the *Rheinische Zeitung,* and under his direction the paper took an even more radical turn until it was finally suppressed by the State Censor in the beginning of 1843. A second series of articles, written during this period, deals with the debates of the Sixth Rhenish Diet on the punishment of wood thieves. Due to the increasing poverty of the rural population, cases of wood theft had steadily increased. The Diet, in which rich landowners held all the power, wanted to sharpen the already severe penalties for this misdemeanor. Marx sensed that there was more injustice in these penalties than is disclosed in a merely juridical consideration, but being unable as yet to cope with the social implications of the problem, he did not go beyond the juridical argument that crime and punishment should be proportionate to each other. Nor did his vehement criticism of property rights

8 *MEGA*, I¹, 210.

lead him to Communism. This appears clearly from an article in the *Rheinische Zeitung* of October 16, 1842, "Communism and the *Augsburger Allgemeine Zeitung,*" in which he defends his newspaper against the *Augsburger Allgemeine*'s accusation of Communist agitation. Not the progressiveness of the *Rheinische Zeitung,* he claims, but the ultraconservative ideas of the *Augsburger Allgemeine* clears the way for Communism. Marx does not want to reject Communism, but he feels insufficiently prepared to discuss the problem at this point. "The writings of Leroux, Considérant, and especially the penetrating work of Proudhon are not to be criticized by the superficial brain waves of the moment, but only after long and thorough study." [9]

Communism was indeed a much discussed topic in France. In 1840, Proudhon had published his book *What Is Property?,* which became the Magna Charta of all later Communism. Proudhon considered private property to be theft, for it forces the laborer to surrender the greatest part of a product which he alone has manufactured to a capitalist who has no right to it. However, Proudhon wanted to preserve a right of possession, consisting in the private use of goods which are not augmented by other people's labor. The distinction between private property and right of possession is rather subtle, since Proudhon neither advocates the abrogation of capitalism as such nor excludes production goods from the right of possession. Proudhon considers his system to be the final synthesis in a historical evo-

---

[9] *MEGA,* I¹, 263. In the Preface of his *Contribution to the Critique of Political Economy,* Marx summarizes his attitude during the *Rheinische Zeitung* period as follows:

> At that time when the good will to go further greatly outweighed knowledge of the subject, a philosophically weakly tinged echo of French Socialism and Communism made itself audible in the *Rheinische Zeitung.* I declared myself against this amateurism, but frankly confessed at the same time in a controversy with the *Allgemeine Augsburger Zeitung* that my studies did not permit me even to venture any judgment on the content of the French tendencies.

(*MEGA,* I¹, li; translated in *Selected Works,* I, 328) .

lution of the right of possession, which started with Communism (thesis), then became private property (antithesis), and in a future stage will reconcile the two previous moments in what he calls the epoch of freedom.

Marx's friend and coeditor on the *Rheinische Zeitung,* Moses Hess, had received Proudhon's book with great enthusiasm as being the first dialectical study on Communism. Hess himself, one of the first German Communists, had always attempted to put his ideas into a neo-Hegelian framework. Proudhon's work taught him that the system of private property constituted the true *alienation* of man. He suspected that Feuerbach's theory of religious alienation (which we will discuss in the next section) did not go to the heart of the matter, and that Feuerbach's humanism was to be complemented by social-economic considerations. Yet, the final synthesis of Communism with Hegelian dialectic was to be made not by Hess but by Marx, and under the influence not of Proudhon but of Feuerbach. However, Marx himself would never have become interested in social philosophy without the influence of Proudhon, Hess, and especially Lorenz Stein.

It is probably through the study of Stein's *Socialism and Communism in Contemporary France (Sozialismus und Communismus des heutigen Frankreichs,* 1842) that Marx first realized the full import of Proudhon's ideas. Stein's work, although written from a conservative point of view, reveals an amazing insight into the origin and essence of Communism. It brings into organic synthesis and sharp expression thoughts more or less confusedly enunciated by several French authors. Stein's basic intuition is that the State depends on the economic structure of society. The modern State is the political framework of a society based on private property. An efficient reform, therefore, must be social and economic, rather than political. Capitalization is the cause of all social and political abuses, for it always produces a proletariat, "the class of those who have neither education nor property as basis for their significance in society, and yet who feel called upon not to remain completely deprived of those goods which constitute the personal value of man." [10] Stein is convinced that private property is indispensable for the free development of man, but social reforms are urgently needed if an imminent crisis is to be avoided. During the French Revolution, the proletariat became aware of its power and ever since it had been trying, through socialistic and communistic movements, to overthrow the whole established social order.

Marx must have read Stein's work shortly after it came out, for it immediately received a favorable review in his own newspaper and it dealt with the sort of social problems which occupied his mind at that time. Stein's work convinced him that the roots of political life are in the social-economic order. Henceforth, his critique of the State would be done from a social, rather than a political, point of view. Stein also provided Marx with the important notion of the proletariat, which was to become central in his revolutionary theory. Finally, Stein's book led Marx to a deeper understanding of French Communism. In 1843, he founded the *German-French Yearbooks* to promote contact with French revolutionary elements. Yet even then, Marx did not openly declare himself for Communism. He restricted his discussion to a sharp, negative criticism of private property, in which he saw, as did the Communists, the cause of all social and political evil. In his *Critique of Hegel's Philosophy of the State,* his arguments against private property and its political superstructure became so devastating that, to remain consistent with himself, he could no longer escape Communism. However, the decisive step was not to be made before the *Economic and Philosophic Manuscripts.* At this time Marx was still seeking a philosophical foundation for his social theories. He was to find it in Feuerbach's *Provisional Theses for the Reform of Philosophy.*

[10] Lorenz Stein, *Sozialismus und Communismus des heutigen Frankreichs* (Leipzig, 1842), p. 7.

Feuerbach's Critique
of Hegel's Philosophy

The Essence of Christianity

In November, 1841, Feuerbach published *The Essence of Christianity (Das Wesen des Christentums)*. In the Preface to the second edition, he describes the significance of his work as follows:

> [It] contains nothing else than the principle of a new philosophy verified practically—i.e. *in concreto*, in application to a special object, but an object which has a universal significance: namely, to religion—in which this principle is exhibited, developed, and thoroughly carried out. This philosophy is essentially distinguished from the systems hitherto prevalent, in that it corresponds to the real, complete nature of man; but for that very reason it is antagonistic to minds perverted and crippled by a superhuman, i.e. anti-human, anti-natural religion and speculation. . . . This philosophy has for its principle, not the Substance of Spinoza, not the *ego* of Kant and Fichte, not the Absolute Identity of Schelling, not the Absolute Mind of Hegel, in short, no abstract, merely conceptional being, but a *real* being, the true *Ens realissimum*—man.[11]

Already in the "Critique of Hegel's Philosophy," Feuerbach had reached the conclusion that philosophy should become anthropology, that is, the science of man in his relation to nature. It is man himself, taken in the concrete environment of his physical nature, that is the first and ultimate reality for man. Whatever is not reducible to man has been estranged from him and will eventually be restored to him. In *The Essence of Christianity*, Feuerbach reached the further conclusion that, just as

---

[11] Feuerbach, *Das Wesen des Christentums*, in *Sämtliche Werke* (ed. by Bolin and Jodl), VII, 282–83; *The Essence of Christianity* (tr. by George Eliot, New York, 1957), pp. xxxiv–xxxv, by permission of Harper & Row, Publishers.

there is only one reality, there is only one *alienation* of this reality—religion.]

In Hegel's philosophy, alienation is the antithesis between the two first moments of the dialectical movement. From their dynamic opposition will eventually arise the synthesis as a provisional reconciliation, which in turn will give birth to a new negation. Feuerbach accepts the concept of alienation along with the dialectical method, but he applies it exclusively to man's relation to the supernatural. God is man's own alienated infinity projected into an imaginary world outside of man.

[Human nature must be infinite, since it has no other limits than the limits of consciousness, and consciousness is infinite.]

> Since to will, to feel, to think, are perfections, essences, realities, it is impossible that intellect, feeling, and will should feel or perceive themselves as limited, finite powers, i.e., as worthless, as nothing. For finiteness and nothingness are identical; finiteness is only a euphemism for nothingness. Finiteness is the metaphysical, the theoretical —nothingness the pathological, practical expression.[12]

For Feuerbach every being is sufficient to itself, and this implies that it is infinite to itself, that it is its own God. To think the infinite is to think oneself. In religion man alienates this consciousness of his own infinite nature.[13]

In answer to the question of why man attributes his own infinity to a being other than himself, Feuerbach points to the opposition between human nature in general and each man's limited individuality. All the attributes predicated of God are derived from man's own nature: there is only as much in God as there is in man. But if the divine attributes are predicates of human nature, their subject, God, must be human nature itself, since the subject contains not more than what is in its predicates. The individual, however, finds that the predicates of human nature apply to himself only in a limited way. To void the

---

12 *Wesen*, VI, 7; *Essence*, p. 6.
13 *Wesen*, VI, 15; *Essence*, p. 12. Needless to say, this argument is a blatant *petitio principii*.

humiliation of acknowledging that his limitations are strictly
his own, individual man projects his own limitation onto the
species and displaces the perfection of the species to a superhuman deity. He thus escapes personal humiliation, but only by
sacrificing the essential attributes of his own nature.

> If [man] makes his own limitations the limitations of the
> species, this arises from the mistake that he identifies him-
> self immediately with the species—a mistake which is inti-
> mately connected with the individual's love of ease, sloth,
> vanity, and egoism. For a limitation which I know to be
> merely mine humiliates, shames, and perturbs me. Hence
> to free myself from this feeling of shame, from this state of
> dissatisfaction, I convert the limits of my individuality into
> the limits of human nature in general.[14]

Thus man projects the consciousness of his own infinite nature
into the fictitious world of religion.

Yet, religion is not all negative. In the second edition of his
book, Feuerbach firmly rejects the accusation that for him religion is an absurdity and a pure illusion.[15] Rather, religion is
the earliest form of man's self-knowledge. It is "the childlike
condition of humanity," in which man first sees himself, but
thinks himself to be another. Insofar as it is the relation of man
to his own nature, religion is true. It is only in its failure to
recognize this nature as man's *own* that religion becomes false.
Without religion man would never have become aware of the
perfections of human nature. Moreover, Christianity's teaching
that God is love and that love is the highest virtue shows man
the way to unite himself with the source of all perfection, since
love is the bond which unites the individual with the human
species. "Love is the middle term, the substantial bond, the
principle of reconciliation between the perfect and the imperfect, the sinless and the sinful being, the universal and the individual, the divine and the human. Love is God himself, and

14 *Wesen*, VI, 8–9; *Essence*, p. 7.
15 *Wesen*, VII, 287. *Essence*, p. xxxviii.

apart from it there is no God. Love makes man God and God man." [16]

Unfortunately, in *faith* Christianity undoes what it has built up in *love*. Whereas love unites men, faith separates them into believers and nonbelievers. In the end it is always faith which gets the upper hand over love: through faith, love becomes Christian love, that is, love which loves only what is Christian. "The Christian must therefore love only Christians—others only as possible Christians; he must only love what faith hallows and blesses. Faith is the baptism of love. . . . The maxim 'Love your enemies' has reference only to personal enemies, not to public enemies, the enemies of God, the enemies of faith, unbelievers." [17]

Just as faith particularizes the love of one's fellow man, so it particularizes the love which is God, making of it one divine attribute among many. Faith transforms the God who is love into a loving person, and thereby destroys the identity of the divine and human nature which love had established. "Faith advances with its pretensions, and allows only just so much to Love as belongs to a predicate in the ordinary sense." [18] Love does away with the self-subsistence of God—faith maintains it. And faith is always the stronger of the two.

The task of anthropology is to awaken man to the truth of religion and to eliminate its falsity: to show that the consciousness of God is the consciousness of the species, and that what man adores is himself. The true view of man is the reverse of the religious view, since "that which in religion holds the first place—namely, God—is . . . in itself and according to truth, the second, for it is only the nature of man regarded objectively; and that which to religion is the second—namely, man—must therefore be constituted and declared the first." [19]

The Provisional Theses for the Reform of Philosophy

In the *Provisional Theses for the Reform of Philosophy* (*Vorläufige Thesen zur Reform der Philosophie*, 1843), Feuer-

---

[16] *Wesen*, VI, 59. *Essence*, p. 48.   [18] *Wesen*, VI, 319; *Essence*, p. 264.
[17] *Wesen*, VI, 305; *Essence*, p. 254.   [19] *Wesen*, VI, 326; *Essence*, pp. 270–71.

bach justifies and completes the anthropology of *The Essence of Christianity*. According to the *Theses,* Hegel's *Logic* is the last refuge, the last rational rampart, of theology. Hegel has converted philosophy into a pseudo-theology. His dialectic, going from the infinite to the finite and back to the infinite, only appropriates philosophy for the religious alienation of man. The concrete, living man is sacrificed to an idea: man is reduced to a mere moment in the evolution of a superhuman Spirit. Thus, Hegel's philosophy never gets beyond the alienated man.[20]

Hegel's Idea replaces God but fulfills exactly the same function. According to Feuerbach,

> Like the divine essence of theology, Logic is the ideal or abstract sum total of all realities, that is, of all determinations, of all finite beings. . . . The essence of theology is the transcendent, the estranged being of man. Similarly, the essence of Hegel's Logic is the transcendent, the thinking of man posited outside man.[21]

Hegel's philosophy contains the same mystification as theology. "Hegel's Absolute Spirit is nothing but the abstract, alienated, so-called finite spirit, just as the essence of theology is nothing but abstract, finite being." [22] His philosophy is abstract; it puts the essence of nature outside nature, the essence of man outside man, the essence of thought outside the act of thinking.

True, Hegel's philosophy affirms the identity of the finite and the infinite: the infinite is real only when it is determinate and therefore finite. But this mediation of the infinite through the finite is mere sleight of hand, for "if the infinite exists and has truth and reality only when it is posited as determinate, that is, not as infinite but as finite, then in fact the infinite is the finite." [23] Hegel vainly tries to reidentify what he has arbitrarily separated. His philosophy pretends to be the science of "what

[20] Feuerbach, *Vorläufige Thesen zur Reform der Philosophie,* in *Sämtliche Werke* (ed. by Bolin and Jodl) , II, 239.
[21] *Thesen,* II, 225–26.
[22] *Thesen,* II, 226.
[23] *Thesen,* II, 230.

is," but succeeds only in estranging *what really is*—the living man of flesh and blood—from himself in the Idea. "The immediate, clear, real identification of man with his own essence, which was estranged from him by abstraction, cannot be deduced from Hegel's philosophy in a positive way, but only as its *negation*. It can be understood and comprehended only as the complete suppression of speculative philosophy." [24] Feuerbach feels that the real science of man, anthropology, starts with an unphilosophical and unspeculative principle—sense experience.[25]

Hegel's philosophy annuls the opposition between thinking and being, "But it annuls the opposition only *within the opposition itself,* within one of the two elements—thought. Thinking for Hegel is being; thinking is the subject, being the predicate." [26] But in Feuerbach's view, "The true relation between thinking and being is where being is the subject and thinking, the predicate. Thinking results from being but being does not result from thinking." [27]

Feuerbach's anthropology reverses Hegel's dialectic. Hegel's second moment now becomes the first: the determination of the notion in its material appearance, rather than being an antithesis, becomes a positive starting point. Whereas for Hegel the final synthesis reintegrates the finite into the infinite, Feuerbach's synthesis reintegrates the infinite into the finite.

At the time when Feuerbach's *Theses* came out, Marx had been working for a whole year on the *Critique of Hegel's Philosophy of the State.* He intended to publish it in the *Anecdota Philosophica,* a collective work scheduled to appear in Switzerland and consisting mainly of articles that were censored from the *Yearbooks.* Apparently Marx's study had not made much progress, for as it has reached us the *Critique* betrays the strong influence of the *Theses.* These *Theses* seem to have supplied Marx with the definitive method for his critique of Hegel. Shortly after their publication, he wrote an enthusias-

24 *Thesen,* II, 237. 26 *Thesen,* II, 238.
25 *Thesen,* II, 235. 27 *Thesen,* II, 239.

tic letter to Ruge in which his only reservation was that Feuerbach "attaches too much importance to nature and not enough to politics." [28] In his own view, the realization of philosophy—the true liberation of man—is to be expected from political reforms rather than from religious critique. A few months later he wrote to Ruge: "Just as religion is the content of all theoretical struggles among men, so is the political State always the main issue of their practical struggles." [29] Under the influence of Stein and Hess, Marx considered the social liberation of man much more fundamental than the religious.

However, at first reading of the *Theses,* Marx did not fully realize how much opposed his own standpoint was to Feuerbach's. It was not until he had applied Feuerbach's method to the solution of social and political problems that Marx became conscious of the novelty of his own philosophy.

[28] *MEGA,* II¹, 308.   [29] *MEGA,* I¹, 574.

4

Marx's Critique of Hegel's Philosophy of the State

SHORTLY AFTER having read Feuerbach's *Theses*, Marx wrote the *Critique of Hegel's Philosophy of the State* (*Kritik des Hegelschen Staatsrechts*, 1843). The unfinished manuscript, which was first published in 1927, may have been preceded by an earlier version. Several months before the *Theses* came out Marx noted that he was working on a critique of Hegel's social theory. At any rate, the text which has reached us was, beyond any doubt, written under the direct impact of the *Theses*. In fact, it betrays so much of Feuerbach's influence that it has usually been dismissed as a mere application of the latter's principles on Hegel's political philosophy.

There is no point in denying this strong influence or the uncertainty of Marx's own social ideas at the time. Nevertheless, in our opinion, the *Critique* is one of the most important writings in the development of Marx's thought. In this first personal confrontation with Hegelianism, Marx decided to accept its method and to reject its content. This decision was to determine the entire future of Marxist philosophy.

Marx's Critique of Hegel's Logical Principles

An Exposition of Marx's Criticism

Hegel's *Philosophy of Right* is based upon the introductory statement: what is rational is real, and what is real is rational.

To a great extent Marx always agreed with that principle. But his interpretation of it differed considerably from Hegel's. Hegel's reality is ideal only insofar as it is a finite, empirical moment of an infinite Idea. According to Marx, this implies that Hegel subordinates reality to thought and that he obtains an identity between the ideal and the real by reducing reality to an appearance, a predicate, of the ideal. Marx, like Feuerbach, protests against this idealization and shows how it deprives the real of its own subsistence. Reality—and not the Idea—is primary. The ideal is in fact a predicate of reality, according to Marx, but in Hegel's philosophy this predicate has taken over the place of the subject. As appearance of an Idea, empirical reality is downgraded to a mere fiction. It stands "not for itself, but for another reality," [1] a logical reality. As Feuerbach had pointed out in his *Theses,* thought for Hegel is no longer an attribute of being; instead, being is an attribute of thought. In Hegel's theory of judgment, as Marx understands it, the real subject is enclosed in the universal predicate. Consequently, the subject becomes a predicate of the predicate—it evaporates into a mere attribute of thought.[2]

Applying this priority of the ideal over the real to political philosophy, Hegel concludes that since the State has a more rational structure than the natural social spheres of family and civil society, the latter owe their origin to the State: "The Idea sunders . . . itself into the two ideal spheres of its concept, family and civil society . . . as in its finitude." [3] The real process by

---

[1] *MEGA,* I¹, 406.

[2] For Marx, on the contrary, the subject of a judgment is a self-sufficient reality, and the predicate is nothing but an intellectual attribute, derived from the subject without adding anything to it. The two terms correspond to two different orders. The subject stands for the whole reality, the predicate is a mental attribute which originates from thinking *about* this reality.

[3] Hegel, *Grundlinien der Philosophie des Rechts,* in *Sämtliche Werke* (ed. by G. Lasson) , VI, 262. This work in the future will be referred to as *R.,* followed by the paragraph numbers, which are the same in all editions in both languages. Our translation is taken from T. M. Knox, *Hegel's Philosophy of Right* (Oxford, 1945) , by permission of the Clarendon Press, Oxford.

which these lower societies pass into the sphere of the State is only the external appearance of "a mediation which the Idea operates on itself and which happens entirely behind the scenes." [4] For Marx this is "logical, pantheistic mysticism," in which family and civil society as moments of a logical Idea lose their independent reality.

Contrary to Hegel's "logical" interpretation, says Marx, the State is the result, rather than the cause, of the social relations in the "lower" spheres. "The political State cannot exist without the natural basis of the family and the artificial basis of the civil society: they are its *conditio sine qua non*. Here, however, the condition is as the conditioned, the determining as the determined, the generating as generated by what it has itself generated." [5]

For Hegel, reality is a mere phenomenon of the Idea, whereas in truth the Idea has no other content than this phenomenon. All the emphasis has been displaced from reality to logic. There is only one science left, the science of the Idea. Physics, chemistry, biology, politics, all have the same abstract logical determinations. The same general Idea shows up everywhere. The specific elements of the various branches of science are entirely lost in this abstract speculation. When, for instance, Hegel writes about the Constitution that "this organism is the development of the Idea to its differences," [6] no mention is made of the specific characteristics of the political Constitution. According to Marx, "The same statement can be made with equal validity concerning the biological and the political organism. How does the biological organism differ from the political? This is not clear from the general definition. But an explanation which does not give the specific difference is no explanation." [7]

Marx contends that the same ideological mystification marks the transition of the lower spheres to the State. The Idea which

4 *MEGA*, I¹, 406.   6 *R.*, 269.
5 *MEGA*, I¹, 407–08.   7 *MEGA*, I¹, 412.

was *in itself* in family and civil society becomes *for itself* in the State.

> The transition has not been deduced from the particular essence of the family, etc., nor from the particular essence of the State, but from the general relation of necessity and freedom. An identical transition is made in the *Logic* from the sphere of essence to the sphere of notion. The same transition again appears in the *Philosophy of Nature,* from inorganic nature to life. The same categories animate now this, now another sphere, and the only important thing is to discover, for the individual concrete determinations, the corresponding abstract ones.[8]

But Hegel's logical mysticism is most evident in his treatment of the State organism. "This organism is the development of the Idea to its differences and their objective actuality. Hence these different members are the various powers of the State." [9] Marx comments: "By adding the word 'hence,' Hegel gives the impression that the different powers are deduced from the proposition about the organism as a development of the Idea. . . . But no predicate justifies the subject 'this organism.' . . . There is no bridge from the universal notion of organism to the determinate notion of the State or the political Constitution, and such a bridge will never exist." [10]

Something similar happens in the case of the monarchy, where the Idea, in order to become concrete, at the end of its evolution conjures up a living individual. Merely contingent elements, such as birth and individuality, have become ideal determinations of the Idea.

> Thus an effect of mystical depth is created. It is very commonplace to say that a man is born, and that this living being, originated by physical birth, grows into a social being and a citizen; all that a man becomes he owes to his birth. But it is profound and impressive that the Idea of the State is born directly, and, in the birth of the mon-

arch, brings itself to empirical existence. . . . It makes a profound, mystical impression to see the Idea posit a particular empirical existence and thus to meet at each stage an incarnation of God.[11]

Through the text quoted above, Marx illustrates Feuerbach's remark that what *is* seems superficial when it is presented as it is, but profound when presented as it is not, that is, as an appearance of itself. Marx argues that by a complicated feint, Hegel gives the impression that his description of the Prussian State is the concrete realization of the ethical Idea. He abstracts some determinations from empirical reality, transposes them into a logical universe, and brings them back to life in an empirical subject, directly deduced from the logical Idea. Thus the State of 1820 receives a mystical, ideal necessity, and the various political institutions within it seem to be derived directly from the Idea.

The most that can be deduced from the notion of the State is that, as Hegel says, sovereignty "comes into *existence* only as subjectivity sure of itself." [12] But, notes Marx, this by no means implies that it exists only in one subject. On the contrary, once one has admitted that sovereignty belongs to the organism as such (that is, to society), it should rather be expected to concretize itself in all of society's members.

For Hegel, the transition from thought to individual reality is the climax of speculative philosophy; for Marx, it means "that the complete contradiction is taken for identity, the highest inconsistency for consistency." Two opposite poles are united here in the name of logic, with the result that logic itself becomes self-contradictory. Hegel tries to justify the leap of thought into reality by referring to the transition from the universal will to the individual act. However, Marx argues that this parallelism does not apply since universal thought undergoes none of the mediations which more and more particularize the universal

11 *MEGA*, I¹, 446–47.   12 *R.*, 279.

will before uniting it with its individual object. The universality of the will is at the same time concrete and determinate and not, like the universality of knowledge, an abstraction of individual data. A comparison with the will would be possible only if individual acts were produced by an abstract universal will.[13]

Marx's assertion that Hegel's notion has no real, universal content does not imply that he rejects every kind of trans-individual reality. More than Hegel or Feuerbach, he is convinced that man is a *generic* being and that his true reality is to be found in society.[14] But this universality of man is real only to the extent that it exists empirically, i.e. in concrete individuals. Marx's social universal, therefore, is not metaphysical, but purely empirical. It is constituted by the dependence of individuals upon each other for the satisfaction of their needs.

Thought does not constitute any part of the real: it is an ideal duplicate of the real and, as such, remains intrinsically dependent upon the empirical, concrete reality. Yet, this dependence does not imply that philosophy is confined to a mere description of the present situation. Human reality is in constant evolution. Reflection, therefore, uncovers not only the present, but also the future implicit in a dynamic present. This enables philosophy to anticipate future developments and to be critical of the actual situation. In its critique of the present, dialectical philosophy merely brings out reality's own dynamism and its immanent oppositions. Through reflection, man has an immediate insight into the dialectical nature of reality. There is no need to "explain" this clear and simple experience by the mystical development of a transempirical Idea.

It is obvious that this interpretation makes Marx's dialectic essentially different from Hegel's. Instead of being the imma-

---

13 *MEGA*, I¹, 440.
14 "Hegel forgets that the essence of the individual person is not his beard, his blood or his abstract *physis*, but his social quality, and that State affairs are nothing but forms of being and operation of man's social qualities. It is evident, therefore, that the individuals, insofar as they are bearers of the powers and interests of the State, must be considered in their social and not in their private aspect." (*MEGA*, I¹, 424.)

nent development of an Idea, the dialectic is now the development of *man*, a being of flesh and blood, determined by external, material conditions. Yet, Marx's reality remains dialectical and, as such, essentially rational.]Whether the dialectical method is compatible with Marx's empiricism is a question that will be considered later.

In his later *Contribution to the Critique of Political Economy* (*Zur Kritik der politischen Oekonomie*, 1859) Marx summarizes the results of the *Critique of Hegel's Philosophy of the State* in the following words: "The conclusion of this critique was that juridical institutions and different forms of the State cannot be explained by themselves, or by a so-called development of the human spirit, but that they are produced by the material conditions of life." [15] It is questionable, however, to what extent Marx in 1843 was able to justify his attitude epistemologically. His commentary is a mere critique of Hegel and does not offer an elaborate criteriology.

On one essential point Marx's ideas were to undergo a major evolution in the two years following the *Critique of Hegel's Philosophy of the State*. Whereas the *Critique* remains purely speculative and, in spite of a more practical approach than Feuerbach's, still attempts to refute philosophy with philosophy, Marx's subsequent writings were to bring out more clearly that the main question is not how to understand reality, but how to bring it to its own perfection, how to *realize* its immanent end. In his doctoral dissertation, he had already announced that philosophy could achieve this task only by annulling itself and becoming a theory of action.

An Evaluation of Marx's Criticism

At this point in our analysis, the reader probably has the feeling that Marx does not always present Hegel's thought correctly. Before entering into the political problems, it will be

[15] *MEGA*, I¹, liv.

useful to compare Marx's interpretation with the original meaning of the texts which he discusses.

Marx criticizes Hegel for *reducing* reality to a merely logical,
nonreal Idea. Marx identifies consciousness with "ideal" and
assumes that both are irreducibly opposed to the real[For Hegel,
however, reality *is* the Idea and the Idea is more than consciousness. Marx is criticizing his own interpretation of Hegel rather
than Hegel himself]when he writes: "The pure ideality of a
real sphere can exist only as knowledge." [16] Indeed, pure ideality
is conscious, but it is much more than that, since it is also the
perfection of the real. The basic assumption of Hegel's philosophy is precisely the identity of the real and the ideal. The content of the State is "the in and for itself rational" insofar as it is
"the *reality* of the substantial will."

Surreptitiously Marx has reintroduced a separation of the
ideal and the real which Hegel could never admit. He understands *reality* in Hegel's philosophy as a *substantial product*
of the Idea. But for Hegel, reality is not a product of the Idea;
it is the Idea itself. Even as nature opposed to consciousness,
reality still retains an ideal character: it is the alienation which
the notion performs upon itself in order to return to itself as
conscious reality (*Idea*). Reality, then, is never a *product* of the
Idea, for the Idea is both substance and subject. Nor is the
State-Idea an ideal framework imposed from without upon political realities: it is the State itself, as it develops along the lines
of its *own* nature. The determinations of the Idea are determinations of the *State*, which, as spiritual being, follows a rational
pattern in its self-explication. There can be no basic opposition
between what *is* and what logically *should* be, for reality is rational in its very essence and develops according to rational
laws. Even at the beginning, the State is what it should be, but,
since development is the law of its being, it grows toward the
perfect realization of itself. The law of growth is the essence of
reality itself. This law does not exist prior to reality in a purely

16 *MEGA*, I¹, 410.

ideal way—it becomes ideal law only when reality is completed. Rather than an empty "logical" schema, the Idea is the self-developing life of a spiritual reality.]

Marx's criticism misses the point when he writes: "The same categories animate now this, now another sphere, and the important thing is to discover, for the individual concrete determinations, the corresponding abstract ones." [17] Hegel's *"categories"* are not abstract, but concrete and dynamic. They are not empty universal concepts, applied indifferently to a number of realities, but *concrete universals* which are particular and individual as well as universal. The same terms return on almost every page, for there is only *one* reality and since it is ideal, it remains consistent with itself in its entire development. But these terms have never exactly the same meaning: reality gradually concretizes its own ideal structures, and consequently gives these structures a new content at each stage of its self-explication. In his *Philosophy of Right,* Hegel says:

> The immanent development of a science, the derivation of its entire content from the concept in its simplicity, . . . exhibits this peculiarity, that one and the same concept . . . which begins by being abstract (because it is at the beginning) maintains its identity even while it consolidates its specific determinations, and that too solely by its own activity, and in this way gains a concrete content.[18]

To call the transition between inorganic nature and life identical with that between the lower spheres and the State, as Marx does, is possible only if one detaches the ideal structures from their content. The identity of the dialectical transitions is the identity of reality with itself, but this identity is dynamic, like the stream which remains the same even though one cannot step into it twice. To disregard the analogy of Hegel's logical determinations is to misunderstand his dialectic. Marx's univocal and formal interpretation of these determinations prevents him from seeing identity wherever there is variety.

[17] *MEGA,* I¹, 409.   [18] *R.,* 279.

Marx's criticism of Hegel's theory of judgment is based on a similar misapprehension of the Idea. To claim that for Hegel the Idea is the subject, and the concrete reality of the State the predicate, is to assume that the *reality* of judgment is entirely on the side of the subject and its ideality on the side of the predicate, and, thus, to reintroduce a separation between the ideal and the real. For Hegel, ideality is as much in the subject as reality is in the predicate: "The subjective interpretation of judgment, as if I ascribed a predicate to a subject, is contradicted by the objective form of judgment: the rose *is* red, gold *is* a metal, etc. . . ." [19] In another passage, Hegel refutes Marx's interpretation of judgment even more clearly:

> It is not correct to consider judgment as a connection of parts, for when speaking of a connection we conceive of the connected elements as independent and without connection. The superficiality of this view is felt even more in the assertion that one constructs a judgment by *adding* a predicate to a subject, as if the predicate existed only in the mind, and from there was added to an external and independently existing subject. This conception of judgment conflicts with the copula. When we say "This rose is red" or "This painting is beautiful," we do not mean that we make the rose red or the painting beautiful, but that red and beautiful are the proper determinations of these objects. [20]

Marx writes: "Hegel gives an independent subsistence to the predicates, the objects, by separating them from their real subsistence, their subject." [21] But from Hegel's point of view it is Marx himself who separates subject and predicate into the two distinct spheres of thought and reality. By confining the predicate entirely to the order of thought, Marx destroys the original identity of thought and being. Thought loses its concreteness and becomes an abstract *duplicate* of reality; reality loses its coherence and becomes an aggregate of unintelligible elements.

---

[19] Hegel, *Encyclopädie der Philosophischen Wissenschaften,* in *Sämtliche Werke* (ed. by G. Lasson, Leipzig, 1913) , V, 167. In future, this work will be referred to as *Enc.,* followed by the paragraph number.
[20] *Enc.,* Appendix, 166.   [21] *MEGA,* I1, 426.

In this separation of thought and reality, the bond which unites the different aspects of reality is dissolved: instead of intimately connected moments, they become juxtaposed *parts* having no intrinsic relation to each other. To be one part is *ipso facto* to be separated from all the others. For Marx the monarchical element of the State as "absolute self-determination" is pure arbitrariness. And, indeed, if the individual moment were really separated from the universal and the particular, as one part is from another, then the will of the monarch would be arbitrary. But Hegel states explicitly that the three moments are always united in the sovereignty; in the monarchy the individual element of self-determination is only its *most characteristic* aspect.

Under the influence of Feuerbach, Marx misrepresents Hegel's thought: instead of being the science of the ideal *in* the real, logic becomes an abstraction from the real. Yet, the correctness of Marx's interpretation of Hegel must not become the criterion for evaluating his own ideas. The entire value of his criticism of Hegel lies in the fact that it prepares a new and less idealistic approach to man's reality. Once he has differentiated his own position from Hegel's, Marx will go on to discover an original dialectic.

Marx's Critique of Hegel's Political Principles

An Exposition of Marx's Criticism

So far we have considered Marx's criticism of Hegel's logical principles and their "application" in the *Philosophy of Right*. The following section outlines Marx's discussion of Hegel's political theories. Here his criticism is much more to the point. It concentrates on the fact that Hegel's idealistic interpretation of the identity of the ideal and the real forced him to give the historical State of his day an ideal necessity, and to justify the existing political structures even if they conflicted with the true nature of the State. For Hegel the possibility that the modern State has basically deviated from its essence is *a priori* excluded. But according to Marx, the modern State has its roots in an asocial and selfish civil society and fails to fulfill its social purpose: it is merely a social mirage of an asocial reality. Hegel, however, considers the asocial situation of modern society as the deepest expression of man's social nature. According to Marx, Hegel's *Philosophy of Right* absolutizes the historical separation between an asocial economic sphere which is real and a social-political sphere which is unreal. Far from expressing man's social nature, the modern State estranges him from it, because it forces man to live his *real* life in a sphere entirely determined by individual interests and leaves his social nature with only a social illusion. The separation of the State from the civil society alienates man from his social nature. Said Marx, "The *political constitution* was, until today, the *religious sphere,* the *cult* of people's life, the heaven of its universality, as opposed to the *earthly existence* of its reality." [22]

Marx here adopts and completes Feuerbach's theory of religious alienation.[23] For Feuerbach, man estranges himself from himself by transposing his own greatness into an external object of worship. He adores what he has taken away from himself. According to Marx, the religious alienation has its origin in the social and economic conditions of life. It is precisely because *he no longer feels at home in this world* that man takes refuge in another world which is above and outside reality. Religion is not the cause but the result of man's alienation. Its real ground lies in an asocial, individualistic society, artificially preserved by the social illusion of a political structure. The true alienation of man, therefore, is ultimately the estrangement of

---

[22] *MEGA*, I¹, 436.
[23] It should be noted, though, that the term "alienation" appears very seldom in the *Critique;* in the *Economic and Philosophic Manuscripts,* it will be used constantly.

the social (the State) from the individual life. Instead of integrating the social into man's reality, the modern State, as a parasite, vegetates on top of man's real life.[24]

> Everyman, therefore, leads a double life: a political one as member of the State, and a private one as member of society. With respect to society the State represents an ideal sphere, just as heaven does with respect to earth. In society man as private person, as selfish individual, leads an existence in disagreement with his nature; only through the State would he be able to bring his existence into accordance with his nature, but here he leads a merely fictitious life, for the State, because of the imperfection of society, cannot offer him more than an illusory existence.[25]

Not only is the State a social illusion, but it is an illusion which protects and legalizes the individualistic reality of the civil society. Since the social sphere has been withdrawn from real life, it no longer has a content of its own, and it is forced to obtain it from the only sphere where reality is to be found, the civil society. Thus, instead of being the expression of man's social nature, the State becomes the social consecration of an individualistic society: it gives a legal status to society's rugged individualism.

It is only in recent times that this alienation has taken on catastrophic proportions. In the Greek *polis,* private life was entirely integrated in the State. "In Greece the *res publica* was the real private concern, the real content of the citizens, and the private man was the slave; the political State *qua* political was the true and only content of their lives and striving." [26] In the Middle Ages, political life lost much of its importance and the corporations became the real center of man's social activity. There was no opposition between a social-economic and a political sphere, since political life, so far as it existed, was part of the economic society: it was an extension of the corporations. Medieval society was as individualistic as modern society, but at

24 *MEGA,* I¹, 436.
25 A. Cornu, *La jeunesse de Karl Marx* (Paris, 1934) , p. 289.
26 *MEGA,* I¹, 437–38.

least it did not separate man's social from his real life.[27] The separation of State and society, which Hegel describes, was not accomplished until the advent of the modern age. Marx proves how each of the three moments of Hegel's State places the social sphere outside man's real life, and thereby estranges man from himself. The living symbol of this alienation is the monarchy, which deprives the people of their sovereignty. Hegel claims that the powers of the sovereignty cannot be held at the same time by the monarch and the people. Marx comments: "If the sovereignty is with the monarch it no longer makes sense to talk about an opposite sovereignty with the people. . . . However, the question is whether the absolute sovereignty of the monarch is not an illusion." [28] It is obvious that a people without a monarch is structureless, *if* one presupposes that a monarch belongs to the essential structure of a society. But is this really the case?

Every Constitution implies a monarchical element. But this does not mean that the government *must* be a monarchy. On the contrary, since the sovereignty lies essentially in the State as a whole, a democratic government would be more logical. A democratic State can do full justice to the monarchical element, but the democratic element, which according to Hegel is equally essential for the State, is entirely lost in the monarchy. It only continues to exist as the inconsistency of an authority which remains with the people after it has been taken away from it. The monarchy estranges the State from the people. In spite of its universal pretentions, the State is no longer everyman's concern: it becomes one man's particular business. In a true democracy, on the contrary, political life is *really* universal.

To obtain this effect, however, it is not sufficient to change the political regime and to replace the monarchy by a republic. A republican government can be as removed from the people as a monarchy, and it is more misleading since it camouflages the separation between real and social life under the disguise of free elections. Not a political democracy, but only a complete reintegration of the social spheres into man's real life will annul the present alienation.

In his treatment of the executive power, Hegel attempts to bring the social sphere back into man's real life. Civil servants and corporations (i.e. trade and professional organizations) are supposed to mediate between State and civil society. But, says Marx, no mediation can bring two contradictory opposites together. The fact that the State can penetrate into the real life of its citizens only through the particular class of civil servants clearly manifests the isolation of the political sphere. Small wonder then that the civil service is permanently in conflict with the representatives of the civil society, the corporations. The corporations are concerned exclusively with their own interests, and would rather have no contact with the universal sphere of the State. Only the fear that other corporations might interfere with their private interests compels them to make concessions to the interests of others.

The discrepancy between political structure and real life also shows in the legislature. Marx attributes Hegel's difficulties in explaining the relation between Constitution and legislative power to the fact that Hegel viewed the Constitution as the legal expression of the formal political State, whereas the legislative is supposed to be the voice of the real people.

But what is worse, according to Marx, is that the legislative does not even represent the people. The true representatives of the people, the Estates, constitute only an unimportant fraction of the legislative branch. Indeed, Hegel writes: "In the legislature as a whole, the other powers are the first two moments that are effective: the monarchy . . . and the executive." [29] Thus the very elements which alienate the social sphere from the people's real life are given the first place in the organism which is supposed to represent the people. The people are reduced to a formal element without political significance. Hegel notes that

[29] *R.*, 300.

the people "means precisely that section [of the State] which does *not* know what it wills," and "that the Estates start from isolated individuals, from a private point of view, from particular interests, and so are inclined to devote their activities to these [interests] at the expense of the general interests." [30] Thus it appears that the Estates are not only superfluous but politically suspect as well. Only the logical necessity to let the universal become "for itself" keeps Hegel from throwing them out altogether. "Hegel admits the luxury of Estates only out of love for the logic." [31] Everything seems to be arranged to give the people a voice in the government, but in such a way that it cannot be heard.

Furthermore, even if the Estates were to take over the whole legislative power, they still would be unable to bring the State closer to real life. To unite State and civil society it is not sufficient, according to Marx, to give social-economic groups some political luster. "The Estates are the synthesis of State and civil society. But how they should unite two contradictory dispositions is not being explained." [32] The Estates show in miniature the internal contradiction of the Hegelian State: as representatives of the people they are opposed to the government, and as part of the government they are opposed to the people. Thus government and people remain opposed within the Estates. "All contradictions of the modern State organization come together in the Estates." [33]

Hegel's Idea-State assumes that State and civil society are in basic agreement with each other. But in the modern State, Marx contends, they are in continuous conflict. Hegel's Idea, then, is one subject with two predicates which exclude each other. In medieval society the social-economic groups had legislative authority *as such:* they were at the same time political Estates.[34] But this situation was radically changed by the national States of the late Middle Ages. The absolute monarchy and the strongly

[30] *R.,* 301.
[31] *MEGA,* I¹, 477.

[32] *MEGA,* I¹, 481.
[33] *MEGA,* I¹, 483.

[34] *MEGA,* I¹, 488.

centralized bureaucracy of the purely political State severed
civil society from its political power. Initially, the national State
was not strong enough to eliminate the medieval structure entirely, and it allowed the Estates to continue an independent
existence within the State. In the French Revolution, however,
the Estates lost their political significance altogether, and with
it the last bond between political and social life. Henceforth
all citizens, regardless of their social rank, became equal for the
State. "Just as Christians are equal in heaven and unequal on
earth, the separate members of a people are equal in the heaven
of their political world and unequal in the earthly existence of
society." [35] When the social-economic groups ceased to be politically significant, they lost their *raison d'être*. Instead of active
social communities, they became individualistic factions determined by wealth and education. The groups which used to
integrate the individuals into the community became classes
which separated the individuals from the community.

Attempts to give these private interest groups political stature
can only result in the contradictory presence of an asocial reality
within an imaginary social sphere. This is most evident in the
class of the landowners, which Hegel has selected to mediate the
civil society with the executive branch. Hegel assumes that finan-
cial independence and the principle of primogeniture predispose
this section of the Estates to political activities more than they
do any other social-economic group. But how could private
property, which creates inequality between those who have and
those who have not, prepare anyone for a function in the State
which has the task of ensuring social equality? Marx comments:

> The primogeniture is not, as Hegel claims, "a shackle on
> the freedom of private right," but rather "the freedom of
> the private right which has rid itself from all social and
> ethical shackles.". . . What makes precisely the *romantic*
> charm of the primogeniture is that private property, and
> therefore also private arbitrariness, shows itself here in its

most abstract form; that the narrow-minded, immoral, brute will here appears as the highest synthesis of the State.[36]

To Hegel's thesis that primogeniture exists only because of the State, Marx opposes his own theory that the modern State is subordinate to the principle of private property. By itself private property is not an inalienable right. Hegel himself admits that nothing is inalienable but "those goods, or rather substantive characteristics, which constitute my own private personality and the universal essence of my self-consciousness. . . . Such characteristics are my personality as such, my universal freedom of will, my ethical life, my religion." [37] Private property is not included in these substantive characteristics. But primogeniture frees private property from all social and personal connections, thus making it into an absolute principle.

By giving private property a political determination, Hegel makes into a public right what is essentially private. Severed from real life, the State no longer has a content of its own, and merely legalizes the principle of the existent civil society. Thus the State becomes a mere instrument to protect the right of property.

"What is the content of the Constitution? " asks Marx.

> The *primogeniture,* the *superlative* of *private property,* the sovereign *private property.* What power has the political State over private property in the primogeniture? It *isolates* it from family and society, it brings it to an *abstract independence.* What then is the power of the political State over *private property? Private property's* own power, its own essence which is brought to existence. What remains of the political State besides this essence? The illusion that it determines, whereas, in fact, it is determined.[38]

Far from being the highest ethical reality, as Hegel claims, the State represents the legalization of man's individualism. By subordinating itself to private property, the State, in fact, sacrifices the highest ethical value, the "universal freedom of will," [39]

[36] *MEGA,* I1, 520–21.   [38] *MEGA,* I1, 519.
[37] *R.,* 66.   [39] *R.,* 66.

which it is supposed to bring into existence. "The *inalienability* of *private property* is at once the *'alienability' of the universal freedom of the will and of ethical life.*" [40]

The political status of primogeniture reverses private property's true relation to freedom: instead of being an attribute of freedom, private property now makes freedom its attribute. The oldest son of the landowner becomes an inheritance of the property. His identity has no importance; the only thing that matters is the integrity of the property. The political significance of the landowners' class is reduced to their property, and the political independence of the State, which is based on this class, is the independence of private property. "The members of the political State receive their independence not from the essence of the political State, but from the essence of abstract private right, from abstract private property." [41]

Hegel defined private right as the right of the abstract personality; but according to Marx, Hegel's own "concrete" ethical State is not more than a social sanction of this abstract right. "Hegel develops private right and morality as abstractions, but he fails to draw the conclusion that the State, the ethical ideal, which is built on them, cannot be more than the society [the social life] of these illusions." [42] Everything, then, becomes private property, not only commerce and industry, but also law and local government, even national identity and science.

In contrast to the ancient State, Marx contends, the Germano-Christian State is an extension of private right. This appears most clearly at its origin, in the feudal epoch. The feudal State *is* the private property of the prince, and right is a privilege given to one person or to one group, but never inherent to society itself. *"Private property* is the *universal existence* of the *privilege,* of right as *exception.*" [43] The Romans recognized the right of property, but never let it interfere with public affairs. Private property was not primarily a right, but an unexplain-

40 *MEGA,* I¹, 521.
41 *MEGA,* I¹, 528.

42 *MEGA,* I¹, 529.
43 *MEGA,* I¹, 530.

able fact. The famous definition *"jus utendi et abutendi"* (the right to use or not to use) was only an attempt to formulate this fact juridically. The private "right" of property always remained subordinated to the *res publica*. With the Teutons, on the contrary, private property gradually conquered the entire State. The sovereignty itself became a hereditary piece of private property.

His reflections on primogeniture and private property led Marx to the conclusion that the modern State, instead of being the sphere in which man lives his universal nature, is entirely determined by an individualistic economic society. This discovery marks a turning point in his political philosophy, for even in the article on wood thefts, published at the end of 1842 in the *Rheinische Zeitung,* he still believed that the modern State had a social function. In the *Critique of Hegel's Philosophy of the State,* his rejection of the modern State is complete. Yet, he does not advocate the abolition of the State, for it is not yet clear to him whether the abuses of the modern State are inherent in the State *as such.* Nor does he know at this point whether private property ought to be abolished, although he feels that it certainly must not be the basis of society.

Marx has not abandoned the Neoclassical concept of society as ethical ideal. He has stripped the ethical glamour from the modern State, but only to restore it to society. He does not question Hegel's assertion that society is the ultimate ethical reality, provided that it is truly social, and not, like Hegel's State, a legalization of individualism. In fact, Marx is so convinced of society's ethical nature that he eliminates Hegel's separate sphere of private morality. For the sphere of morality is needed only because modern society does not fulfill its moral purpose.

> Hegel has repeatedly been attacked for his development of morality. But he only develops the morality of the modern State and of modern private right. Attempts have been made to detach morality from the State, to emancipate it more. But what does that prove? That the separation be-

tween the contemporary State and morality is moral, that morality is apolitical, and that the State is amoral.[44]

For Marx, authentic morality coincides with ethics and is realized in the perfect society.

An Evaluation of Marx's Criticism

With remarkable insight, Marx has seen the weakness of the modern State as it is described and absolutized in Hegel's system. Since the rise of the national State, there has been a split between political and real life. The French Revolution has not succeeded in restoring the harmony of the Ancient State: instead the complete leveling of all citizens in the political State caused a break with the existing social structures. Marx correctly concludes that this has led to an increasing individualism: the State has become an empty organism and the civil society has lost its social reality.

The absence of a social dimension in modern life was acutely felt as the economic upsurge of the nineteenth century caused a social crisis. Even now, however, Marx's considerations have not entirely lost their importance, for although social legislation has brought the political and economic spheres closer together, it often seems that most of the existing social laws were partial concessions, obtained under pressure, which failed to reform the social structure of the State itself. In many instances, social legislation exists not *because* but *in spite* of the modern State: the nineteenth-century State was the juridical expression of a society in which those who had risen to economic power made the law.

Marx's insights on this point will be further developed in his theory of the class struggle. At this moment, however, he is not yet able to determine to which social-economic forces the

44 *MEGA*, I¹, 529.

political State owes its origin. Only the class struggle, first announced in the *Introduction to the Critique of Hegel's Philosophy of Right* and worked out in *The German Ideology*, will show *how* the State was alienated from society, how it became a legal instrument by which one *particular class* subjects society to its own interests.

Another point which Marx will develop further is the concept of alienation. The whole *Critique of Hegel's Philosophy of the State* turns on it. Yet, it is hardly ever mentioned by name and remains undefined. With Feuerbach, Marx agrees that the real alienation is not the alienation of consciousness but the alienation of man. But contrary to Feuerbach, he thinks that man's alienation consists in the estrangement of his real, social nature rather than in the extrapolation of man's strivings in a supernatural world. Religion is only a result of man's basic frustration in society.

However, it is not clear at all in what this *social alienation* consists. Marx's concept of man remains as abstract as Feuerbach's. He is aware that man is a *generic* being. Yet, man's *generic* nature is never defined—it remains a mere assumption, not less abstract than Hegel's universality.[45] It is only in the *Economic and Philosophic Manuscripts* that Marx's concept of man will receive concrete form and shape through the *relation to nature*. This will also clear up the notion of alienation: man's alienation is his *estrangement from nature* expressed in the institution of private property.

---

[45] Heinrich Popitz, *Der Entfremdete Mensch* (Basel, 1953) , p. 88.

5

Marx's Humanism: The Writings of the Paris Period

The *German-French Yearbooks*

AT THE END of 1843, Marx made another step away from the Young Hegelians. He moved to Paris to edit the *German-French Yearbooks (Deutsch-Französische Jahrbücher)*, of which only one issue was to appear. Besides some letters, it contained Marx's *Introduction to the Critique of Hegel's Philosophy of Right* and an article in which Marx attacks Bruno Bauer's position on the Jewish question.

The Jewish Question

As Bruno Bauer presented it, the emancipation of the Jews is basically a religious problem. It can be solved only by a religious emancipation of society by which the Jews cease to be Jews and the Christians to be Christians. As long as the Jews continue to consider themselves a religious group, they have no ground to claim equal rights from non-Jews, for the latter will refuse their request on the same religious basis used by the Jews themselves. For Christians only one religion can be right, and hence there is no reason to concede religious privileges to another sect. The same argument holds for a secular State: citizens who have emancipated themselves from religion will never recognize a group which is in fundamental disagreement with the secular State. The Jews' only recourse, therefore, is to drop their religious status and to cooperate with others in a society recognizing neither Jews nor Christians.

The fallacy of this argument is obvious, and Marx did not hesitate to point it out: Bauer confused political rights with religious recognition. All that the Jews asked for was political emancipation, and this could be granted without any religious commitment on the part of the Christian or the secular state. But the very fact that political emancipation could be achieved with retention of the religious alienation showed that neither the political nor the religious emancipation is the true emancipation of man. "We do not, therefore, say to the Jews as Bauer does: 'You cannot be politically emancipated unless you emancipate yourselves from Judaism.' We say, rather, to them: 'Since you can become politically emancipated without abandoning Judaism completely, political emancipation will not bring you human emancipation.' "[1]

In the United States, wrote Marx, the political regime has emancipated itself entirely from religion: the State grants equal rights to all religious groups. Such a solution escapes between the horns of Bauer's dilemma, for the Jews are allowed to keep their religious privileges and have the same rights as other American citizens. Nevertheless, the United States has a Jewish problem. This proves Bauer wrong in assuming that the problem can be solved by a secularization of the State. The laicization of the State does not lead to the liberation of man. Religion is never the cause but always the effect of man's alienation. It arises from a social *maladjustment,* a cleavage between man's social and his individual existence. His social reality has been taken away from him, and he is reduced to an impoverished, isolated existence. In his frustration, he seeks the fulfillment of his nature in the imaginary world of religion. Man takes refuge in

[1] *MEGA,* I¹, 591; Marx, *A World without Jews (Zur Judenfrage,* tr. by Dagobert Runes, New York, 1959), p. 21, by permission of Philosophical Library. This selection will hereafter be referred to as "Runes."

religious illusions because in the modern State social illusion has taken the place of social reality. This situation cannot be remedied by a change in the religious attitude of the State. The State itself is a result of the same alienation which gives rise to religion. In that sense the State is always religious.

> The members of the political State are religious by means of a dichotomy between their individual lives and the lives of the species, between their life in civil society and their political life. They are religious insofar as man is related to life in the State—which lies beyond his real individuality—as to his true life; they are religious insofar as religion is the spirit of civil society and expresses the separation and alienation of man from man.[2]

The secular State is even more religious than the Christian, for the secular State absorbs religion in itself—it *identifies* itself with the religious illusion.

> The State that continues to profess Christianity as a religion does not yet profess it in political form because it still behaves religiously toward religion. This means that it is not a genuine fulfillment of the human basis of religion, because it is still the product of unreality, of the imaginary shape of the human nucleus.[3]

Bauer claims that as long as the Jew is Jewish (in the religious sense) his limited nature as Jew will always prevail over his human nature, by which he is a social being and a member of the State. He thereby assumes that the modern State is social. But this assumption is wrong, for the State is based on individualistic principles. And with this individualism the Jewish mentality is in perfect accord. Far from being an outcast of society, the Jew is the purest representative of a society in which man is alienated from his true nature. Money and selfish individualism, rather than religion, are the foundation of modern Judaism. And this individualism anticipates the ideal to which our "Chris-

[2] *MEGA*, I¹, 590 (my translation).
[3] *MEGA*, I¹, 587; Runes, p. 16.

tian" society tends.[4] "Christianity sprang from Judaism; it has now dissolved itself back into Judaism."[5] The only way for Jews to emancipate themselves is to become *social* beings and contribute to the social liberation of society.

An Introduction to the Critique of Hegel's Philosophy of Right

Marx's contact with the French Communist movement and his social studies had given him two new insights: (1) that a revolution is the only way to achieve social justice; and (2) that this revolution must be *social* and not political. In the *Introduction to the Critique of Hegel's Philosophy of Right* (*Zur Kritik der Hegelschen Rechtsphilosophie*, 1844) Marx first stated his revolutionary theories. Although this *Introduction* was written only a few months after the unfinished *Critique of Hegel's Philosophy of the State*, Marx's ideas in the meantime had undergone a strong evolution. Through his contact with the French socialist movement, he had come to realize the importance of the proletariat for social reforms. Also, as a result of the *Critique*, his thought had taken a more and more pragmatic turn: action, not speculation, was needed for the liberation of society. He therefore abandoned the publication project of the still speculative *Critique* and integrated its conclusions in the argument of his *Introduction*.

Marx starts his article with a survey of what has been accomplished by the religious (or as he puts it, irreligious) critique in Germany. "The basis of irreligious criticism is: *Man makes religion*, religion does not make man. In other words, religion

[4] Robert Tucker, in *Philosophy and Myth in Karl Marx* (Cambridge, Eng., 1961), p. 110, rightly draws attention to an earlier article by Moses Hess which indicates the connection between monetary exchange and "Jewish Christianity." Both are expressions of the same alienation—the former practical, the latter theoretical. It is almost certain that Marx has been influenced here by Hess's ideas.
[5] *MEGA*, I¹, 605; Runes, p. 43.

is the self-consciousness and self-feeling of man, who either has not yet found himself or has already lost himself again." [6]

The critique of religion has to be made because it is the basis of all critique. Yet, it is not sufficient—it fails to explain *why* man repeatedly turns to the religious illusion. Feuerbach's psychological explanation is obviously inadequate: it is based on abstract man. Real man is man living in the world, and this world is not primarily man's physical environment, as Feuerbach thinks, but his social relations in State and society. "Man is no abstract being, squatting outside the world. Man is the world of man, the State, society." [7]

Feuerbach mentions "mankind" as the deeper reality of man, but he is unable to concretize this concept. Despite all his talk about the concreteness of man, he becomes extremely abstract when he deals with other than sexual relations.[8] His philosophy is humanistic, for it restores man to his central place, yet it remains abstract. The critique truly begins where Feuerbach's religious critique leaves off.

When the *beyond* (*Jenseits*) *of truth* has vanished, the task of history is to *constitute the truth of the present* (*Diesseits*). Once the *sacred simulacrum* of man's alienation is unmasked, philosophy, the servant of history, must unmask the alienation in its *unholy shapes*. Thus the critique of heaven is transformed into a critique of earth, the *critique of religion* into a *critique of right*, the *critique of theology* into a *critique of politics*.[9]

[6] *MEGA*, I¹, 607; partial translation in Marx and Engels, *Basic Writings on Politics and Philosophy* (ed. by Lewis Feuer, New York, 1959), p. 262. Henceforth this will be referred to as Feuer.

[7] *MEGA*, I¹, 607; Feuer, p. 262.

[8] A year later in Brussels Marx will formulate his criticism more sharply in his *Theses on Feuerbach*. In the sixth thesis he reproaches Feuerbach for a twofold abstraction. First, his considerations on religion are based on a concept of man as an isolated individual; secondly, the social aspect of man is limited to purely "natural" relations. "Feuerbach resolves the essence of religion into the essence of *man*. But the essence of man is no abstraction inherent in each separate individual. In its reality it is the *ensemble* (aggregate) of social relations." (*MEGA*, I⁵, 535; tr. by R. Pascal, *The German Ideology* [New York, 1960], p. 198, by permission of International Publishers Co., Inc.)

[9] *MEGA*, I¹, 608.

In the final analysis, however, this critique is not different from a critique of religion which goes to the roots: it explains *why* man projects his perfection into another world. What prevents man from finding his happiness and perfection in this world and forces him to look for it in the beyond? If man is so constituted that he can eventually reach his true destination, as Feuerbach proclaims, why is it that he cannot do so from the very beginning? Whence come adversity and unhappiness in Feuerbach's optimistic philosophy?

Only an insight into the social nature of man enables us to answer these questions. For the misery which drives man into religious illusions results from his social condition in economic society and State.

> This State, this society produce religion, a *perverted world consciousness,* because they are a *perverted world.* . . .
> Religious distress is at the same time the *expression* of real distress and the *protest* against real distress. . . .
> The abolition of religion as the *illusory* happiness of the people is required for their *real* happiness. The demand to give up the illusions about its condition is the *demand to give up a condition which needs illusions.*[10]

After this introduction, Marx measures the political situation in Germany against its philosophy. Germany was politically the most backward State of Western Europe; yet its philosophy was of the most revolutionary character. The Germans were the philosophical but not the historical contemporaries of their time. And yet, for Marx, philosophy is essentially pragmatic: its purpose is to be *realized.* Dialectical philosophy is potential revolution; it reaches its completion only when it is actualized in political reality.

But is Germany in its present political stage able to realize its philosophy? Philosophy alone never starts a revolution. "The weapon of the critique is not a substitute for the critique of the weapons; material power must be overthrown by material

10 *MEGA,* I¹, 607–08; Feuer, pp. 262–63.

power. Yet, theory also becomes material power as soon as it gets hold of the masses." [11] To become action, philosophy must penetrate the masses, but to do that, it must correspond to their actual needs. "It is not sufficient that thought tend toward its realization: reality must also tend toward thought." [12]

The whole question, then, is: Is Germany ripe for the realization of its radical philosophy? From this point of view Germany's situation looks more promising, for it has reached a point where nothing less than a radical overthrow of the established order can remedy it. The German people have none of the intermediate political emancipations which other European countries have won. They have witnessed the emancipation of other peoples—shared their sufferings and needs, but had no part in their rewards. Germany has undergone "restorations" without ever having seen an emancipation. It suffers under the abuses of the *ancien régime* as well as those of the modern State, without enjoying the advantages of either one. Of constitutional monarchy it knows the illusions only, and not the reality. A synthesis of all political and social frustrations, Germany can be freed only by throwing off all its political shackles at once.

Marx criticizes the Utopians as envisioning for Germany "not the *radical* revolution, not the *universally human* emancipation, but rather the partial, the *purely* political, revolution, the revolution which leaves the pillars of the house upright." [13] Marx argues that all that a partial revolution emancipates is that fraction of society which comes to power. This fraction would indeed liberate all the others if they shared its own particular situation. But since they never do, the momentary agreement of all opposition groups, which alone makes a revolution possible, is based on an illusion. The emancipation of the bourgeoisie in the French Revolution would have led to the liberation of all classes if all had lived under the same social conditions. In fact, however, the Revolution merely emancipated the

[11] *MEGA*, I¹, 614.   [12] *MEGA*, I¹, 616.   [13] *MEGA*, I¹, 617.

bourgeoisie. Like all political revolutions, it simply shifted the power from one class to another. The very fact that a revolution is political shows that it is not universal and will keep intact the previous state of affairs.

But a partial, political revolution has no chance in Germany. None of the existing classes has become sufficiently self-conscious to challenge the present order. Nor is any class recognized by the others as representing the entire society. No class is able to present its particular interests as the interests of society. They all lack "the breadth of soul that identifies itself, even for a moment, with the soul of the nation, the geniality that inspires material might to political violence, or that revolutionary daring which flings at the adversary the defiant words: *I am nothing, but I must be everything.*" [14] Germany's social and political degradation has prevented the rise of a leading class. All classes suffer from frustration, but not one has the determination from which a revolution originates. For that reason there is no prospect of a partial revolution in Germany.

The situation will become more and more critical until for the majority of the people, revolution is the only means to survival. Yet, even at that time, a revolution must be achieved by one class. Marx therefore predicts that a new class will be formed for which, unlike for the existing classes, revolution becomes an inescapable necessity, a matter of sheer survival. This class will suffer from all the evils of modern society *at once*. It will have no positive characteristics but will represent, paradoxically, the total deprivation of all human values, the dissolution of the class idea itself. Marx describes it as

> a class with *radical chains,* a class of civil society which is not a class of civil society, an estate which is the dissolution of all estates, a sphere which has a universal character by its universal suffering and claims no *particular right* because no *particular wrong* but *wrong generally* is perpetrated against it; . . . a sphere, finally, which cannot eman-

cipate itself without emancipating itself from all other spheres of society, and thereby emancipating all other spheres of society, which, in a word, is the *complete loss* of man, and hence can win itself only through the *complete rewinning of man.* This dissolution of society as a particular estate is the *proletariat.*[15]

The proletariat embodies the complete dehumanization of man in modern society. Other classes free themselves by subjecting the rest of mankind, but the proletariat, which suffers from *all* the evils of the existing order, can emancipate itself only by emancipating the whole society. Its revolt is not against some particular alienation, but against alienation as such. It alone can start a social revolution. Other classes make political revolutions: they direct their attacks against some flaw in the political order which hurts their particular interests. The proletariat attacks the *entire* political system.

The proletariat must not be confused with the class of the poor. Stein, in his book on French Communism, had already made it clear that the proletariat is a result of the capitalist industrialization and not of any particular social disorder. Not material poverty, but poverty resulting from industrialization characterizes the proletariat. Germany's agricultural society has many paupers but no proletarians. "Not the *naturally arising* poor but the *artificially impoverished* . . . form the proletariat." [16]

The function of the future proletarian class is to convert the German revolutionary philosophy into *action.* Philosophy becomes revolution as soon as it penetrates the proletariat. "The *head* of this emancipation is *philosophy,* its *heart* is the proletariat." [17] In the proletarian revolution, philosophy will finally realize itself and thus suppress itself. Of course, the existence of

---

[15] *MEGA,* I¹, 619; Feuer, pp. 264–65.
[16] *MEGA,* I¹, 620; Feuer, p. 265. The importance of the proletariat for the social revolution was first brought to Marx's attention by Stein's work. Marx's later contact with the social movement of the French workers confirmed Stein's conclusions.
[17] *MEGA,* I¹, 621; Feuer, p. 266.

a proletariat is entirely dependent on social-economic conditions. Yet, economic factors alone will never lead to a revolution. Philosophy is needed to make those who suffer under the economic conditions *conscious* of their power. The revolutionary power, therefore, ultimately depends on the infiltration of the masses by philosophy. Marxism was to be more than an economic or sociological theory—in spite of its emphasis on sociological and economic factors, it remained essentially a *philosophy of action*. This was to become entirely clear to Marx after his first serious contact with economy, in the *Economic and Philosophic Manuscripts*.

"The King of Prussia and Social Reform"

However, before considering the *Manuscripts,* a few words must be said about an article published in August, 1844, in the *Pariser Vorwärts,* in which Marx further elaborates the idea that the proletariat is and must remain a social class rather than a political group. In "The King of Prussia and Social Reform," he attacks his former friend and coeditor of the *German-French Yearbooks,* Arnold Ruge, for his criticism of the weaver revolt in Silesia. According to Ruge, all social revolts in Germany were doomed to failure, since Germany had not yet developed political consciousness, as France and England had. He implied that *social* reforms could be achieved only by means of *political* revolutions. According to Marx, just the opposite is true: the gradual emancipation effected by political revolutions never leads to the total emancipation of society. It is precisely when the proletariat is *politically* conscious that it wastes its blood and energy in partial revolutions from which another minority class will reap all the profit. A politically conscious proletariat will try to modify the established political regime instead of overthrowing the State itself. An example of this was the revolt of the workers of Lyon, who, instead of being "soldiers of socialism," became "soldiers of the republic." "The political insight deceived them on the origin of their social misery, distorted the consciousness of their real goal, and lied to their social instincts." [18]

A political revolution is always particular. A social revolt, however limited, attacks the entire social order. It protests against the alienation of the rights of *man*. A political revolt attempts to re-establish the rights of one particular class: it accepts the State as a given and only seeks to install a new class to rule the old government structure, while firmly maintaining the system which perpetuates social alienation.

> A *social* revolution takes place on the level of the *totality* because, even though it might be limited to *one* factory district, it is a protest of man against the dehumanized life, because its starting point is *the one, real individual,* because the communal nature from which the individual does not want to be severed is the *true* communal nature of man, the essence of man. On the contrary, the *political* soul of a revolution consists in the tendency of the politically powerless classes to put an end to their isolation from the State and its authority. Its level is that of the State, an abstract totality whose whole being is to be separated from real life, an abstract totality unthinkable without the organized opposition between the universal Idea and the individual existence of man.[19]

In that respect the Silesian revolt was more important than many successful revolts in politically conscious countries. The stronger the State, the more politically conscious are the people, and the less disposed to consider the principle of the State as socially evil. The example of England is there to illustrate this point. It is typical that this politically progressive country is also the traditional cradle of pauperism, and that the State has always blamed a deficient administration or the "laws of nature," but never itself, for the existing social abuses. The more alive

[18] *MEGA*, I³, 20.   [19] *MEGA*, I³, 22.

the State, the more inclined are social groups to take on a political character, and the less inclined to accuse the State as the
source of social evil.

The *Economic and Philosophic Manuscripts*

In 1844 Engels published his "Outlines of a Critique of Political Economy" ("Umrisse zu einer Kritik der Nationaloeko-
nomie") in the *German-French Yearbooks*. This article and the
subsequent contact with its author had a decisive influence on
Marx's further development. In the *Introduction* Marx had
reached the conclusion that philosophy is dependent on certain
social-economic conditions for its practical realization. From
Engels' article he now learned that the laws which rule an economic system escape all human control. As soon as a particular
system is accepted, man has no further control over its operation.

This discovery opened a new avenue to social problems. Social reforms cannot be achieved without cutting out the very
roots of social evil, the existing political economy. Under the
present economic system, all attempts at social reform are vain
since man's social relations are determined by his economic conditions, and these conditions cannot be changed: economy follows its own laws. Only a radical overthrow of the whole system
can lead to social changes. What must be criticized, then, is not
individual economic factors, but the entire economic system of
contemporary society.

But such a critcism can only come from a total philosophy of
man. The economist is enclosed within the present system; he
takes it for granted. Only philosophy can criticize the system itself and show how, far from furthering man's free development,
the system leads to his alienation. Once man lives in a certain

economic system he is subject to its laws, but the system is ultimately made by man and can be rejected in its totality.

Although Marx from now on concentrates on the study of economy, his work remains inspired by ethical concerns. He studies the classical economists to discover the influence of economic laws on society and to criticize the system from a humanistic viewpoint. In this philosophical critique of the economy, he reveals himself as a great and original thinker. All the results of his previous studies are brought together in one powerful synthesis to which he remains basically faithful in his later works.

Yet, this synthesis would not have been possible without a return to Hegel's dialectic. Before the Paris *Manuscripts,* Marx's attitude toward Hegel had been mainly negative: he was convinced that Hegel's idealism had profoundly corrupted his philosophy. Feuerbach had attempted to rescue the dialectic from Hegel's System by restoring man to the central place held by the abstract Idea. But his "man of flesh and blood" was no less abstract than Hegel's Idea. Marx had tried to remedy this by replacing Feuerbach's man in his concrete social environment. The results were not satisfactory. The dialectic was no longer the vital movement of man's evolution which it was in Hegel, but an artificial framework, imposed from without. Hegel's dynamic relation among the dialectical moments was entirely lost in Feuerbach's and Marx's own humanism. Marx thus came to the conclusion that Hegel's method could not easily be detached from his philosophy. So once more he returned to Hegel himself, but this time he turned to the *Phenomenology,* in which the original impulse of the dialectical movement was not yet weakened by the conservatism of the later System. The result of this renewed contact with Hegel was the unpublished manuscripts of 1844.

Marx's Critique
of Hegel's Concept of Alienation

Marx discovered that, amazingly enough, Hegel's dialectic provided the only adequate criticism of man's present situation. He also realized that he had never understood the full significance of alienation, even though he had used the notion often enough. For Hegel alienation was the driving force of the dialectical development. For Marx, on the contrary, alienation had had no positive meaning: it was a mere negation of which man had to rid himself. But a second reading of Hegel now convinced him that alienation is highly positive: it is the forward movement which makes man a self-creating process, rather than a static being. With the same necessity the dialectical development simultaneously leads to the negation *and to the annulment of the negation.*

> The outstanding thing in Hegel's *Phenomenology* and its final outcome—that is, the dialectic of negativity as the moving and generating principle—is thus first that Hegel conceives the self-genesis of man as a process, conceives objectification as loss of the object, as alienation and as transcendence of this alienation, that he thus grasps the essence of labor and comprehends objective man . . . as the outcome of man's own labor.[20]

Two elements of Hegel's thought are important here. (1) Labor is conceived of as the activity through which man realizes his own essence. "Labor is man's coming to be for himself." [21] Man is not a static being—he *becomes* himself through his labor. Hegel's view of man provides the philosophical foundation of the economic thesis that labor is the essence of economic value. (2) This becoming oneself is realized "within alienation." According to Hegel, labor itself constitutes this alienation.

[20] *MEGA*, I³, 156; Karl Marx, *Economic and Philosophic Manuscripts of 1844* (tr. by Martin Milligan, Moscow, 1959), p. 151. Henceforth this will be referred to as "Milligan."
[21] *MEGA*, I³, 157; Milligan, p. 151.

To some extent, Marx accepts both views. For him also, man realizes his essence in labor, and he becomes himself through a process of alienation. But Marx rejects the identification of labor *itself* with alienation. This identification results from Hegel's idealistic presupposition that man is *essentially* a conscious being and that the object of consciousness is merely self-consciousness objectified. From this presupposition it follows that any relation to an *extrinsic* object, any involvement with an *external* world, is an alienation of man. Labor then, insofar as it is an outgoing movement, estranges man from himself in Hegel's philosophy.

> Objectivity as such is regarded [by Hegel] as an estranged human relationship which does not correspond to the *essence of man*, to self-consciousness. The *re-appropriation* of the objective essence of man, begotten in the form of estrangement as something alien, has the meaning therefore not only of annulling *estrangement*, but *objectivity* as well. Man, that is to say, is regarded as a *non-objective*, spiritual being.[22]

Thus the whole humanization process, according to Hegel, becomes an evolution from consciousness of the object to self-consciousness, and the genesis of man is reduced to a reappropriation of objectivity. The final outcome is a spiritual, non-objective being. Marx feels that Hegel's idealistic concept of man misled him about the nature of man's alienation. Hegelian alienation is merely an alienation of consciousness: it "is the thought, the consciousness of alienation." For Hegel, man alienates himself in his labor and establishes thinghood. But this establishment of thinghood is not really creative for Hegel, for thinghood is an independent reality only in appearance: it is not a real thing, but an abstraction entirely dependent on the subject and without any real substance. Man's alienation is his very involvement with the external world; his estrangement is the estrangement of self-consciousness.[23] By identifying man with

[22] *MEGA*, I³, 157; Milligan, pp. 152–53.
[23] *MEGA*, I³, 157; Milligan, p. 152.

consciousness, says Marx, Hegel has made man into a spiritual, unworldly being and severed his vital relation to nature. Nothing is gained, therefore, when the object of Hegel's alienation is reincorporated into consciousness. Hegel correctly described the alienation process but he mistook an alienation of consciousness for man's alienation.

> Hegel having posited man as equivalent to self-consciousness, the estranged object—the estranged essential reality of man—is nothing but *consciousness*, the thought of estrangement merely—estrangement's *abstract* and therefore empty and unreal expression, negation. The annulment of the alienation is therefore likewise nothing but an abstract, empty annulment of that empty abstraction—the *negation of the negation.*[24]

But man is not only a subject, argues Marx; he also is an objective, natural being. He belongs to nature by origin and essence. He is endowed with objective powers by which he exteriorizes himself in the objective, natural world, and constitutes himself as an objective being. This relation to the world is passive as much as active, for man not only shapes the world, but, as part of the world, is also shaped by it.

> *Man* is directly a *natural being*. As a natural being and as a living natural being he is on the one hand furnished with *natural powers of life*—he is an *active* natural being. These forces exist in him as tendencies and abilities—as *impulses*. On the other hand, as a natural, corporeal, sensuous, objective being he is a *suffering*, conditioned and limited creature, like animals and plants. That is to say, the *objects* of his impulses exist outside him, as *objects* independent of him; yet these objects are *objects* of his *need*—essential *objects*, indispensable to the manifestation and confirmation of his essential powers. To say that man is a *corporeal*, living, real, sensuous, objective being full of natural vigour is to say that he has *real, sensuous objects* as the objects of his being or of his life, or that he can only *express* his life in real, sensuous objects. To be objec-

tive, natural and sensuous, and at the same time to have object, nature and sense outside oneself, or oneself to be object, nature and sense for a third party, is one and the same thing.[25]

The science of man is part of natural science. History, for instance, should be subsumed under natural history, i.e. the process of nature coming to be man.[26] Man and nature are the two terms of the same relational reality. Any psychology which considers man an isolated being is abstract and incorrect, for man is essentially related to nature. The practical part of the new science of man and nature is industry, "the exoteric revelation of man's essential powers." Industry reveals the natural essence of man and the human essence of nature.[27]

Marx's Theory of Alienation

Man's true alienation is the opposite of what Hegel thought: it does not consist in man's relation to nature but in his estrangement from nature, in his *inhuman* relation to nature. This estrangement takes a threefold form: man is alienated from the product of his work, from the act of producing, and from his own social nature. In a society based on private property, particularly in industrialized capitalism, the worker is a mere instrument in the production process of external goods. What he produces is a *thing*, alien to himself. His labor becomes part of an external object, entirely independent of himself and to be consumed by a stranger.

> The *alienation* of the worker in his product means not only that his labor becomes an object, an *external* existence, but that it exists *outside him,* independently, as something alien to him, and that it becomes a power on its

25 *MEGA*, I³, 160–61; Milligan, pp. 156–57.
26 *MEGA*, I³, 123; Milligan, p. 111.
27 *MEGA*, I³, 122; Milligan, p. 110.

own confronting him; it means that the life which he has conferred on the object confronts him as something hostile and alien.[28]

Rather than liberating him, such a form of labor enslaves man: it reduces him to an object. The more he produces, the more his personal value decreases, for his value consists entirely in his contribution to the production of external goods, and these goods devaluate as their number increases. "The worker becomes all the poorer the more wealth he produces, the more his production increases in power and range. The worker becomes an ever cheaper commodity, the more commodities he creates. With the *increasing value* of the world of things proceeds in direct proportion the *devaluation* of the world of men." [29]

Nature provides man with his means of subsistence. But the more the worker appropriates nature, the less he receives from it. He is reduced to the bare minimum that is necessary to keep him active in the production process. "The worker's needs are but the one *need*—to maintain him *whilst he is working* insofar as may be necessary *to prevent the race of laborers from dying out*. The wages of labor have thus exactly the same significance as the *maintenance* and *servicing* of any other productive instrument." [30] Whatever exceeds the satisfaction of his most immediate needs is a waste of production capital. Political economy, the science of wealth, is for the great mass of men the science of self-denial. Thrift becomes the major virtue of the capitalistic society. The more the worker can deny himself, the better for the production which is the ultimate goal of capitalism. Whatever is not needed for his productive labor is luxury: not only culture and recreation, but even fresh air and procreation of children beyond the number needed for future production are wasteful extravagances. The ideal worker of the capitalist society is the man who has no human needs and saves even the little money that he makes for further investment. Capitalism's

[28] *MEGA*, I³, 83–84; Milligan, p. 70.   [30] *MEGA*, I³, 97–98; Milligan, p. 85.
[29] *MEGA*, I³, 82–83; Milligan, p. 69.

advice to man is: "The less you eat, drink and read books; the less you go to the theatre, the dance hall, the public-house; the less you think, love, theorize, sing, paint, fence, etc., the more you *save*—the *greater* becomes your treasure which neither moths nor dust will devour—your *capital.*" [31]

But the capitalist system estranges man from his *producing activity* even more than from the *results* of it. The worker's activity is no longer determined by his personal benefit (his self-creation), but by his physical or mental dispositions for the benefit of the objective product. Labor, instead of being man's self-realization, becomes his self-negation. "The worker only feels himself outside his work, and in his work feels outside himself. He is at home when he is not working, and when he is working he is not at home. His labor is therefore not voluntary, but coerced; it is *forced labor.*" [32] Instead of being an expression of himself, it becomes a burden which he is *forced* to assume in order to keep himself alive. "As soon as no physical or other compulsion exists, labor is shunned like a plague." [33] The more man works, the less human he becomes. As a result he only feels at home in the mere animal functions of eating, drinking, and procreating. The very labor which was to liberate his humanity has reduced him to an animal.

A third aspect of the alienation in the capitalist society is the estrangement of the worker from his fellow man. As a conscious being, man in his creative activity transcends the mere satisfaction of his individual, physical needs. "Man (like the animal) lives on inorganic nature; and the more universal man is, compared with an animal, the more universal is the sphere of inorganic nature on which he lives." [34] Consciousness provides man with the perspective necessary for looking at objects from a distance. As a result, man is able to produce beyond the immediate means of his subsistence, and the entire world becomes a possible object of his activity in art, science, and technology. But in

[31] *MEGA,* I³, 130; Milligan, p. 119.   [33] *MEGA,* I³, 86; Milligan, p. 72.
[32] *MEGA,* I³, 85–86; Milligan, p. 72.   [34] *MEGA,* I³, 87; Milligan, p. 74.

this production beyond his immediate, individual needs, man produces with and for the entire human race. Any cultural production is a common enterprise, to be shared by the entire human community. Unlike the animal, man produces as a universal being.

In the capitalist society, however, the very labor through which man becomes a universal, a species-being, is estranged from him and turned into animal labor. The universal productive impulse is deprived of its universal character and deformed into a mere means to satisfy individual physical needs. Man's life activity becomes fully determined by physical necessity, like an animal's. No longer does he mold the object of his work to his own inspiration. "In degrading spontaneous activity, free activity, to a means, estranged labor makes man's species life a means to his physical existence. . . . Estranged labor turns thus man's *species being*, both nature and his spiritual species property, into a being *alien* to him, into a means to his individual existence." [35] Through the alienation from his life activity, man is estranged from his fellow man. His fellow man becomes a stranger—another individual competing with him for the satisfaction of his own needs. And both are strangers to each other because they are alienated from their universal human activity.

But there is more. In capitalist society, man's fellow man becomes another means for satisfying individual needs. Supposedly, there is a "social aspect" to capitalist economy—the division of labor. But this is merely the social form of man's alienation. Division of labor is the exploitation of the diversity of man's abilities for a production process which gradually deprives him of all human and social dignity. "The division of labor is nothing else but the estranged, alienated positing of human activity as a *real activity of the species* or as activity of man as a species being." [36]

"Division of labour and exchange are the two phenomena in connection with which the political economist boasts the social

[35] *MEGA*, I³, 89; Milligan, p. 76.   [36] *MEGA*, I³, 139; Milligan, p. 129.

character of his science and in the same breath gives expression to the contradiction in his science—the establishment of society through unsocial, particular interests." [37] Division of labor results from exchange, which even the classical economists admit originates from purely egoistic drives. Adam Smith says:

> Man has constant occasion for the help of others, and it is in vain for him to expect it from their benevolence only. He will be more likely to prevail if he can appeal to their personal interest and show them that it is for their own advantage to do for him what he requires from them. We address ourselves not to other men's humanity but to their self-love. . . .[38]

On such a basis, says Marx, no true society can ever be built. The means of exchange, money, takes the life out of all authentic human relations: it allows me to buy anything which I do not yet possess—even love and respect. Money secures the dominion of the object over the person. The person is reduced to what he can buy or sell. His human value is marked down to the value of his money, like merchandise. His power is his buying power.[39]

In the capitalist society, labor sacrifices the worker to the material wealth of the nonworker. But the real god is the capitalist system, for the nonworker is also its victim. Private property is as much an alienation of his life as it is of the worker's. The capitalist is not the master but the slave of his capital. Capital is its own master, and can only serve its own increase to the detriment of man.

The identification of man's alienation with alienation of labor which Marx makes in the *Economic and Philosophic Manuscripts* signals a new departure in his thought. Until now he has seen private property as the ultimate *cause* of alienation. In the *Manuscripts* he reaches the conclusion that private property is only the *result* of man's estrangement from his own labor.

[37] *MEGA*, I¹, 144; Milligan, p. 134.
[38] *MEGA*, I³, 139; Milligan, p. 130.
[39] *MEGA*, I³, 145–49; Milligan, pp. 136–41.

True, it is as a result of the *movement of private property* that we have obtained the concept of *alienated labour* (of alienated life) from political economy. But on analysis of this concept it becomes clear that though private property appears to be the source, the cause of alienated labour, it is really its consequence, just as the gods in the beginning are not the cause but the effect of man's intellectual confusion. Later this relationship becomes reciprocal.[40]

Marx owes his new insight into the nature of man's alienation to Hegel's *Phenomenology* and to the classical economists Smith and Ricardo. Through their works he comes to see that man is estranged from his *act* of self-creation as well as from the product of his act. Adam Smith interiorized the whole economic process by declaring labor the ultimate economic value. Property itself takes all its value from the amount of labor that man puts into it. Smith thus understands the economic process as a *human* process. Marx compares this interiorization of economy with the religious interiorization of the Reformation.

Just as Luther sublated *external* religiosity by making religiosity the *inner* substance of man—just as he negated the priest outside the layman because he transplanted the priest into laymen's hearts, just so with wealth: wealth as something outside man and independent of him, and therefore as something to be maintained and asserted only in an external fashion, is done away with; that is, this *external, mindless objectivity* of wealth [of the economists before Smith] is done away with, with private property being incorporated in man himself and with man himself being recognized as its essence. But as a result man is brought within the orbit of private property, just as in Luther he is brought within the orbit of religion. Under

---

[40] *MEGA*, I³, 91–92; Milligan, p. 80. It has been said that this is a *petitio principii*. Since Marx analyzes the estranged labor within the context of an economic system which is based on private property, it is obvious that from this analysis he can in turn deduce the principles of private property. See H. Popitz, *Der Entfremdete Mensch* (Basel, 1953), p. 142. However, Marx's argument is not logical but anthropological. The priority of the estrangement of labor is not so much that of a cause with respect to its effect, as that of the more *interior* principle (a man himself—in his operation) with respect to its external manifestation.

the semblance of recognizing man, the political economy whose principle is labor is really no more than the consistent implementation of the denial of man, since man himself no longer stands in an external relation of tension to the external substance of private property, but has himself become this tensed essence of private property.[41]

What previously was considered exterior to man has now become man's own act of self-expression.

Private property reveals the contradiction of the present economic system insofar as it makes labor into the subjective essence of all property and leaves the laborer without property. But the essence of labor is man, and so, in an economic system based on private property, man is alienated from himself. This alienation is still hidden in feudal society, where private property adopts the form of landed property and labor with economic value is limited to agricultural work exclusively. But in the industrial era *any* form of labor becomes an object of private property and, consequently, man becomes *entirely* estranged from his self-creation. Industrialization has completed the *reification* of man which is inherent in private property: man has become an instrument to make things.

The Reintegration of Human Labor

From the estrangement of labor and man Marx turns to their reintegration. Most Communist theories try to suppress private property by making it into *common* property. But such a solution still maintains the basic principle of private property: it considers material possessions and not man's self-realization as the end of labor.

In negating the *personality* of man in every sphere, this type of communism is really nothing but the logical expression of private property, which is this negation [of the person]. General *envy* constituting itself as a power is the

[41] *MEGA*, I³, 107–08; Milligan, p. 94.

disguise in which *avarice* re-establishes itself and satisfies itself, only in *another* way. . . . How little this annulment of private property is really an appropriation [of what was estranged from man] is in fact proved by the abstract negation of the entire world of culture and civilization, the regression to the *unnatural* simplicity of the *poor and undemanding* man who has not only failed to go beyond private property, but has not yet even attained to it.[42]

Private property should be suppressed, not by returning to communal property, but by abolishing the alienation itself of which it is the expression. Through this positive transcendence of private property, the object of man's activity again becomes a *human* object. Man appropriates the world in a human way: his relation to it is no longer one of *having* but of *being*. His work is no longer a means to an end outside himself but an expression of his entire being, in which he objectifies *himself* without losing himself (as he did in private property). Nature becomes human and man becomes natural.

The transcendence of private property is therefore the complete *emancipation* of all human senses and attributes; but it is this emancipation precisely because these senses and attributes have become, subjectively and objectively, *human*. The eye has become a *human* eye, just as its *object* has become a social, *human* object—an object emanating from man for man. The *senses* have therefore become directly in their practice *theoreticians*. They relate themselves to the *thing* for the sake of the thing, but the thing itself is an *objective human* relation to itself and to man, and vice versa. Need or enjoyment have consequently lost their *egotistical* nature, and nature has lost its mere *utility* by use becoming *human* use.[43]

Man's objectification of himself in nature creates a genuine culture only when he uses nature in a truly human way.

In humanizing his relation to the material world, man will suppress all forms of alienation. Religion and the State are only

42 *MEGA*, I³, 112; Milligan, p. 100.
43 *MEGA*, I³, 118–19; Milligan, pp. 106–07.

partial expressions of the one fundamental estrangement of man from nature and are bound to disappear simultaneously with their cause. But a religious or political emancipation alone can never liberate man. The religious critique merely fights the *consciousness* of man's alienation and leaves the roots of the alienation intact. "Communism begins from the outset with atheism; but atheism is at first far from being *communism;* indeed, it is still mostly an abstraction." [44] The same holds true for the political critique: not political reforms but only a reintegration of man with nature can return him to his true essence.

This reintegration will also restore the bond between man and his fellow man, for the humanization of nature is essentially a social task. "Activity and consumption, both in their content and in their *mode of existence,* are *social: social activity* and *social* consumption." [45] "Social" refers of course to more than merely work which is done in immediate cooperation with others. Even the lonely task of the scientist is social, for the material on which he works as well as his personal life are a product of the community. His consciousness is "the theoretical shape of that of which the living shape is the real community." [46] There is a mutual causality between man and society. The society which man creates through his work will in turn create him. "Just as society itself produces *man as man,* so is society *produced* by him." [47] "Thus society is the consummated oneness in substance of man and nature—the true resurrection of nature— the naturalism of man and the humanism of nature both brought to fulfillment." [48]

[44] *MEGA,* I³, 115; Milligan, p. 103.
[45] *MEGA,* I³, 116; Milligan, p. 103.
[46] *MEGA,* I³, 116; Milligan, p. 104.

[47] *MEGA,* I³, 116; Milligan, p. 103.
[48] *MEGA,* I³, 116; Milligan, p. 104.

A Critique of the Economic
and Philosophic Manuscripts

In the *Manuscripts,* Marx has entirely abandoned Hegel's speculative Logic. Instead of an Idea, the moving force of the universe is man—and this man is not an abstract, isolated individual, as in Feuerbach's anthropology, but a concrete being essentially related to nature and to his fellow man.

At the same time, the *Manuscripts* show a definite return to Hegel, not the Hegel of the System, it is true, but the Hegel of the *Phenomenology.* Having found his own way, Marx is now in a better position to appreciate the dialectical method in its unadulterated form. In clarifying his own ideas, Marx has finally discerned what can be retained from Hegel's philosophy: henceforth he confidently employs the dialectical method without being inhibited by Hegel's idealism.

Many questions remain after the *Manuscripts.* The most important is *why* man becomes alienated from his labor. Feuerbach had situated man's alienation in religion. In his *Critique of Hegel's Philosophy of the State,* Marx proved that the religious alienation was only an expression for man's social alienation, resulting from private property. Now the *Manuscripts* show that private property itself results from the warping of man's relation to nature: his work is no longer a creation in and through nature, but a bondage to nature which reduces him to a thing. How does man ever reach this state of bondage? The manuscript in which Marx announces his answer to this question breaks off unfinished.

Another problem that still awaits its final solution at the end of the *Manuscripts* is the nature of Marx's Communism. His description of *positive Communism* remains extremely vague. Marx's break with the past is radical enough, but his view of the future never becomes entirely clear. It reveals the influence of Hegel's notion of historical necessity. Private property is not just the alienation of man—it is a *necessary* alienation of man. Positive Communism can appear only as a sequel to a social structure based on private property. "On the one hand, human life required private property for its realization and on the other hand it now requires the supersession of private property." [49] However, Marx fails to show *how* the same necessity which causes man's estrangement will also cause his liberation. His commitment to the dialectical method makes it clear enough that this necessity exists. But at the time of the *Manuscripts,* he merely concentrates on the alienation and its social-economic causes. His economic studies have not proceeded far enough to make the supersession of private property more than a dialectical assumption. Marx is unable to point to concrete social and economic facts which make it more than a *logical* necessity. For this reason his treatment of positive Communism remains a vague description of an unsubstantiated ideal, contrasting with the stringent analyses of alienation.

A final question which one might well ask is whether the *Manuscripts* are not, after all, a mere application of Hegel's theory of alienation.[50] Marx certainly criticizes Hegel's theory of labor often enough, but the question remains whether his criticism is correct and whether his own theory is as original as he believes it to be.

Marx is certainly mistaken in his objections to the abstract, spiritual character of Hegel's notion of labor. Hegel did not overlook the concrete, physical aspects of labor. Nor is it correct to say that the dialectic of work in the *Phenomenology* annuls the subject-object opposition of man and his world. It is true that the opposition is annulled on the *immediate* stage of the ego-nonego relation, but it reappears on a more reflective level. It is therefore not annulled *altogether* but *sublated,* that is, negated and then elevated to a higher level. One may say that the subject-object opposition has become interiorized, but not that it has disappeared. This opposition is never overcome: it is the

---

49 *MEGA,* I3, 144; Milligan, p. 134.
50 This is somewhat the tendency of Popitz's excellent book, *Der Entfremdete Mensch.* For a criticism, see J. Hommes, *Der Technische Eros* (Freiburg, 1955) , p. 265.

hinge on which Hegel's dialectic turns. In considering nature as a part of man, Hegel merely affirms that man cannot become himself except in dialogue with the world, and that the world through man's work takes on a human character. But this thesis is no less basic for Marx than for Hegel. It is true that in Hegel all the emphasis is on consciousness. But then Hegel's *Phenomenology* differs from Marx's anthropology in purpose: the former describes only the genesis of consciousness and does not pretend to be a complete philosophy of man.

Nevertheless, Marx's criticism of Hegel is not altogether unjustified. For if one understands the *Phenomenology* through its later developments, as Marx did, one hardly escapes the impression that the identification of the real with the ideal *in the Spirit* ultimately eliminates the otherness of nature. Marx senses that Hegel's spiritual monism prevented him from taking the alienation seriously. If the real as well as the ideal is a moment of the Spirit, then any opposition between them takes place within the basic identity of the Spirit with itself. Nature is no longer the *other* when it is merely the *otherness of the Spirit*. It is not surprising, then, that the element of struggle becomes weaker and weaker in Hegel's later works. The dialectic becomes a process of self-development in which the Spirit passes smoothly through its own oppositions, without being alarmed by them.

For Marx as for Hegel, man develops himself in a dynamic relation to nature. But this relation to nature is not reducible to a relation of the Spirit to itself. The two different terms—nature and man as conscious being—remain opposed, and this creates the possibility of real strife. Man depends on *another* (in the real sense of the word) for his own realization. It is the *otherness* of the term to which man is related which makes it possible for the relation to become a true alienation. In Hegel's philosophy this possibility does not exist: the two terms are dialectical moments of the same Spirit. The alienation in his dialectic merely consists in the *distinction* between the two terms, in the fact that they do not coincide in complete identity. But a real *opposition* between two terms of the same reality is impossible.

Here one might object that the two terms, consciousness and nature, are ultimately unified even in Marx's thought: even as conscious being, man remains a part of nature. This is true, but Marx strongly affirms that man is a very unique part of nature, which, through consciousness, has detached itself from the whole. Man does not belong to nature as minerals or animals do, for nature *becomes* through man what it *was not* through itself. On the other hand, man's essence is such that, in order to become himself, he must constantly become more than himself, and he can do this only by maintaining a dynamic relationship to a term which is *different* from himself.

The relation between consciousness and reality will be further elaborated in Marx's next writing, *The Holy Family,* and will receive its definitive treatment in *The German Ideology.* Critical conclusions on this point will thus be postponed until after the analysis of both these works.

The Holy Family

In November, 1844, Marx completed *The Holy Family: The Critique of the Critical Critique (Die heilige Familie, oder die Kritik der Kritischen Kritik)*, his first published book after the doctoral dissertation.[51] To the reader of the *Manuscripts, The Holy Family* is somewhat disappointing: Marx shows himself a penetrating and sarcastic polemicist, but he adds little to his previous theories. Not until *The German Ideology* are the ideas of the *Manuscripts* further developed. In *The Holy Family* Marx mainly answers the attacks on Engels and himself by

---

[51] Engels' name also appeared on the title page, but he had contributed only an insignificant part.

Bruno Bauer and the "cenacle" of the critical journal *Die all-gemeine Literaturzeitung.*

The greater part of the work is devoted to Szeliga's critical interpretation of Eugène Sue's *Les Mystères de Paris* (1842–43), a novel which today is almost as completely forgotten as Szeliga's farfetched philosophical commentary. Marx has little trouble proving that Szeliga's speculative constructions are based on a misreading of the novel. But he takes the opportunity to destroy Sue's own religious and social paternalism at the same time.

Marx's Defense of Proudhon

The most valuable part of *The Holy Family* consists of the marginal notes to Edgar Bauer's German translation of Proudhon's *What Is Property?* (*Qu'est-ce que la propriété?*, 1840). Marx goes to the defense of Proudhon, whose ideas had been betrayed by Bauer's translation and critical commentaries. It is somewhat questionable whether Marx's interpretation of Proudhon is more faithful to the original than Bauer's, but at least it elucidates Marx's ideas at the time. In Marx's view, Proudhon was the first to question the basic principle which all national economists presuppose as a matter of course—private property. Proudhon shows that private property, instead of being the *human* foundation of the economic process, is human only in appearance. It is true that private property seems to correspond to a basic need of human nature, but, once accepted, it becomes uncontrollable and leads to the most inhuman conditions of life. This is obvious enough in the case of the salaried worker. His wages seem to be determined by a free agreement of the employer and the employed, but in fact he is forced by the economic pressure of the private property system to accept a salary in which neither he nor the employer has any choice. The economists themselves feel these contradictions, and vacillate between the human aspect of their science and its deterministic, nonhuman laws.

In his discussion of Proudhon, Marx, for the first time, clearly enunciates the dialectical struggle between the possessing class and the proletarians. Proletariat and wealth are "the two forms of the world of private property." Wealth is the positive side of the antinomy, the proletariat the negative. The proletariat works for its own suppression, which at the same time is the suppression both of the institution which produces proletarians (private property) and of its positive counterpart, the class of the possessors. Private property leads to its own abolition through the conscious and free action of its negative side, the proletariat. "The proletariat carries out the sentence which private property, by creating the proletariat, passes upon itself, just as it carries out the sentence which wage-labor, by creating wealth for others and poverty for itself, passes upon itself." [52]

Again it is clear that Marx does not believe in a mechanistic economic liberation of man. He never questions the inescapable necessity of this liberation, but neither does he forget that this *necessity* itself depends on man's intervention. Private property can be abolished only through the free action of the proletarians. But this free revolutionary action is made inevitable by the economic situation and by philosophy's inexorable infiltration of the masses. The selfish objectives of single individuals in the proletarian class are unable to inhibit this revolutionary movement.

> It is not a matter of knowing what this or that proletarian, or even the proletariat as a whole, *conceives* as its aims at any particular moment. It is a question of knowing *what* the proletariat *is,* and what it must accomplish in history according to its *nature.* Its aim and its historical activity are ordained for it, in a tangible and irrevocable way, by its own situation, as well as by the whole organization of present-day civil society.[53]

Like Hegel, Marx believes in the practical power of ideas. But he rejects Hegel's belief that the *Idea* develops from its own

[52] *MEGA*, I³, 206.   [53] *MEGA*, I³, 207.

intrinsic power. Ideas become powerful only when they become flesh and blood in living people. A revolution is a conscious protest of the masses, rather than a necessary development of the Idea. History is not a "separate entity, a metaphysical subject of which real human individuals are mere representatives," and in which the absolute Idea proves its own truth. History does not make man, but man makes history. "History . . . does not use man to realize its own ends, as if it were a particular person: it is nothing but the activity of man pursuing his own objectives." [54]

The Role of the Masses
in the Emancipation of Man

For this reason Marx rejects any philosophy which, like Bauer's, secludes itself from the mass of mankind in a little cenacle of its own. A philosophy opposed to the people cannot be true, for the truth of philosophy is action, and this can never be achieved by speculative philosophers who pride themselves that the masses, the only center of real power, are unable to understand them. Ideas make history, but only when they are *realized* by the living people—the masses. "Ideas never lead beyond the established situation, they only lead beyond the ideas of the established situation. In fact, ideas cannot realize anything. The realization of ideas requires men who apply a practical force." [55] This again requires that the ideas respond to the problems of the masses. If they do, nothing can stop their practical impact. It is an illusion of the ivory-tower philosopher that the masses are incapable of absorbing ideas. The French Revolution was a social failure not because the revolutionary ideas were watered down once they reached the masses, as Bauer assumes, but, on the contrary, because they never reached the masses. The revolutionary impulse originated in a limited group whose aspira-

[54] *MEGA*, I³, 265.   [55] *MEGA*, I³, 294.

tions were too far removed from the real needs of the people to awaken more than a momentary interest.

Bauer's distinction between the "philosophical" elite and the mass of people is a secular reappearance of the Teutonic-Christian contrast between pure spirit and sinful matter. A few individuals represent this pure spirit and separate themselves contemptuously from the spiritless matter of the masses. "All the progress of the spirit up till now has been directed against the mass of mankind, which has been thrown into a less and less human situation." [56] It is true that history has developed apart from the masses, but only because the few who were in possession of consciousness of purpose (the driving of history) deliberately kept it from the masses to lead events to their private advantage.

How the historical "emancipation of man" has developed apart from the real people is well illustrated by the *Déclaration des droits de l'homme*. The alleged recognition of *human* rights was in fact a recognition of the rights of one class of people, the bourgeoisie. The "emancipation of man" turned out to be the enslavement of the masses to the desires of the few. Modern man has been "emancipated" only from restrictions on ruthless individualism, and the only society set free is a *civil society* destructive of all true social life. "The basis of the *modern* State is civil society and the *individual* of civil society, that is, the independent individual, whose only link with other individuals is private interest." [57]

Marx feels that Bauer was naive in believing that the suppression of privilege leads to the liberation of man. Just the opposite is true. The suppression of privileges has merely universalized abuses which formerly were restricted to a few instances. The suppression of trade and corporation privileges has not stopped the industrial upsurge but has rather accelerated it. The same is true for landed property and commerce; both started expanding after they were freed from the fetters of com-

[56] *MEGA*, I³, 256.   [57] *MEGA*, I³, 288.

mercial privileges and property restrictions. Even religion, the favorite example of Bauer, has not died after the abolition of religious privileges; on the contrary, it has received a vigorous impulse from its new independence, as the example of the United States shows. The suppression of privileges has emancipated the privileged object but not the unprivileged man. Rather, what is liberated is all that enslaves man.

The real liberation of man is to be achieved by the masses and not by a few individuals or groups of individuals who consider themselves the representatives of the "spirit of the epoch." The distinction between a material and a spiritual element of society, between the masses and the philosophical elite, must disappear if man is to be liberated at all. And it will disappear; for the masses have reached the depths of human degradation, and "in the midst of degradation [is born] the *revolt* against degradation, a revolt to which the masses are forced by the contradiction between their *humanity* and a situation which is an open, clear and absolute negation of this humanity." [58]

Marxist Humanism and French Materialism

Marx's defense of the masses in *The Holy Family* is another aspect of the integral humanism for which he had laid the foundation in the *Economic and Philosophic Manuscripts*. History has never been *man's* history (i.e. the history of the *people*) and philosophy has never stated *man's* purpose of action. A true humanism implies the reappropriation of all human reality into man so that there is no opposition between man, on the one hand, and God, history, philosophy, or nature, on the other.

Only by keeping this humanism in mind can one understand Marx's defense of French "materialism." This topic is introduced in *The Holy Family* in reply to Bauer's assertion that

[58] *MEGA*, I³, 205.

the materialist movement in France was basically rationalistic in inspiration. According to Bauer, French materialism is directly deduced from Spinoza's metaphysical monism. Marx, on the contrary, believes that it is an antimetaphysical and antitheological humanism which, like Feuerbach's anthropology, had its roots in a new theory of man rather than in speculation on the nature of the universe. French materialism, while influenced by Descartes and Locke (rather than Spinoza), owes more to Bayle's irreligious scepticism. For Bayle showed "that a society consisting only of atheists is possible, that an atheist can be a respectable man, and that, rather than by atheism, it is by superstition and idolatry that man debases himself." [59]

But materialism received its main impetus from its own practical humanism. Helvetius' and D'Holbach's theories are primarily social philosophies, founded on the natural goodness and equality of all men, the idea of progress, and the omnipotence of education. A direct link connects those thinkers with the later French Communists. It is the humanistic and social conclusions which captivate Marx's interest; the materialistic premises he merely tolerates.

> If man draws all his knowledge, sensation, etc. from the world of the senses and the experiences gained in it, the empirical world must be arranged so that in it man experiences and gets used to what is really human, and so that he becomes aware of himself as man. If interest correctly understood is the principle of all morality, man's private interest must be made to coincide with the interest of humanity. If man is unfree in the materialist sense, i.e. is free not through the negative power to avoid this or that, but through the positive power to assert his true individuality, crime must not be punished in the individual, but the antisocial source of crime must be destroyed, and each man must be given social scope for the vital manifestation of his being. If man is shaped by his surroundings, his surroundings must be made human. If man is social by nature, he will develop his true nature only in society, and the

[59] *MEGA*, I³, 303–04.

power of his nature must be measured not by the power of separate individuals but by the power of society.[60]

For Marx, French materialism is basically an assertion of man's essential relation to nature and a denial of any sort of superhuman transcendence. The ontological implications of this materialism (the nature of matter and spirit) do not interest him. As we shall see in *The German Ideology,* his own historical materialism is essentially a theory of action, which systematically avoids becoming a theory of being.

[60] *MEGA,* I[3], 307–08.

6

Marx's Historical Materialism: The German Ideology

German Ideology and History

In February, 1845, Marx was expelled from France at the request of the Prussian government, and was allowed to settle down in Brussels after promising to abstain from political activity. His Brussels period lasted until the Belgian government expelled him for participating in the revolution of 1848. While there, Marx continued his economic studies and started a life-long collaboration with Engels. Their first joint product was *The German Ideology* (*Die deutsche Ideologie*, 1845). Marx has left an account of its demise:

> The manuscript in two solid octavo volumes had long reached the publisher in Westphalia when we received information that conditions had so changed as not to allow of its publication. We abandoned the manuscript to the stinging criticism of the mice the more readily since we had accomplished our main purpose—the clearing up of the question to ourselves.[1]

The publication of this work by the Marx-Lenin Institute in 1932 has caused a real revolution in the interpretation of Marx's later works. Its importance is quite surprising in that the *Ideology* is largely polemic, and was originally conceived

---

[1] *Werke*, XIII, 10; *Contribution to the Critique of Political Economy* (tr. by N. I. Stone, Chicago, 1904), p. 14.

as a refutation of Max Stirner's almost forgotten work, *The Ego and His Own* (*Der Einzige und sein Eigentum,* 1844). Later, the project escalated into a general attack on the Young Hegelian movement, including Bauer and Feuerbach as well as Stirner. It became a final rejection of all "ideology"—any interpretation of history which is based on a dialectic of ideas divorced from the social-economic realities in which those ideas originate.

The first part, entitled "Feuerbach" although only a few pages refer to him, is by far the most important. Marx here, for the first time, develops the theory which will later be called "historical materialism," and which is the heart of the Marxist philosophy. We may assume that Engels' contribution to this first part was insignificant, for he himself has repeatedly asserted that Marx's materialist theory of history was already formed when their collaboration started.

A Critique of the Young Hegelians

The section on Feuerbach opens with the following description of the philosophical situation in Germany.

As we hear from German ideologists, Germany has in the last few years gone through an unparalleled revolution. The decomposition of the Hegelian philosophy, which began with Strauss, has developed into a universal ferment into which all the "powers of the past" are swept. In the general chaos mighty empires have arisen only to meet with immediate doom, heroes have emerged momentarily only to be hurled into obscurity by bolder and stronger rivals. It was a revolution beside which the French Revolution was child's play, a world struggle beside which the struggles of the Diadochi appear insignificant. Principles ousted one another, heroes of the mind overthrew each other with unheard-of rapidity, and in the three years 1842–1845 more of the past was swept away than normally in three centuries. All this is supposed to have taken place in the realm of pure thought. Certainly it is an interesting event we are dealing with: the putrescence of the absolute spirit.[2]

The world revolution of the Young Hegelians from Strauss to Stirner was, in fact, not more than a harmless demythologization of Hegel, criticizing one aspect of his philosophy by means of another without ever coming to grips with the system itself. The Young Hegelians merely converted Hegel's philosophy into a negative theology. Their entire critique consists in denouncing law, State, and morality as religious phantoms, and it concludes with the hope that after this negative canonization all abuses will automatically disappear from the world.

> The Old Hegelians had *comprehended* everything as soon as it was reduced to an Hegelian logical category. The Young Hegelians *criticized* everything by attributing to it religious conceptions or by pronouncing it a theological matter. The Young Hegelians are in agreement with the Old Hegelians in their belief in the rule of religion, of concepts, of an abstract general principle in the existing world. Only, the one party attacks this dominion as usurpation, while the other extols it as legitimate.[3]

The supremacy of consciousness remains sacrosanct, and the critical revolution simply replaces the religious consciousness with the profane. The critical reformers never dream of altering the material conditions of life, from which all religious phantoms arise. "In spite of their allegedly 'world-shattering' statements, [they] are the staunchest conservatives."[4]

The Basis of History

To the religious world history of "St. Bruno" (Bauer) and "St. Max" (Stirner), Marx opposes his own, secular views. Instead of reforming reality through ideas, he intends to reform

---

[2] *MEGA*, I⁵, 7; Marx and Engels, *The German Ideology* (tr. by R. Pascal, New York, 1960), p. 3, by permission of International Publishers Co., Inc. Henceforth this will be referred to as *G. I.*
[3] *MEGA*, I⁵, 9; *G. I.*, p. 5.
[4] *MEGA*, I⁵, 9; *G. I.*, p. 6.

ideas through reality. History presupposes as its basic fact the existence of living human individuals, and these individuals, because of their physical being, are determined by their relation to nature. This might seem to place men on a par with animals. However, unlike animals, men actively transform nature in order *to produce* their means of subsistence. The basic requirements for subsistence are provisions for "eating and drinking, a habitation, clothing and many other things." [5] But as soon as these fundamental needs are satisfied, other needs arise, which man, with his newly acquired instruments, is equally able to satisfy. The creation of needs and their subsequent satisfaction constitute the first historical act of man. In the production of luxury he becomes a *human,* i.e. a civilized being. Because there is no limit to the needs he can create, or to the means of satisfying them, man continually transcends himself. Through this transcendence he becomes more and more human. The production process then is at once man's self-expression and his self-creation. "As individuals express their life, so they are." [6] Man's essence depends on his productive activity, and this activity is determined by nature.

But there is still a third basis of human history. Man not only produces his own life from day to day, he also *reproduces* it in his children. This procreation process, involving the cooperation of man and wife, introduces the social factor into human history. From their merely reproductive function, social relations soon pass into productive functions and expand far beyond their original cell of the family. This social expansion is entirely determined by man's material needs and the state of his production powers: social relations mark the extent to which man's productive forces are developed. But the opposite is also true. New social relations give rise to new forms of production. Social life and production determine each other: a change in one causes a change in the other.

[5] *MEGA,* I[5], 17; *G. I.,* p. 16.   [6] *MEGA,* I[5], 9; *G. I.,* p. 7.

Division of Labor: The Alienation of Man

Up to the present, social cooperation in the production process has always taken the form of specialization, of *division of labor*. This leads to private property, for the division of labor "determines also the relations of individuals to one another with reference to the material, instrument, and product of labor."[7] The product no longer belongs to the one who has worked on it, but to the one who owns the instruments of production. Wages replace the original link between labor and product, between production and consumption. The result is that those who contribute most to the production receive the least enjoyment from the actual product. By depriving the worker of the product of his work, the division of labor also estranges him from his own activity. He no longer freely determines his work for his own benefit: it is determined by his given physical or mental dispositions for the benefit of a product to which he contributes but in which he has no claim. Social cooperation is essential for the production process, but as soon as the form of cooperation is determined by the product rather than by the producer, it becomes inhuman.

> As long . . . as activity is not voluntarily, but naturally,[8] divided, man's own deed becomes an alien power opposed to him, which enslaves him instead of being controlled by him. For as soon as labor is distributed, each man has a particular, exclusive sphere of activity, which is forced upon him and from which he cannot escape. He is a hunter, a fisherman, a shepherd, or a critical critic, and must remain so if he does not want to lose his means of livelihood.[9]

What was referred to in the *Manuscripts* as the "alienation of man from his *productive activity*" is here expressed in economic terminology as "division of labor." But no matter what

---

[7] *MEGA*, I5, 11; *G. I.*, p. 9.
[8] According to the worker's mental or physical talents for production and not according to his own well-being.
[9] *MEGA*, I5, 22; *G. I.*, p. 22.

terminology is used, each is considered responsible for the alienation of man from the *product* of his work—private property. "Division of labor and private property are . . . identical expressions: in the one the same thing is affirmed with reference to activity as is affirmed in the other with reference to the product of the activity." [10] Alienated labor is crystallized in private property, and private property is nothing but the disposal of another man's labor.

As in the *Manuscripts,* Marx states that the division of labor estranges man from his fellow man, for it arises from the drive to produce and exchange as much as possible, rather than from the intrinsically social character of labor. It is adopted not for humanitarian but for purely egoistic motives. The division of labor brings out the always imminent conflict between private and universal interests. These universal or communal interests are real, as real as the dependence of the individuals upon each other. Since man is essentially social in his productive activity, the dissociation of individual from communal interests causes a profound cleavage in his whole life. The communal interests cannot be abolished, since production itself is a social activity, however much it may be exploited for the benefit of one individual. Man depends on others for the attainment of even his most private goals. In an illusory way, modern man recognizes the social nature of his activity by attributing a separate existence to his communal interest. "The latter takes an independent form as the *State,* divorced from the real interests of individual and community, and at the same time as an illusory communal life." [11] But the individualistic production process, which uses the social forces for the purpose of the product and not of the producer, must also have a *real* communal aspect. This is the *class,* the community which is based not on the communal character of the productive activity, but on the special task which individual members have been assigned through the division of labor. The State is the social illusion—the class,

[10] *MEGA,* I[5], 22; *G. I.,* p. 22.   [11] *MEGA,* I[5], 23; *G. I.,* p. 23.

the social reality of an individualistic society. In the class, man turns the social powers of his production process to his private interests. He remains a social being, but a frustrated one.

The Inevitability of Class Struggles

A society whose social groups stem from individualistic drives will necessarily have conflicts among those groups. Such conflicts are always *class struggles,* for the class is the only *real* unit in an individualistic society. Political oppositions, which alone receive all the attention of the historians, merely cover the deeper, apolitical oppositions among the classes. "All struggles within the State, the struggle between democracy, aristocracy and monarchy, the struggle for the franchise, etc., etc., are merely the illusory forms in which the real struggles of the different classes are fought out among one another." [12]

Each class, in its struggle to dominate other classes, tries first to conquer the State, the political power, "in order to represent its interest as . . . the general interest." [13] In fact, the "general" interest of the State is no more than the interest of one class. That is why every intervention of the State appears to all nonruling classes "not as their own united power but as an alien force existing outside them." [14]

The State is an illusory community: the real interindividual commerce takes place in the economic sphere of life. It is in the civil society, not in diplomatic parleys or on political battlefields, that the real struggles of history are fought.

> Already here we see how this civil society is the true source and theatre of all history, and how nonsensical is the conception of history held hitherto, which neglects the real

[12] *MEGA,* I⁵, 23; *G. I.,* p. 23.
[13] *MEGA,* I⁵, 23; *G. I.,* p. 23.
[14] *MEGA,* I⁵, 24; *G. I.,* p. 24. By introducing the concept of class struggle, Marx reinterprets his theory of the State in the *Critique.* We shall see that the suppression of the political alienation also differs from what it was in the *Critique.*

relationships and confines itself to high-sounding dramas of princes and states. Civil society embraces the whole material intercourse of individuals within a definite stage of the development of productive forces. It embraces the whole commercial and industrial life of this stage and, insofar, transcends the State and the nation, though, on the other hand again, it must assert itself towards foreign peoples as nationality, and inwardly must organize itself as State.[15]

The effects of the division of labor may be summarized as follows: the division of labor leads to private property, and this in turn creates social inequality, class struggles, and the erection of political structures. Marx illustrates this conclusion by showing how the evolution of property and of social classes throughout the ages runs parallel with the division of labor in the productive process.

The Stages of History

In a first, undeveloped stage of production, people live by hunting, fishing, herding, or, in the highest stage, by farming. All property belongs to the tribe, and the division of labor is very elementary, hardly more pronounced than in the family. After tribal ownership follows State or communal ownership, represented mainly by the economic system of the ancient city-state. Private property—first movable, then immovable as well —begins to exist alongside communal property. But it remains basically subordinate to communal property: the slaves still belong primarily to the community. The division of labor is not well developed, nor is the class opposition: the only producing class is that of the slaves. Gradually, however, an opposition between town and country arises and the class opposition grows simultaneously: some people become "town animals," others "country animals," with conflicting interests.

15 *MEGA, I*[5], 25–26; *G. I.,* p. 26.

The third form of ownership, the feudal or estate property, originates as a result of the barbaric invasions and the destruction of the ancient production forces. The towns become depopulated, and trade and industry all but disappear. In this situation, landed property becomes predominant, and the serfs replace the slaves as the productive basis of society. The class of the landowners completely dominates the others. But with the growth of new towns, they are increasingly challenged by the guilds. Thus the old division into town and country dwellers reappears. Even at this stage, however, there is no division of labor in the modern sense of an industrial economy, for each town has to supply all the demands of its people, and each man is expected to master all of his craft. This, of course, is even more the case for agriculture.

The change to a new stage, the capitalist era, is caused by the increasing power of the towns, on the one hand, and the separation of production and commerce, on the other.

> With commerce [being] the prerogative of a particular class, with the extension of trade through the merchants beyond the immediate surroundings of the town, there immediately appears a reciprocal action between production and commerce. The towns enter into relations *with one another,* new tools are brought from one town into the other, and the separation between production and commerce soon calls forth a new division of production between the individual towns, each of which is soon exploiting a predominant branch of industry.[16]

Out of this contact among the towns arises a new class: the bourgeoisie. As all landed property becomes gradually transformed into industrial and commercial property, the bourgeoisie becomes the sole possessing class.

The division of labor between the towns, as well as the extension of commerce, leads to an accumulation of capital, mak-

[16] *MEGA,* I⁵, 42; *G. I.,* pp. 47-48.

ing manufacturing possible. Manufacturing in turn accelerates commerce and capital concentration. The rising colonies provide industry and commerce with a world market, thus precipitating a struggle for trade among the nations. By colonial expansion and a commercial fleet one country manages to secure most of the world trade. Soon the demands for its manufactured products become so great that they can no longer be met by existing productive forces. But in the meantime the advance of technology has caused an industrial revolution, and machines are ready to take over where manpower is deficient.

The machine industry inaugurates a new economic era. It effects an unprecedented concentration of people in large industrial cities and brings the division of labor to such an extremity that it loses "the last semblance of its natural character."[17] It sweeps away the old opposition among nations and launches an international class struggle.

> While the bourgeoisie of each nation still retained separate national interests, big industry created a class, which in all nations has the same interests and with which nationality is already dead; a class which is really rid of all the old world and at the same time stands pitted against it.[18]

The international capitalist class is born, and with it its negative counterpart, the international proletariat.

Marx's historical analysis confirms his thesis that conditions of production and social relations shape each other.

> It follows from this that a certain mode of production, or industrial stage, is always combined with a certain mode of co-operation, or social stage, and this mode of co-operation is itself a "productive force." Further, that the multitude of productive forces accessible to men determines the nature of society, hence that the "history of humanity" must always be studied and treated in relation to the history of industry and exchange.[19]

[17] *MEGA,* I⁵, 50; *G. I.,* p. 57.
[18] *MEGA,* I⁵, 50; *G. I.,* pp. 57-58.

[19] *MEGA,* I⁵, 19; *G. I.,* p. 18.

History and Ideology

This conclusion implies an entirely new concept of history. For Marx, history is not determined by ideas but by social-economic relations. Whereas German philosophy of history descends from the heaven of ideas to the earth of realities, Marx's theory ascends from earth to heaven. Not what men *think* or imagine but what they *are* determines history. Ideology (morality, religion, metaphysics), far from being a determinant factor in human history, is a mere sublimate of a life process which depends on material production and material commerce. "Life is not determined by consciousness but consciousness by life." [20] To attack man's "religious phantoms" with other brain phantoms, as Bauer and his friends do, shows a basic misunderstanding of history.

Four factors shape the reality which makes history: the production of means of subsistence, the creation of new needs, the family as the first social unit, and the division of labor extending beyond the family with the increase of production. Only after these four basic factors do we meet the only one considered by the ideologists—consciousness. Consciousness is not an independent factor; it is determined by language, and language arises out of social relations, which themselves depend upon the material production. "The production of ideas, of conceptions, of consciousness, is at first directly interwoven with the material activity and the material intercourse of men, the language of real life." [21] Hegel had already stressed the social aspect of consciousness in the Master-Slave section of the *Phenomenology*. Marx goes further: "Consciousness is . . . from the very beginning a social product, and remains so as long as men exist at all." [22] Moreover, since social relations are determined by man's relation to nature, consciousness is always "consciousness of nature"; it is "conditioned by a definite development of

[20] *MEGA*, I⁵, 16; *G. I.*, p. 15.   [22] *MEGA*, I⁵, 20; *G. I.*, p. 19.
[21] *MEGA*, I⁵, 15; *G. I.*, pp. 13–14.

man's productive forces and of the intercourse corresponding to these." Nevertheless, consciousness originates a new and essential relationship, distinct from the previous two—a relationship to oneself. Without this reflective movement into himself man would not be aware that he is living in a society at all, nor would he be able to transform his passive relation to nature into an active one. By constituting a different relation, consciousness obtains a certain independence, so much so that it can make a pretense of autonomy. This becomes obvious when in a developed stage of society the division between physical and mental labor appears.

> From this moment onwards consciousness *can* really flatter itself that it is something other than consciousness of existing practice, that it is *really* conceiving something without conceiving something *real;* from now on consciousness is in a position to emancipate itself from the world and to proceed to the formation of "pure" theory, theology, philosophy, ethics, etc. But even if this theory, theology, philosophy, ethics, etc. comes into contradiction with the existing relations, this can only occur as a result of the fact that existing social relations have come into contradiction with existing forces of production.[23]

The division between mental and physical labor has severed consciousness from its vital source, the process of life production. It has generated intellectuals and speculative philosophers. Yet, even the most abstract speculation, which seems to rise above all earthly concerns, is deeply rooted in the material conditions of life. For it is nothing more than the ideal expression of the social relations underlying the rule of the dominating class. As soon as one class obtains control over the means of material production, it immediately falls heir to the "means of mental production" and starts imposing its own ideas on the entire society.

> Insofar . . . as they [i.e., the ruling individuals] rule as a class and determine the extent and compass of an epoch,

[23] *MEGA,* I⁵, 21; *G. I.,* p. 20.

it is self-evident that they do this in their whole range, hence among other things [they] rule also as thinkers and producers of ideas, and regulate the production and distribution of the ideas of their age: thus their ideas are the ruling ideas of the epoch.[24]

Of course, the division of labor also separates, within the ruling class, the thinkers from the men of action, and this separation may even lead to conflicts. But those collisions are harmless, for as soon as an ideology endangers the dominance of the class, it automatically disappears, and thus "vanishes the semblance that the ruling ideas were not the ideas of the ruling class and had a power distinct from the power of this class." [25]

The error of modern historiography, and even more of the philosophy of history, is that it abstracts the ideas from the class in which they originated and attributes to them an independent existence. This ideological abstraction serves a highly practical purpose in the class struggle: it gives the ruling ideas a semblance of universality in order to make them acceptable to the rest of society. The ideas of the ruling class are presented as a universal and independent force which brought this class to power, rather than as the conceptual solidification of power already acquired.

The class concept also explains why the ideals of a new epoch are always more universal and abstract than those of the previous one, why freedom and equality are considered more important in capitalist societies than loyalty and honor, which were predominant in the feudal period. To rise to power, a class must rally all other classes in its fight against the ruling class. It can do this only by proposing its own interests as the interests of the entire society. Originally, the "entire society" was limited to the few classes which were socially conscious, but gradually it came to include all classes. To appeal to more people, the liberation slogans had to become ever more universal. The new class which comes to power

[24] *MEGA*, I⁵, 35–36; *G. I.*, p. 39.   [25] *MEGA*, I⁵, 36; *G. I.*, p. 40.

appears as the whole mass of society confronting the one ruling class. It can do this because, to start with, its interest really is more connected with the common interest of all other non-ruling classes, because under the pressure of conditions its interest has not yet been able to develop as the particular interest of a particular class. Its victory, therefore, benefits also many individuals of the other classes which are not winning a dominant position, but only insofar as it now puts these individuals in a position to raise themselves into the ruling class. When the French bourgeoisie overthrew the power of the aristocracy, it thereby made it possible for many proletarians to raise themselves above the proletariat, but only insofar as they became bourgeois.[26]

As long as the class system prevails, history will always be written in ideological abstractions instead of social realities. However, the ideological mystification will come to an end when the power is seized by that class which represents the interests of man rather than of a particular class, and which will abolish the whole class system—the proletariat. With no dominating class to impose its own particular interests in the form of universal ideals, history will be seen as the interaction between the production process and the social relations determined by this process. This historiography of the future is the only true one for Marx.

> Our conception of history depends on our ability to expound the real process of production, starting out from the simple material production of life, and to comprehend the form of intercourse connected with this and created by this (i.e. civil society in its various stages), as the basis of all history; further, to show it in its action as State; and so, from this starting-point, to explain the whole mass of different theoretical products and forms of consciousness, religion, philosophy, ethics, etc., etc., and trace their origins and growth, by which means, of course, the whole thing can be shown in its totality (and therefore, too, the reciprocal action of these various sides on one another).[27]

[26] *MEGA,* I⁵, 37; *G. I.,* p. 41.   [27] *MEGA,* I⁵, 27; *G. I.,* p. 28.

A new concept of history also implies a new concept of man. Man, as Hegel had shown in his *Phenomenology*, is a historical being. But the question is: what does history consist of? As long as one sees it as a development toward self-consciousness, as do the ideologists, man remains an ideal being. Only when history is seen as the interaction of productive forces and social patterns does the historical nature of man become a concrete reality.

The Communist Revolution

In the final section of the first part of the *Ideology*, Marx describes the Communist revolution and its effects on society. Since this is Marx's clearest and most complete analysis of a central aspect of his philosophy, it calls for careful study. We have already learned that big industry requires an accumulation of labor which, in turn, leads to an extreme division of labor. These factors cause an *opposition between the instruments of labor and labor itself.*

> The division of labor implies from the outset the division of the *conditions of labor,* of tools and materials, and thus the splitting up of accumulated capital among different owners, and thus, also, the division between capital and labor, and the different forms of property itself. The more the division of labor develops and accumulation grows, the sharper are the forms that this process of differentiation assumes.[28]

The Dialectic of Productive Forces and Production Relations

But since capital, like all private property, is nothing but accumulated labor, the opposition between capital and labor becomes an opposition within labor itself, an *opposition between*

[28] *MEGA*, I5, 56; *G. I.*, p. 65.

accumulated labor and actual labor. The productive forces (accumulated labor) become independent of the producing individuals (actual labor). This leads eventually to a fundamental opposition between *productive forces* and *production relations.*

Production relations are the social conditions under which the production takes place. As we saw in the previous section, a certain social structure corresponds to each way of producing. At regular intervals new production methods are discovered. But since social relations soon stabilize themselves, they do not keep pace with these changes in the production process.

From this lag there inevitably arises an opposition between the productive forces and the existing social conditions. The latter are no longer felt as *essential* by the producing individuals; instead of furthering the production process from which they originated, they now stand as an obstacle.

> These various conditions, which appear first as conditions of self-activity, later as fetters upon it, form in the whole evolution of history a coherent series of forms of intercourse, the coherence of which consists in this: that in the place of an earlier form of intercourse, which has become a fetter, a new one is put, corresponding to the more developed productive forces and, hence, to the advanced mode of the self-activity of individuals—a form which in its turn becomes a fetter and is then replaced by another. Since these conditions correspond at every stage to the simultaneous development of the productive forces, their history is at the same time the history of the evolving productive forces taken over by each new generation, and is therefore the history of the development of the forces of the individuals themselves.[29]

Marx will express the same idea in his later *Contribution to the Critique of Political Economy,* where he says that at a certain stage of their development, the material forces of production in society come into conflict with the existing relations of production, "or—what is but a legal expression for the same

[29] *MEGA,* I⁵, 61–62; *G. I.,* pp. 71–72.

thing—with the property relations within which they had been at work before."[30] The forms of intercourse must be adapted to the new production conditions. But since the evolution of social relations moves very slowly and since they are sustained by a self-created political organism, the power of outdated forms of intercourse can be broken only by a revolution.

According to Marx, all revolutions in history have their origin in the contradiction between the productive forces and the forms of intercourse.[31] Up to the present, these revolutions merely readjusted the existing forms of intercourse to the state of the productive forces without modifying the basic relationship between productive forces and producing individuals. Now this is no longer possible: as a result of the extreme division of labor, the forces of production have been transformed into independent material powers standing over against the producing individuals and threatening their existence. No possible readjustment of the forms of intercourse can adapt man's social life to the present form of production. It is and remains inhuman. Nor can man ignore it and start the production process on an entirely new basis, for the division of labor has made people so dependent upon one another that they are unable to survive without the complex machinery of the present production process. No sooner would they abolish the existing production powers than a similar complex system would arise.

> Thus, on the one hand, we have a totality of productive forces which have, as it were, taken on a material form and are for the individuals no longer the forces of the individuals but of private property, and hence of the individuals only insofar as they are owners of private property themselves. Never, in any earlier period, have the productive forces taken on a form so indifferent to the intercourse of individuals as individuals, because their intercourse itself was formerly a restricted one. On the other hand, standing over against these productive forces, we have the majority

30 *Werke*, XIII, 9; *Contribution to the Critique of Political Economy*, p. 13.
31 *MEGA*, I⁵, 63; *G. I.*, p. 73.

of the individuals from whom these forces have been wrested away, and who, robbed thus of all real life-content, have become abstract individuals.[32]

The Inevitability of Revolution

The division of labor has delivered man to the mercy of these impersonal productive forces. Gradually, he has become estranged from the very powers through which he was to create himself. In their present stage the productive forces fail to provide the majority of men with even a material subsistence, and their reappropriation is no longer a matter of choice but of physical survival. Communism therefore becomes a necessary and inevitable result of the present economic conditions. "Communism is for us not a stable state which is to be established, an *ideal* to which reality will have to adjust itself. We call communism the *real* moment which abolishes the present state of things. The conditions of this movement result from the premises now in existence." [33]

The Communist revolution will be entirely different from all previous revolutions. In one sense all revolutions in the past have been social, for they were always caused by an opposition between productive forces and production relations. The opposition was solved in that the class of most importance in the production process brought the existing social relations into proportion with this importance by acquiring full control over that part of the productive forces which it directed. Accordingly, the social advantages gained by the revolution were limited to this one class. For all other classes the situation became worse than before, since the appropriation of capital by one class led to its greater accumulation and, consequently, aggravated the division of labor.

[32] *MEGA*, I⁵, 57; *G. I.*, pp. 65–66.   [33] *MEGA*, I⁵, 25; *G. I.*, p. 26.

In all revolutions up till now the mode of activity [i.e. of producing] always remained unscathed and it was only a question of a different distribution of this activity, a new distribution of labor to other persons, whilst the communistic revolution is directed against the preceding *mode* of activity [and] does away with *labor*.[34]

The proletarian revolution alone reappropriates all production powers to the entire society. It eliminates once and forever the forced division of labor which results from the exclusive possession of capital by one class, and thus brings to an end the inhuman opposition between actual labor and accumulated labor.

Such a revolution will be accomplished *in the present time*, because only at the present level of industrialization have the productive forces developed to their *totality*, and only now has social intercourse become universal. It will be carried out *by the proletariat*, because the proletariat is a universal rather than a particular class. It is "a class which forms the majority of all members of society. [It is] the expression of the dissolution of all classes . . . within present society." [35] The proletariat epitomizes the total dehumanization of man, and thus represents the entire society in a negative way.[36] But it is universal in a positive way as well, for, more than all other classes, it is international. The proletarians have reached a state of dejection where national feelings can no longer exist and where the only possible brotherhood is that of partners in distress.

The revolution of the proletariat is inevitable; yet, as we learned in the *Introduction* and in *The Holy Family*, it will not be accomplished by a mere economic process. To be successful, the proletarians must first *unite*, which requires that they become *conscious* of their situation and of the necessity of revolution. The revolutionary consciousness of the proletarians is

[34] *MEGA*, I[5], 59; *G. I.*, p. 69. The word "labor" here is to be interpreted as work in an economic system based upon the division of labor. It obviously does not mean that the Communist revolution will do away with work.
[35] *MEGA*, I[5], 59; *G. I.*, p. 69.
[36] J.-Y. Calvez, *La Pensée de Karl Marx* (Paris, 1956), pp. 490–91.

the mediating factor which brings the present economic process to its end.[37] It differs from any revolutionary ideology in that it knows itself to be dependent on economic conditions. That is why it remains essentially realistic and *social-economic.* Revolutionaries in the past had only a very dim notion of the social-economic implications of their activity. "The individuals who started the revolutions made illusions about their own activity according to their degree of culture and the stage of historical development." [38] They fought mostly for political emancipation, at best for class emancipation. The proletarians consciously fight for the emancipation of the entire society. Their destiny is to initiate a true social consciousness and, by means of the revolution, to communicate it to all men—and ultimately to create a new man. It is obvious, then, that the revolutionary consciousness of the proletariat goes beyond the existing social structures. Yet, it never becomes ideological, for it remains dependent on these structures and merely gives conscious expression to the negative forces at work in the present economy. A new *positive* consciousness can evolve only by means of the revolution itself and the subsequent change in social relations. To see the new man as the creation of a conscious effort alone is an ideological error. This is precisely the mistake of Stirner's anarchistic theory in *The Ego and His Own.*

Stirner's Individual

Stirner, like Marx, felt that Feuerbach's notion of *humanity* was as remote from the real man as the religious illusion which he tried to demolish. But after this common criticism, their ways part. For Marx, the real man is man living in a society determined by economic conditions. For Stirner, society is as much a religious illusion as philosophy, politics, or morality. The real man is the *single individual* whom Stirner calls "I"; his emancipation consists in becoming disengaged from all

---

[37] Calvez, pp. 483–85.   [38] *MEGA*, I5, 63; *G. I.,* p. 74.

moral, religious, and social ties and satisfying his individual interests. Marx, Engels, and Hess considered Stirner's anarchism a threat to adequate social action, all the more so because of their common criticism of Feuerbach's abstract humanism. They felt that Stirner's *Ego* merely added one more abstraction to the list by the German ideologists. His presentation of the individual's development from child to man simply ignores the physical and social factors by which the process of consciousness is determined. He made the same mistake, Marx argued, in his theory of history, which merely follows the stages of the individual consciousness and thereby becomes one more chapter in the sacred history of religious illusions. But above all Marx resented Stirner's attack on the Communist movement. Stirner saw the Communist ideals as inspired by a morbid desire to sacrifice the individual's innate egoism to the religious phantom of the community. But, Marx points out, the Communists do not want to bring sacrifices to "society"—at the most they want to sacrifice the existing society itself. Furthermore, Communism is not a social ideal—it is an economic reality which exists in society right now and of which the proletarians only have to become conscious. It is not the Communists but Stirner who believes in religious phantoms—what else could one consider the concept of a *single individual* who realizes himself independently of all social and economic ties?

Stirner contended that the world will not change so long as the people remain the same, and that social revolutions are useless unless the people who make them first undergo an internal revolution—a revolution of consciousness. Marx flatly denies this: the "alteration [of men] can only take place in a practical movement, a *revolution*." [39] Fundamental change in man's attitude will be an *effect* of the revolution, not its *cause:* to change man, one must first change the social and economic conditions which determine his conscious life. It is precisely to produce a new man that the proletarians prepare a revolution.

[39] *MEGA*, I[5], 60; *G. I.*, p. 69.

The indefatigable propaganda of the proletarians, their daily discussions, prove sufficiently that they by no means want to remain "the same," and that, speaking in general, they very little desire all men to remain "the same." They would remain "the same" only if, with Saint Max [Stirner], "they found the fault in themselves." But they know too well that they will not cease to be "the same" unless the conditions change, and they are determined to modify these conditions at the first opportunity. In the revolutionary activity the change of oneself coincides with the modification of the conditions.[40]

The Results of the Revolution

Marx felt that it would be an ideological error to predict what the "new man" will be like. But he did describe the economic conditions under which he will live, since these conditions would be a necessary result of the inevitable revolution:

1. The limited social intercourse determined by the *division of labor* will become an unlimited intercourse of *persons.*
2. Labor will be transformed into self-activity.
3. Private property will be abolished.

The revolution's first result will determine the other two. Through the division of labor, production relations have become more and more estranged from man's true social life. "There appears a division within the life of each individual, insofar as it is personal and insofar as it is determined by some branch of labor and the conditions pertaining to it." [41] With the emergence of the *class* (that is, the social group which is determined exclusively by its function in the production process), this division grows into an *opposition* between personal and class life: the social conditions which are forced upon the great majority of men stand in *full contradiction* to their personal lives. To preserve his personal life, the proletarian has no

[40] *MEGA,* I[5], 193.   [41] *MEGA,* I[5], 65; *G. I.,* p. 76.

other choice than to abolish the very conditions of his present existence—the division of labor—and to establish a truly *human* production process which will lead to truly social relations. Henceforth, he will no longer be a member of a class but a member of a *human* community. To make such a community possible, the production powers must be restored to the community.

This reappropriation also implies, and this brings us to the second point, that work in the new community no longer will be determined by external productive forces but by the free self-development of its members. "[The community of proletarians] puts the conditions of the free development and movement of individuals under their control—conditions which were previously abandoned to chance and had won an independent existence over against the separate individuals." [42]

Marx does not say that in the Communist society there will be no division of tasks or that everybody will just do what he likes, but only that there will be no more *division of labor,* i.e. no distribution of tasks determined by impersonal productive forces rather than by man himself. Since the means of production are to be controlled by the community itself, the members of the community will have a chance to cultivate all their talents. Thus work becomes a creative act, instead of an act of enslavement to inhuman powers.

> In communist society, where nobody has one exclusive sphere of activity but [where] each can become accomplished in any branch he wishes, society regulates the general production and thus makes it possible for me to do one thing today and another tomorrow, to hunt in the morning, fish in the afternoon, rear cattle in the evening, criticize after dinner, just as I have a mind, without ever becoming hunter, fisherman, shepherd or critic.[43]

In all previous economic phases, freedom and society have been opposed to each other—an individual being able to de-

---

[42] *MEGA,* I[5], 64; *G. I.,* p. 75.   [43] *MEGA,* I[5], 22; *G. I.,* p. 22.

velop his freedom only if he belonged to the ruling class and, even there, only within the externally determined relationships of this class. In the Communist stage man will become free through society. This, of course, presumes that he disposes of the illusory society, the State, which is based on class opposition and division of labor, and which prevents individuals from becoming truly social. "In order, therefore, to assert themselves as individuals, they must overthrow the State." [44]

Marx hardly mentions the abolition of private property in the Communist society, because it is a natural sequel to the community's appropriation of all productive forces. The mistake of all previous Communist theoreticians, as Marx had pointed out in the *Manuscripts,* was precisely that they failed to see the intrinsic relationship between property and labor in the capitalist system, and championed the suppression of private property without giving sufficient attention to the social conditions which had led to it. None of the French Communist writers realized that private property with its abuses ultimately derives from the division of labor and from the existence of productive forces independent of the human community.

True Socialism

Still, Marx rates the contributions of the French social reformers infinitely higher than those of their German critics, the "true socialists." The third part of the *Ideology* is devoted entirely to a discussion of true socialism.[45] Marx considered true socialism

[44] *MEGA,* I5, 67; *G. I.,* p. 78.
[45] It is difficult from the *Ideology* alone to form a clear idea about the nature of the movement. One reason is that Hess, who had initiated the movement, was abandoning it just at that time, and the *Ideology,* even though it attacks his previous writings, takes great pains to separate him from his followers Gruen, Luening, and Kriege. In a letter to Marx, dated July 28, 1846, Hess admits that he is convinced by Marx's arguments and that he is going to concentrate on the study of political economy. But there is reason to believe that Hess began to revise his position much earlier, for one long section of the *Ideology* is written in his handwriting. This collaboration ex-

to be a movement not of the working class but of "pseudo-philosophers and literary hacks." It was based not on the political or economic situation, he felt, but exclusively on the philosophies of Hegel and Feuerbach. One of its representatives writes: "The French arrived at communism by way of politics—the Germans arrived at socialism by way of metaphysics, which eventually changed into anthropology (Feuerbach)." [46] The German socialists were not interested in the needs of a particular class and time, but in "the most reasonable" social order for mankind. Proletarian Communism for them was too one-sided a party system to satisfy the needs of the "human race." In his earlier writings, Hess had made it clear that Communism was not a proletarian movement but a movement of humanity. "How could communists preach the ideal of classlessness and still appeal to *one* class against another? How could the ideal values of communism be regarded as the concern *only* of the proletariat when they really flowed from the real nature of man?" [47] Hess conceded that as a revolutionary force the proletarians would have an important role in the liberation of man, but he insisted that the movement itself went beyond them.

Communism was an ethical ideal for the German socialists, not an economic fact, as it was for Marx. It was to be effected by a moral revolt and by the philosophical education of the masses —not by an economic necessity. For Marx, true socialism was just another expression of German ideology, basically similar to the critical philosophy of Bauer and Stirner. It showed the same contempt for facts and earthly realities that is found in all idealist systems. Marx satirizes this superficial analysis of the present society:

---

cludes any actual association of Hess with the true socialists at the time of the *Ideology*. For an authoritative discussion of Hess, true socialism, and Marx's critique of it, see Sidney Hook, *From Hegel to Marx* (New York, 1958) , pp. 186–219. However, I am not convinced, as Hook is, that the attack on German socialism in *The Communist Manifesto* is directed against Hess.
[46] *MEGA*, I⁵, 441–46; *G. I.,* p. 83.
[47] Hook, p. 198.

It is a fact that proletarians exist and that they work mechanically. Why are proletarians driven to "mechanical forms of production"? Because of the corrupt essence of the rentiers. Why is the essence of the rentier corrupt? Because "present-day society is so barbarous." Why is it so barbarous? Ask thy Maker.[48]

And the true socialists need not worry about how to effect the revolution, for "the recognition of the essence of man has as a necessary and natural result a life which is truly human." [49]

On a practical level the true socialists are so simple-minded, argues Marx, that they actually join the ranks of the reactionaries. They fight the liberal reform plans of the bourgeoisie on the ground that a revolutionary must be antibourgeois, without realizing that in the present state of Germany the middle class is the only effective instrument against the feudal nobility. Because in France the working class fights the bourgeoisie, they think that the same must be done in Germany. They forget that the class system itself depends on the actual stage of development of industry. True socialism offers only universal solutions—no practical principles.

The same abstractionism appears in the true socialists' critique of the French Communist theories. It detaches the ideas from the real movement in which they originated and takes them for universal truths. Says Marx: "These 'socialists' . . . consider foreign communist literature not as the expression and the product of a real movement but merely as a set of theoretical writings; it has been evolved, they imagine, by a process of 'pure thought,' after the fashion of the German philosophical systems." [50] The German socialists mistakenly transform relations of particular individuals into "human" relations, and interpret the thoughts of these particular individuals on their relations into thoughts about "mankind." For Marx and Engels there are no universal solutions. What man is depends on the society in which he lives, and this society depends on the state

[48] *MEGA,* I⁵, 447; *G. I.,* p. 91.   [50] *MEGA,* I⁵, 435; *G. I.,* p. 79.
[49] *MEGA,* I⁵, 452; *G. I.,* p. 96.

of the production powers. Moral principles which are not firmly rooted in existent social and economic relations are abstract and ineffectual.

As for man's relation to nature, the true socialists turn it into a mystic bond. According to Matthäi—in "Cornerstones of Socialism," *Rhenish Annals (Rheinische Jahrbücher,* 1845) —society has loosened this bond with nature, but a philosophical reeducation of man will help him to live once more in peaceful communion with the universe. Marx and Engels point out, first of all, that the harmony of the universe is romantic nonsense. There is as much struggle in nature as there is in human society. When Mathai invites his readers to consider the lilies of the field, the authors of the *Ideology* answer: "Yes, consider the lilies of the field, how they are eaten by goats, transplanted by man into his button-hole, how they are crushed beneath the immodest embraces of the dairy maid and the donkey-driver." [51] Furthermore, the German socialists' concept of nature is entirely abstract. Nature is considered as an entity by itself, of which man, just like plants and animals, was originally a part and to which he should return. But, as Marx shows in the first part of the *Ideology,* nature is not independent of man, nor is man a mere part of nature. Man and nature stand in an essential relation to each other: man makes nature and nature makes man. In trying to abolish the dichotomy between the two, true socialism in fact suppresses the relation, and the whole romantic theory turns out to be another version of shallow materialism.

Marx's "Materialism"

Materialism or Humanism?

In the *Manuscripts,* Marx's social philosophy had grown into a full-fledged theory of man in relation to nature and his fellow man. This dialectical humanism was definitive; Marx was

[51] *MEGA,* I⁵, 456; *G. I.,* p. 102.

not to change it any more. Yet, several questions remained un-answered. If man is a self-creating, historical being, what factors determine his historical evolution? What is the precise relation between consciousness and nature? Which social-economic fac-tors in society are responsible for the alienation described in the *Manuscripts?*

Marx attempts to answer these questions in the *Ideology,* which, in that sense, may be considered as a continuation of the *Manuscripts.* It contains a complete philosophy of history and concretizes the notion of alienation in a social-economic theory on the division of labor. Yet the way in which the *Ideology* an-swers the questions raised by the *Manuscripts* has led many readers to believe that Marx has basically shifted his position. His attacks on the "ideologists" and his social-economic inter-pretation of human alienation seem to announce a more mate-rialistic trend in his thinking.

Up to and including the *Manuscripts,* Marx had always dis-cussed social problems in terms of man; in the *Ideology* and his later works, he mentions only productive forces. In the *Manu-scripts,* ideas seemed to be the driving force of history; in the *Ideology* they are merely the results of the production process, or, as Marx calls them later, "superstructures." Up to and in-cluding the *Manuscripts,* philosophy was considered the lever of the social revolution; in the *Ideology,* philosophy is dis-missed as having no impact on reality.

The continuity between Marx's earlier and his later writings (starting with *The German Ideology*) has been under discussion for several years and is of vital importance for the interpretation of Marx's philosophy as a whole. Are there really two "Marx-isms," one humanistic, the other materialistic; one accepted in certain existentialist milieus, the other adopted by the Com-munist party in the U. S. S. R. and in China? [52]

52 In his excellent book, *Philosophy and Myth in Karl Marx* (Cambridge, Eng., 1961), Robert Tucker has already given an answer to this question. We agree with his conclusions:

At first sight, certain passages seem to prove Marx's materialism beyond question.

> We set out from real, active men, and on the basis of their
> real life-process we demonstrate the development of the
> ideological reflexes and echoes of this life-process. The
> phantoms formed in the human brain are also, necessarily,
> sublimates of their material life-process, which is empiri-
> cally verifiable and bound to material premises. Morality,
> religion, metaphysics, all the rest of ideology, and their
> corresponding forms of consciousness, thus no longer re-
> tain the semblance of independence. They have no his-
> tory, no development; but men, developing their material
> production and their material intercourse, alter, along with
> this their real existence, their thinking and the products
> of their thinking.[53]

It is obvious that products of consciousness have no autonomous
value for Marx—they are conditioned by the development of
material production and the corresponding social intercourse.

Yet, Marx never discusses the nature or origin of the mind itself. He may in fact have believed that the mind is made of the
same substance as nature, but this view, if present at all, does
not interfere with his argument. Ontological problems are never
brought up by Marx, and whenever they appear, as in the discussion of French materialism, they are reinterpreted in the
humanistic terms of *historical* materialism. This historical materialism consists essentially in a rejection of idealism.

---

1. There is no fundamental break between the early and the mature writings of Marx.
2. Marx was never a materialist in the mechanistic sense of that word—
his "materialism" is opposed not to humanism but to idealism (considered in the *Ideology* and later writings to include all speculative philosophy). Dialectical materialism as a theory of nature apart from human history is a development of the scholastic period of Marxism
which started with the later writings of Engels.
3. The economic terminology of the *Ideology* and later works is an organic development stemming from the alienation theory in the early
writings.

53 *MEGA*, I5, 15–16; *G. I.*, pp. 14–15.

Marx insists that consciousness is *conditioned* by social relations, which in turn are conditioned by the forces of production. But he never implies that these social relations are the *cause* of consciousness. In a sense, they depend as much on consciousness as consciousness depends on them. Marx says explicitly that "man's consciousness of the necessity of associating with the individuals around him is the beginning of the consciousness that he is living in society at all." [54] It is obvious, then, that man could no more be a social being without consciousness than a conscious being without social relations. True, Marx sees consciousness primarily as a function of man's social nature: it takes the place of "social" instincts in animals and, originally, it is merely herd-consciousness. But it is *not* an instinct, and the difference is crucial.

The same mutual conditioning is found in man's relationship to nature. Marx says that mental production is determined by material production. But this is still a far cry from a determination of consciousness by matter. Material production presupposes an *active* relationship with nature in which man, from the very beginning, takes as much initiative as nature does, and this is possible only if man is not a mere product of nature, or, in the language of the *Manuscripts,* if he is a part of nature which opposes itself to nature. Man is made by his material environment, but at the same time, he makes this environment. To say that man is made by his circumstances is correct only if one adds that he himself makes the circumstances. "The materialistic doctrine concerning the changing of circumstances and education forgets that circumstances are changed by men and that the educator himself must be educated." [55]

---

[54] *MEGA,* I⁵, 20; *G. I.,* p. 20.
[55] *MEGA,* I⁵, 534; Thesis III, *Theses on Feuerbach,* in *G. I.,* pp. 197-98.

The Theses on Feuerbach

Marx's repeated attacks on "materialism" can be understood only within the context of his previous theory (*Manuscripts*) that man is a *relational being*, who creates himself in a continuous, active dialogue with nature. Ordinary materialism *reduces* man to nature and, as a result, excludes any real *human history*. Marx's "materialism" *relates* man to nature and excludes only *ideological history*.[56]

This is quite clear from his critique of Feuerbach in the *Ideology*, and in the *Theses on Feuerbach*, both of which were written in the same year (1845). For Feuerbach, man's relationship with nature is entirely passive—it is one of contemplation and feeling. The world shapes man, but man does not shape the world. "[Feuerbach] does not see how the sensuous world around him is not a thing given direct from all eternity, ever the same, but the product of industry and of the state of society; and, indeed, in the sense that it is an historical product, the result of the activity of a whole succession of generations, each standing on the shoulders of the preceding one, developing its industry and its intercourse, modifying its social organization according to the changed needs." [57]

Feuerbach forgets that the nature which he contemplates is a product of man. Modern man's material environment is entirely different from prehistoric nature. If human activity were interrupted for only one year, Feuerbach would not be able to survive in this world on which he claims to depend entirely. Even though man was originally produced by nature in a "spontaneous generation," he became truly human only when he started opposing himself to nature in productive activity. Historical man, who alone attracts the interest of Marx, is more a producer of nature than a product of it. Wherever Feuerbach discusses man's activity, he forgets his basic thesis, man's passive dependence on nature, and lapses into the opposite extreme by

[56] *MEGA*, I[5], 37–38; *G. I.*, p. 38.   [57] *MEGA*, I[5], 32; *G. I.*, p. 35.

making man *purely* active, but active only in the realm of the mind. Opposed as these two approaches are, they both originate in the same idealist attitude of viewing reality as an object of contemplation, rather than as an object of action.[58]

It is to this idealism that Marx opposes his "materialism." Nature and consciousness are irreducible but intimately connected realities. One cannot be understood without the other.[59] Consequently, any attempt to explain the reality of man apart from nature is doomed to failure. But this is precisely what all ideologists try to do: they detach consciousness from nature, and, by means of this ideological abstraction, explain man's historical development. Nature itself is transformed into a concept, a pure brain figment which has nothing in common with reality. That is why the ideologist never changes anything in the world, in spite of his revolutionary phrases. His reform plans are limited to the reform of ideas. But ideas cannot be changed without fundamental changes in the underlying social structures and productive forces. Contrary to the materialist, the idealist philosopher believes in history, but in disconnecting history from nature, he reduces it to a mere fiction.

Marx wants to overcome the antithesis between history and nature.[60] His historical materialism is as far removed from materialism as it is from idealism. "It does not have a physical or mechanical or physiological connotation, nor does it question

---

[58] In his first thesis on Feuerbach, Marx shows materialism and idealism to be opposite poles of the same speculative attitude.

> The chief defect of all materialism up to now (including Feuerbach's) is, that the object, reality, what we apprehend through our senses, is understood only in the form of the *object* or *contemplation;* but not as *sensuous human activity,* as *practice;* not subjectively. Hence, in opposition to materialism, the *active* side was developed abstractly by idealism—which, of course, does not know real sensuous activity as such.

(*MEGA*, I[5], 533; Thesis I, *Theses on Feuerbach,* in *G. I.,* p. 197.)
[59] As we pointed out before, prehistoric nature, for Marx, has almost nothing in common with the nature in which man lives.
[60] *MEGA*, I[5], 28; *G. I.,* p. 30.

the reality of conscious mind. It does not refer to a theory about the nature of the stuff of which the universe is composed although Marx assumed that this is material stuff." [61] It concentrates on the dialectical relation of man to nature in the productive process. Any ontological consideration of what consciousness or nature are *in themselves* is *per se* abstract and lapses into idealism or materialism, for neither consciousness nor nature can be taken by itself; each depends on the other. Materialism and idealism are both ideologies; they are *static* and, by reducing one term to the other, they eliminate the dynamic relationship between man and nature. Only a theory which preserves this dynamic relationship enables man actively to transform the world. "The philosophers have only *interpreted* the world differently; the point is, to change it." [62] This transformation of man and his world will be achieved by Communism.

A Critical Conclusion

With the *Ideology,* Marx's "philosophical" period comes to an end. He has shown that man's social-economic activity is at the basis of all human values, the theoretical as well as the practical. The production process and the concomitant social relations of an epoch determine its leading ideas, its ethical and juridical standards, even its aesthetic creations. Understanding of man's cultural life will not be obtained from philosophy or from any speculative science, but from a historical study of man's social-economic conditions. These conditions contain the roots and causes of all that man thinks, admires, hopes for, and even of what he freely strives for.

This conclusion, however, will not convert Marx to pure economy or sociology, for both these sciences lack the over-all view of history which places their data in proper perspective. They

[61] Tucker, p. 178.
[62] *MEGA,* I⁵, 535; Thesis XI, *Theses on Feuerbach,* in *G. I.,* p. 199.

merely register and synthesize human praxis—man's activity—insofar as it is dialectically related to nature in a particular period, under particular conditions.[63] Neither one of them offers a total explanation of the praxis itself. The economist considers his laws to hold universally true, and forgets that they are true only within certain *social* conditions which are subject to change. The sociologist, for his part, will tend to isolate the social data from the productive forces which determine them. What is needed is a science that synthesizes social and economic data, and, most important, shows their historical dialectic.

But there is one more aspect which differentiates historical materialism from all other sciences. Since the praxis is at the origin of all theory, historical materialism refuses to be merely a science—it is a theory of action, founded in action, and returning to action. A purely theoretical science, even if it is based upon positive facts, is bound to turn into an ideology. Unless it can be converted into action, theory becomes estranged from praxis, and since praxis alone contains the truth of man, theory alone becomes *eo ipso* false. Historical materialism, then, both expresses and participates in the active relation between consciousness and nature which constitutes man's reality. It may be called a philosophy insofar as it takes an *a priori* position toward the empirical data of the positive sciences and provides a framework in which they can be integrated. But it also is the abolition of all philosophy, insofar as it refuses any *speculative a priori:* it is exclusively based upon and directed toward action. These two aspects do not contradict each other, because the living praxis is *a priori* with respect to both speculative and empirical sciences. Historical materialism becomes self-contradictory only when it posits itself as a pure theory, severed from

---

[63] Of course, sociology as a science was not established until years after the *Ideology.* Auguste Comte may be considered its founder. Nevertheless, long before sociology had become an independent science, Marx was acutely aware of the existence of social factors as distinguished from economic ones. The rest of this paragraph merely suggests what Marx's views on the future science would have been.

action. At that moment it loses the right to be *a priori*, since the only *a priori* which it can accept is that of action.

In the next chapter we shall see how Marx applies this new method in a work intended to be both an interpretation of history and a theory of action—*The Communist Manifesto*. Yet, before going into that, a few words must be said about *The Poverty of Philosophy*, in which Marx applies insights early acquired to a critique of economic theory.

7

Applications of Historical Materialism

The Poverty of Philosophy

EARLY IN 1846, Marx organized a Communist propaganda committee in Brussels and invited Proudhon to join it as correspondent from France. In a long letter Proudhon replied that his disagreement with Marx's principles did not allow him to collaborate with the committee. Proudhon declared himself opposed to any revolutionary action and advocated instead a scientific education of the masses in a spirit of tolerance and peace. At the same time he announced the forthcoming publication of his new book, *The Philosophy of Poverty* (*Philosophie de la misère*, 1846). A few days after he received it, Marx started writing a refutation in French of Proudhon's theories. It was published in 1847 under the title *The Poverty of Philosophy* (*Misère de la Philosophie*) and forever ended Marx's friendship with Proudhon.

Until Proudhon's second book appeared, Marx's attitude toward him had always been somewhat ambiguous. In *The Holy Family* he had defended *What Is Property?* against Edgar Bauer's criticism, and even in his later days, Marx preserved a certain admiration for Proudhon's early work. It was written in the language of a prophet rather than that of a scientist. In the eyes of Marx, Proudhon's genuine feeling of indignation compensated for his lack of originality and the shallowness of his economic theories. But Marx had more serious qualms about the underlying conservatism. Proudhon believed that all social problems could be solved within the existing economic conditions. In an article published in *Der Sozialdemokrat* of February, 1865, Marx concisely formulated his early criticism:

> In spite of all his apparent iconoclasm one already finds in *What Is Property?* the contradiction that Proudhon is criticizing society, on the one hand, from the standpoint and with the eyes of a French small peasant (later petty bourgeois) and, on the other, with the standards derived from his inheritance from the socialists.[1]

Proudhon's Dialectical Economy

The ambiguity of Proudhon's ideas became even more obvious to Marx in *The Philosophy of Poverty*. Proudhon was now dabbling with economic theories of which he had only the most superficial knowledge and to which he opposed his own "scientific discovery." As it turned out, this discovery consisted partly of views which had already been expressed much better by the classical economists and partly of contradictions invented by Proudhon. The deficiencies of the content were no longer camouflaged by the emotional and stylistic qualities of his former work, and indeed were even accentuated by rhetoric and would-be scientific pretentiousness. The prophet had become a charlatan. But what irritated Marx most was the pseudo-Hegelian philosophy which connected Proudhon's ramshackle ideas. In 1844, when Marx had first met him in Paris, Proudhon knew nothing about German philosophy except what he had gathered from French translations of Kant. So Marx introduced him to the philosophy of Hegel. Some twenty years later Marx remarked wryly: "In the course of lengthy debates often lasting all night, I infected him to his great injury with Hegelianism, which, owing to his lack of German, he could not study prop-

[1] *Werke*, XVI, 26; letter to Schweitzer, in Appendix to Marx, *The Poverty of Philosophy* (New York, 1936), p. 165, by permission of International Publishers Co., Inc.

erly." [2] After Marx's expulsion from Paris, the "true socialist" Karl Gruen took over Proudhon's education, and *The Philosophy of Poverty* was the result of this secondhand philosophical training.

In Marx's view, Proudhon treated economic categories the way the German ideologists had treated religion, culture, and human relations—only less competently. "Instead of conceiving them as the *theoretical expressions of historical relations of production, corresponding to particular stages of 'development in material production,* he transforms them by his twaddle into *eternal ideas* existing prior to all reality." [3] Thus nothing had been gained by Proudhon's economic approach to social reforms; economy itself had become one more chapter of ideology.

In a letter to Pavel Annenkov, a Russian correspondent in Paris, written just after he finished reading *The Philosophy of Poverty,* Marx outlines the criticism which he gives in *The Poverty of Philosophy:* Proudhon, like all bourgeois economists, overlooks the historical growth of economic categories and regards them as *eternal laws.* Yet, at the same time, he favors social reforms and realizes that they have something to do with changes in the economy. To justify development and progress in his static economic world, he turns to Hegel's dialectic and treats economic laws as expressions of a self-developing Absolute Idea. As a result, economic systems come and go, not according to the laws of their intrinsic evolution (for in his conception they do not evolve) but according to the development of a supereconomic and superhuman Idea, until they reach the stage where Proudhon wants them to be. The Hegelian philosophy is a mere substitute for insight into the economic development itself.

M. Proudhon, incapable of following the real movement of history, produces a phantasmagoria which presumptuously claims to be dialectical. . . . The *evolutions* of which Proudhon speaks are understood to be evolutions such as are accomplished within the mystic womb of the Absolute Idea. If you tear the veil from this mystical language, what it comes to is that M. Proudhon is offering you the order in which economic categories arrange themselves inside his own mind. It will not require any great exertion on my part to prove to you that it is the order of a very disorderly mind.[4]

In the first part of *The Poverty of Philosophy*, Marx discusses Proudhon's "scientific discovery," the new theory of economic value; in the second part he attacks Proudhon's metaphysics of political economy. Marx's ideas in the book (although important for a correct understanding of his value theory in *Capital*) mostly lie beyond the scope of our analysis.

Proudhon's Theory of Economic Value

Proudhon sets out from the classic distinction between use value and exchange value, and pretends that they are inversely proportional to each other. He then identifies use value with supply, and exchange value with demand. This identification is too simplistic, argues Marx, for the consumer himself offers a certain supply in exchange for what he receives, and the supplier also makes certain demands in return for his supply. Furthermore, Marx notes, the use value is not entirely determined by the product supplied, but also by the estimation of the demander (which Proudhon relegates entirely to the exchange value). Proudhon explains the difference between use and exchange value as the result of a free agreement between the buyer and the producer. To reduce the exchange value to the use value of the product, and thereby to remove the opposition between them, it suffices that the buyer make up his mind about the price he is *willing* to pay. However, as Marx points out, the freedom of the buyer is a mere fiction, for the producer has no

---

[4] *Werke*, XXVII, 454; letter to Annenkov, in Appendix to *Poverty*, p. 154.

control over the means of production, and the consumer can buy only according to his means and needs, which do not depend on his free will but on his economic position. Moreover, the needs themselves depend on the organization of the production and not on the estimation of the individual consumer.

The problem of the "fair price" is solved by Proudhon's theory of synthetic value—that is, the value of a product based on the labor time which is incorporated in it. The production cost in labor time is the absolute norm which should determine the price (or exchange value) of the product, and not the relative standard of supply and demand. But, Marx objects, if the value of a product is determined by the labor time required to produce it, then it also follows that the value of labor itself, if measured by wages, is determined by the labor time required to produce the wages. By valuing labor in terms of wages, Proudhon in effect treats labor as a commodity and thereby subjects it to the fluctuations of supply and demand. "Labor, inasmuch as it is bought and sold, is a commodity like any other commodity, and has, in consequence, an exchange value." [5] But an exchange value depends on the variable state of the commodity market rather than on the fixed measure of the commodity itself. The price of labor varies with the varying price of food and shelter, and the supply and demand of workers. Now, this is precisely the present situation, described by Ricardo not as an economic ideal but as the basic fact determining the very economic system which Proudhon wishes to reform. Only if supply and demand happen to be in perfect balance will the absolute standard of labor time determine the exchange value of a product. But it is quite utopian to expect that labor time as the norm of value will balance supply and demand. In fact, in an industrial society, supply outruns demand and reduces the laborer to a level of bare subsistence. "Thus relative [exchange] value, measured by labor time, is inevitably the formula of the present en-

[5] *MEGA*, I⁶, 141; *Poverty*, p. 50.

slavement of the worker, instead of being, as Mr. Proudhon would have it, the 'revolutionary theory' of the emancipation of the proletariat." [6]

But Marx goes even further: Actual labor time cannot even be a partial value standard, for what counts is not "the time taken to produce a thing, but the *minimum* time it could possibly be produced in, and this minimum is ascertained by competition." [7] A product which takes two hours of labor time depreciates in value the moment it can be made in one hour. Marx concludes that a price proportionate to actual labor cannot be reestablished within the framework of the existing economy, no matter what standard is applied. In the past there existed a certain proportion between price and labor, because demand always preceded and regulated supply. But in the industrial era supply dominates and creates demand. This causes an anarchy of production which can be prevented only by community control of production, which implies the elimination of individual exchange.

Marx's critical comments on Proudhon's *value* theory should not obscure the fact that he agrees with Proudhon on some very basic points. Marx's theory in *Capital* (*Das Kapital,* 1867) also starts out from the distinction between use and exchange value. And his suggested norm for the *exchange value* of a product is also *labor time.* But since this norm in itself is abstract—it varies with the social conditions of every society and of every particular stage of a society's development—Marx interprets it in terms of the *total* work force of a given society at a given stage. Labor time therefore is merely the time which is necessary *in this particular society as a whole* to produce a certain product. Yet, even this concrete definition remains a norm for establishing exchange value only as long as the latter is in balance with the use value. At a certain point, however, as a result of the extreme division of labor and the consequent increase of exchange, the exchange value goes up so high that it loses all proportion to

---

[6] *MEGA,* I[6], 136; *Poverty,* p. 45.   [7] *MEGA,* I[6], 147; *Poverty,* p. 57.

the use value. The exchange value of a product, then, becomes an autonomous economic value, and the social and human aspect of exchange, which was based on the use value of products, disappears altogether. At this point, economic value turns into a *fetish*, a superhuman determination which is expressed in money. The capitalist system is entirely based on money because everything is reduced to its exchange value. Nothing less than the abolition of individual exchange can restore the balance between use value and exchange value.

Proudhon's Static Categories

In Marx's view, the main inadequacy of Proudhon's theory is a total lack of insight into the historical evolution of economic categories. Treating them as static and independent entities, Proudhon has no way of connecting them except by an abstract, logical process which remains outside the historical development of the categories themselves. Marx shows this in several instances. One of the most interesting is the division of labor, with which Proudhon starts his series of economic evolutions. He takes the division of labor as a discrete phenomenon that appears all at once in economic history. It is a completely abstract and univocal concept that remains the same for all historical periods.

> Thus the abstraction, the idea, the word, has to suffice for him to explain the division of labor at different historical epochs. Castes, corporations, manufacture, large-scale industry have to be explained by the single word *divide*. First study carefully the meaning of "divide," and you will have no need to study the numerous influences which give the division of labor a definite character in every epoch. Certainly, things would be made much too easy if they were reduced to M. Proudhon's categories. History does not proceed so categorically.[8]

---

[8] *MEGA,* I⁶, 193; *Poverty,* p. 108.

Proudhon always follows the same pattern. He accepts the ready-made categories of production from the classical economists and, instead of explaining how these categories themselves have been produced historically, he merely puts them in a "rational" order of succession. But as Marx had said already in his letter to Annenkov: "The categories are no more eternal than the relations they express. They are historical and transitory products. For M. Proudhon, on the contrary, abstractions and categories are the primordial cause. According to him they, and not men, make history." [9] Just as Hegel reduced religion, morality, and right to abstract logic, Proudhon has made logic out of political economy. He fails to see that the social relations of production are just as much produced by men as are linen and flax. Their history is the step-by-step evolution of man's productive forces, and not the development of an absolute economic Idea.

Moreover, complains Marx, Proudhon is a poor dialectician as well, for the order in which he gives his economic categories is not the order in which they actually engender one another.

> What then does M. Proudhon give us? Real history, which is, according to M. Proudhon's understanding, the sequence in which the categories have manifested themselves in order of time? No! History as it takes place in the idea itself? Still less! That is, neither the profane history of the categories, nor their sacred history! What history does he give us then? The history of his own contradictions.[10]

The Communist Manifesto

"Wage Labor and Capital"

Near the end of his sojourn in Brussels, Marx became more and more involved in direct political propaganda. One of the most interesting documents of that period is a series of lectures

---

[9] *Werke*, XXVII, 459; *Poverty*, p. 160.   [10] *MEGA*, I⁶, 183; *Poverty*, p. 97.

given to the German Workingmen's Club of Brussels, which were later published in the *Neue Rheinische Zeitung,* under the title "Wage Labor and Capital." [11]

In this work, Marx gives a definition of capital which is different from that of the classical economists and which was to be developed in *Capital.* Classical economy had defined capital exclusively in terms of production goods: raw materials, instruments of labor, and means of subsistence of all kinds. But this definition fails to mention the specific conditions under which the means of production become capital and is, therefore, merely tautological. "A cotton-spinning jenny is a machine for spinning cotton. It becomes *capital* only in certain relations. Torn from these relationships, it is no more capital than gold in itself is *money,* or sugar the price of sugar." [12] Means of production become capital only under the social conditions prevalent in a bourgeois society. Capitalism is a social concept as well as an economic one: it is a mode of exchanging as much as a way of producing. A characteristic of a capitalist society is that capital is erected when the exchange value of labor is preserved and accumulated in such a way as to become a social power independent of, and in conflict with, the actual labor power. This presupposes the existence of a separate class of owners which dominates the producing class and gradually deprives it of the means of production. It is primarily this class theory which Marx was to work out in *The Communist Manifesto.*

The Class Struggle

In 1847 the Communist League in London, an organization heavily infiltrated by German workers, asked Engels and Marx to write up a program for the Communist party. Engels prepared a first draft in question-and-answer form, but Marx was

---

[11] *MEGA*, I⁶, 473–99; "Wage Labor and Capital," in Marx and Engels, *Selected Works* (Moscow, 1950) , I, 74–97.
[12] *MEGA*, I⁶, 482; *Selected Works*, I, 83.

not satisfied with the presentation and rewrote the program entirely. The remarkable conciseness and expressive force of this definitive version has made *The Communist Manifesto* (1848) into one of the world's most famous documents. As Isaiah Berlin writes in his biography of Marx:

> No other political movement or cause can claim to have produced anything comparable with it in eloquence or power. It is a document of prodigious dramatic force; in form it is an edifice of bold and arresting historical generalizations, mounting to a denunciation of the existing order in the name of the avenging forces of the future, much of it written in prose which has the lyrical quality of a great revolutionary hymn, whose effect overwhelming even now, was probably greater at the time.[13]

But the *Manifesto* is more than a powerful social pamphlet: it is the conclusion to Marx's theory of alienation. In his earliest writings he had shown how religious alienation is rooted in man's political alienation; later he had reduced this political alienation to an alienation of man's self-expression of labor. *The German Ideology* then narrowed the concept of alienation down to the division of labor. But the ultimate cause which touched off the historical process of alienation had never been discussed. The class theory of the *Manifesto* attempts to clarify this point. Marx shows that the formation of classes is a social-economic necessity and, at the same time, that the very notion of class implies struggle and alienation.

The notion of class is not defined in the *Manifesto,* and the definitions in Marx's other works do not agree with one another. At times the class seems to be a purely social-economic structure, independent of class consciousness. But at other times Marx implies that a class is constituted as class only when its members are class-conscious. In the *Ideology* the concept of class is exclusively determined by the division of labor. But in *The Eighteenth Brumaire of Louis Bonaparte* (1852), Marx brings in the

---

[13] Isaiah Berlin, *Karl Marx—His Life and Environment* (New York, 1959), p. 157.

element of consciousness, which was lacking in his earlier definition.

> Insofar as millions of families live under economic conditions that separate their mode of life, their interests, and their culture from those of other classes and put them in hostile opposition to the latter, they form a class. Insofar as there is merely a local interconnection among these small-holding peasants and the identity of their interests begets no community, no national bond, and no political organization among them, they do not form a class.[14]

In addition to its social-economic content, the notion of class here requires a formal element, the consciousness of sharing certain interests, a certain culture, and a way of life with other people. Without this collective consciousness, a group is unable to strive for domination of other groups.

Marx always considered the class *struggle* to be inherent in the class concept, for it is precisely through this struggle that a class attains its identity. Even in the *Ideology,* where consciousness is not explicitly mentioned as a requirement for class identity, the class struggle is already considered essential to the constitution of a class: "The separate individuals form a class only insofar as they have to carry on a common battle against another class." [15] It is this element of class struggle which has gained importance in the *Manifesto,* and which becomes the key to Marx's theory of alienation.

Class struggles have existed at least since the dawn of written history.

> In the earlier epochs of history we find almost everywhere a complicated arrangement of society into various orders, a manifold gradation of social rank. In ancient Rome we have patricians, knights, plebeians, slaves; in the Middle Ages, feudal lords, vassals, guild masters, journeymen, ap-

---

[14] *Werke,* VIII, 198; *The Eighteenth Brumaire of Louis Bonaparte,* in *Selected Works,* I, 303.
[15] *MEGA,* I⁵, 43; Marx and Engels, *The German Ideology* (tr. by R. Pascal, New York, 1960), pp. 48–49, by permission of International Publishers Co., Inc.

prentices, serfs; in almost all of these classes, again, subordinate gradations.[16]

Yet, class struggles in all preceding social-economic stages were
different from those of capitalist society because they affected
only a limited segment of society. As Marx will point out later,
in ancient Rome the class struggle took place between only the
very rich and the very poor, while most of the productive manpower—the slave class—was not involved in it. But the essential
difference between the capitalist stage and all preceding epochs
is that in the capitalist society the class antagonisms have become universally polarized. "Society as a whole is more and
more splitting up into two great hostile camps, into two great
classes directly facing each other: Bourgeoisie and Proletariat." [17]

In *The Class Struggles in France,* most of which was written
shortly after the *Manifesto,* Marx summarizes how this polarization process gradually took place in France:

> Little by little we have seen peasants, petty bourgeois, the
> middle classes in general, stepping alongside the prole-
> tariat, driven into open antagonism to the official republic
> and treated by it as antagonists. Revolt against bourgeois
> dictatorship, need of a change in society, adherence to
> democratic-republican institutions as organs of their move-
> ment, grouping round the proletariat as the decisive revo-
> lutionary power—these are the common characteristics of
> the so-called social democracy, the party of the red repub-
> lic. . . . So swiftly had the march of the revolution rip-
> ened conditions, that the friends of reform of all shades,
> the most moderate claims of the middle classes, were com-
> pelled to group themselves round the banner of the most
> extreme party of the revolution, round the red flag.[18]

The Communist Manifesto analyzes the social-economic fac-

---

[16] *MEGA,* I⁶, 526; *Manifesto of the Communist Party,* in *Selected Works,*
I, 33. Henceforth this will be referred to as *C. M.*
[17] *MEGA,* I⁶, 526; *C. M.,* pp. 33–34.
[18] *Werke,* VII, 87–88; *The Class Struggles in France, 1848–1850,* in *Selected
Works,* I, 201–02. On the absorption of the French peasantry into the proletariat, see *Werke,* VIII, 198–203; *Selected Works,* I, 302–07.

tors which will drive all classes into the camp of the bourgeoisie or the proletariat. Today's ruling class, the bourgeoisie, is the result of a long economic development. Emerging with the medieval towns, the new class gained momentum through the discovery and colonization of East India and America, the increase in the means of exchange, and a manufacturing system based on the division of labor. It reached its apex in the epoch of industrialization: wherever productive forces outgrew the production relations and the mode of intercourse of the feudal society, the bourgeoisie imposed its rule and dominion. The new class had a revolutionary start and has remained the most revolutionary class up to the present. "It has accomplished wonders far surpassing Egyptian pyramids, Roman aqueducts, and Gothic cathedrals; it has conducted expeditions that put in the shade all former Exoduses of nations and crusades." [19] The very essence of the bourgeoisie class is revolution: it cannot exist without constantly changing the instruments of production and, with them, production relations.

Yet, the revolutionary surge of the bourgeoisie will ultimately lead to its own destruction. "Modern bourgeois society with its relations of production, of exchange, and of property, a society that has conjured up such gigantic means of production and of exchange, is like the sorcerer who is no longer able to control the powers of the nether world whom he has called up by his spells." [20] The same opposition between productive forces and productive relations which brought the bourgeoisie to power will cause its downfall. Slowly the productive forces are outgrowing the conditions of bourgeois property which are the basis of the bourgeois society. Economic crises of overproduction threaten the very existence of today's social structures. The bourgeoisie is no longer able to cope with the increasing problems: its only solution—expanding markets—will lead to even more violent crises in the future.

[19] *MEGA*, I⁶, 528; *C. M.*, p. 35.   [20] *MEGA*, I⁶, 531; *C. M.*, pp. 37–38.

The Rise of the Proletariat

Out of these crises emerges the bourgeoisie's negative counterpart, the proletariat. The proletariat is created by the wage system, which in turn results from the opposition between labor and capital. The wage system reduces the worker to one item in the production cost of a commodity. The producer is obliged to keep the cost of labor low in order to compete with other producers. "Hence the cost of production of a workman is restricted, almost entirely, to the means of subsistence that he requires for his maintenance and for the propagation of his race." [21]

But the most degrading aspects of the capitalist system are the working conditions. *The German Ideology* described how the division of labor leads to higher production, but only by empoverishing the individual productive power of the worker: the less he thinks, the more he is able to fulfill his limited task correctly. This situation becomes even worse when machines take the place of the hand tool.

The revolution of the machine modifies the division of labor without in any way improving the condition of the laborer. What had been a lifelong dedication to a tool now becomes a lifelong dedication to a machine, even more inhuman. Whereas in the manufactural system the worker exercised a variety of skills, in the factory the worker's movements are determined by the machine, and the worker becomes merely a part of the machine. "He becomes an appendage of the machine, and it is only the simplest, most monotonous, and most easily acquired knack, that is required of him." [22] Apart from the growing monotony, the use of machinery has the effect that muscular power is no longer needed and, consequently, that women and children can be employed extensively in the labor market. This in turn leads to a depreciation of the value of manpower. "The less the skill and exertion of strength implied in manual labor, in other

<hr />

[21] *MEGA*, I⁶, 532; *C. M.*, p. 39.   [22] *MEGA*, I⁶, 532; *C. M.*, p. 39.

words, the more modern industry becomes developed, the more is the labor of men superseded by that of women. Differences of age and sex have no longer any distinctive social validity for the working class." [23] In Chapter XV of *Capital,* Marx will sketch a forceful picture of the moral abuse and the deterioration of family life to which the labor of women and children has led in an industrialized country like England.

A further result of the use of machinery is the lengthened working day: the more hours a day a machine is used, the quicker it reproduces its own value and the less chance it has of becoming obsolete before it is physically depreciated. Legal restrictions on the working day do not solve this problem for as soon as the law sets a time limit, the laborer's task is arranged in such a way that he has to make up in intensity what is lost in work hours.[24]

The class of men reduced to these conditions is constantly augmented, for the classes between proletariat and bourgeoisie gradually disappear. Only those who produce at the lowest possible cost survive the system of free competition. All the losers—and capitalism makes an ever greater number of them—drift into the one, undifferentiated mass of the proletariat. This class has no positive consciousness of unity. It is a mere negation of the bourgeoisie, and its existence can be defined only in reference to the bourgeoisie. In the initial stage of its formation, the proletarians do not even consider themselves as a separate class but as the more unfortunate members of the bourgeoisie. They fight the bourgeoisie's enemies and are unaware of the basic opposition of their own interests to those of the bourgeois class. To be sure, the proletarians are dissatisfied with their working conditions, but their animus is not directed against the bourgeoisie or against the capitalist system which produced it. They attack the instruments of production, rather than the *capitalist* use of these instruments, and mistakenly believe that the

23 *MEGA*, I⁶, 533; *C. M.*, p. 39.
24 See *Das Kapital,* in *Werke*, XXIII, 426–40; *Capital* (tr. by S. Moore and E. Aveling, New York, 1906) , pp. 441–57.

elimination of modern production techniques (particularly machinery) will enable them to restore the working conditions of
the past. The absence of class consciousness prevents them from
seeing themselves as a homogeneous and powerful group.

> If anywhere they unite to form more compact bodies, this
> is not yet the consequence of their own active union, but
> of the union of the bourgeoisie, which class, in order to
> attain its own political ends, is compelled to set the whole
> proletariat in motion [against the finance aristocracy], and
> is moreover yet, for a time, able to do so.[25]

In *The Class Struggles in France,* Marx shows how in this initial stage the proletariat actively participates in subjecting other
classes to the rule of the bourgeoisie. In the French revolution
of February, 1848, the workers took the side of the bourgeoisie
against the finance aristocracy. As was to be expected, the bourgeoisie alone profited from the revolution and the proletarians'
lot was worse than before. To avenge their interests they staged
another revolution a few months later. They were defeated by
the same bourgeoisie which they had helped to come to power.
Yet, the June revolution was a decisive step forward in the evolution of the proletariat. In the head-on collision with the bourgeoisie it finally became aware of its basic opposition to the class
which had created it. Another effect of the workers' defeat was
an increase in the ranks of the proletariat. The petty bourgeoisie, imagining that they shared the same interests, had fought
on the side of the industrial bourgeoisie to crush the proletarian
revolt. After the revolution, however, they found out that they
had merely consolidated the position of big capital and destroyed their own.

> No one had fought more fanatically in the June days for
> the salvation of property and the restoration of credit than
> the Parisian petty bourgeois—keepers of cafés and restau-
> rants, *marchands de vins,* small traders, shopkeepers, handi-
> craftsmen, etc. The shopkeeper had pulled himself to-

[25] *MEGA,* I⁶, 533; *C. M.,* p. 40.

gether and marched against the barricades in order to restore the traffic which leads from the streets into the shop. But behind the barricade stood the customers and the debtors; before it the creditors of the shop. And when the barricades were thrown down and the workers were crushed and the shopkeepers, drunk with victory, rushed back to their shops, they found the entrance barred by a savior of property, an official agent of credit, who presented them with threatening notices: Overdue promissory note! Overdue house rent! Overdue bond! Doomed shop! Doomed shopkeeper! *Salvation of property!* But the house in which they lived was not their property; the shop which they kept was not their property; the commodities in which they dealt were not their property.[26]

Defeats such as the one suffered in the June revolution are necessary for the proletariat to find its class identity. Yet the necessary class struggle between bourgeoisie and proletariat depends on the industrialization of a society. Big industry concentrates the workers in centers. It depresses wages, causes economic crises through overproduction, and improves the means of communication which unite the workers. As a result, the collisions between capitalists and workers become more frequent and are carried out on a wider scale. The workers begin to organize trade unions, and the conflict now takes the form of a struggle between two united classes.

Yet, the occasional victories of the proletariat at this stage are not decisive. Their only important effect is to bring the proletarians closer together, and thus to prepare them for the final revolution. The complete solidarity needed for the ultimate victory of the workers is a most difficult goal to accomplish, partly because of the competition among the workers and partly because of the conservative outlook of the middle-class elements of society which are continuously reduced to the ranks of the proletariat. Yet, in spite of the constant threat of division, the revolutionary movement will progress. The bourgeoisie itself will advance this by providing the proletariat with all the sup-

[26] *Werke,* VII, 37–38; *Selected Works,* I, 155.

port it needs. In its struggle with finance aristocracy, petty bourgeoisie and, particularly, bourgeois competition from other countries, the bourgeoisie is forced to bring the proletariat into the political arena. "It supplies the proletariat with its own elements of political and general education: in other words it furnishes the proletariat with weapons for fighting the bourgeoisie." [27]

As Marx wrote in *The Holy Family*, bourgeoisie and proletariat are opposite faces of the same reality. The proletariat is the negation of everything the bourgeoisie stands for. The bourgeois has property—the proletarian has not. The bourgeois lives by a rigid code of family relations—the proletarian has wife and children, but scarcely any family relations. The bourgeois believes in law, order, and some sort of religion—for the proletarian, "law, morality, religion are . . . so many bourgeois prejudices, behind which lurk in ambush just as many bourgeois interests." [28] But precisely because it is the total negation of all accepted human values, the proletariat is bound to become an eminently positive force. Its emancipation will not lead to a new class order with slightly different values: it will create an entirely new society and a new man. The lack of traditional values makes for the strength of the proletarian.

The proletariat can create nothing short of total revolution. Other classes have merely consolidated the class system by appropriating the instruments of production. But the proletarians' only chance to control the productive forces consists in abolishing property itself, and thereby reappropriating them to the entire society. In this total reappropriation the eternal succession of class dominion will be broken. The proletarian revolution will liberate society from the class system itself. It is the revolution of the majority for the liberation of *man*.

All previous historical movements were movements of minorities, or in the interest of minorities. The proletarian movement is the self-conscious, independent movement of

[27] *MEGA*, I⁶, 535; *C. M.*, p. 41.   [28] *MEGA*, I⁶, 536; *C. M.*, p. 42.

the immense majority, in the interests of the immense majority. The proletariat, the lowest stratum of our present
society, cannot stir, cannot raise itself up, without the
whole superincumbent strata of official society being
sprung into the air.[29]

In the *Manifesto,* as in the *Ideology,* Marx shows that the proletarian revolution is inevitable. The proletariat has no hope of
outgrowing its servitude by a gradual improvement of its living
conditions. In fact, the capitalist system becomes less and less
able to provide a living for the oppressed class. "The modern
laborer . . . instead of rising with the progress of industry,
sinks deeper and deeper below the conditions of existence of his
own class. He becomes a pauper." [30] Pauperism will grow until
revolution is the only possible outcome.

The Role of the Communist Party

But if the Communist revolution is inescapable, why must
there be an active Communist party? How can a movement justify itself if its goal is inevitable anyway? In the second section
of the *Manifesto,* Marx answers these questions.

Communism, he states, is not a separate party, opposed to
other groups of the working class. The Communists are merely
the most advanced members of the proletariat, who, more than
their fellow workers, have understood the meaning of the present social and economic situation. "The Communists . . . have
over the great mass of the proletariat the advantage of clearly
understanding the line of march, the conditions, and the ultimate general results of the proletarian movement." [31] Their objectives are those of the proletarian class itself: to unite all proletarians by a strong class consciousness which will allow them
to overthrow the bourgeois supremacy. The revolutionary power

[29] *MEGA,* I⁶, 536; *C. M.,* pp. 42–43.   [31] *MEGA,* I⁶, 538; *C. M.,* p. 44.
[30] *MEGA,* I⁶, 537; *C. M.,* p. 43.

of the proletariat results from an irresistible social-economic movement, of which the Communists are merely the vanguard. The Communist party, then, is not an ideological movement, initiated by a social reformer. It is rather an expression of the necessary consciousness of, and free cooperation with, an economic process which inevitably leads to revolution. True enough, without the conscious and free determination of the proletariat, the revolution could never take place, for the political coups which lead to its realization require free acts and deliberate planning. Yet, these also are a result of the economic forces at work in the present society, for the economic development is such that ultimately the proletarian can no longer escape the consciousness of his true situation. Economic pressure will bring him to the point where to survive he has no choice other than revolt.

The Communist movement, then, is at once the *self-expression* and the *moving force* of the proletariat. It represents the proletariat's first awareness of what *is,* that is, the "actual relations springing from an existing class struggle." [32] And it provides the workers with the principles and organizational structure required for revolutionary action. The revolution will come in any case, but an active Communist party will achieve unity and class consciousness much sooner than could an unorganized proletariat.

The party always heeds the interests of the proletariat as a *whole.* Occasionally it may have to sacrifice its immediate interests in one country in order to accomplish lasting achievements over a broader area. The same principle of totality may also require that the party even cooperate with reactionary political groups or abandon its name and conceal its true objectives. The Communists will support any movement which threatens the established order, regardless of who initiated it. "The Communists fight for the attainment of the immediate aims, for the enforcement of the momentary interests of the

[32] *MEGA,* I⁶, 538; *C. M.,* p. 44.

working class, but in the movement of the present they also represent and take care of the future of that movement."[33]

The Communist Society

Marx's description of the Communist society clarifies what he means by the abolition of private property, which was mentioned, but not worked out, in the *Ideology*. Communism does not need to confiscate the property of the artisan and the small peasant; the industrial revolution has already taken care of that. Nor will it confiscate the worker's property, for the worker has no property. The profit of his labor goes, in greater part, into capital as accumulated labor: his wages represent a small fraction of the economic value which his work creates.

> The average price of wage labor is the minimum wage, i.e. that quantum of the means of subsistence which is absolutely requisite to keep the laborer in bare existence as a laborer. What, therefore, the wage laborer appropriates by means of his labor merely suffices to prolong and reproduce a bare existence. We by no means intend to abolish this personal appropriation of the products of labor, an appropriation that is made for the maintenance and reproduction of human life, and that leaves no surplus wherewith to command the labor of others. All that we want to do away with is the miserable character of this appropriation, under which the laborer lives merely to increase capital, and is allowed to live only insofar as the interest of the ruling class requires it.[34]

The only property that Communism wants to abolish is capitalist property. But for the great majority of people this can only be a gain, for the capitalists have already swallowed up nine-tenths of all property. By making all capital common property, Communism converts accumulated labor from a mere means for accumulating more labor into a direct boon to the laborer himself.

[33] *MEGA*, I[6], 556; *C. M.*, p. 60.   [34] *MEGA*, I[6], 539–40; *C. M.*, pp. 45–46.

To the objection that Communism does away with freedom, law, and culture, Marx answers: the freedom of the bourgeoisie is not human freedom—it is merely the license to exploit other classes; the law of the capitalist society is not the law of human nature—it is the bourgeoisie's legalization of its own greed; bourgeois culture is not human culture—it is the universalization of bourgeois ideals. Cultural values change every time a new class emerges, but there is no reason why the culture of Communist society should be inferior to that of capitalism.

It is true that Communism will effect a more drastic change than any previous revolution, but then all societies in the past, however different from one another, still shared the same basic feature: one part of society was exploited by another.

> No wonder then that the social consciousness of past ages, despite all the multiplicity and variety it displays, moves within certain common forms, or general ideas, which cannot completely vanish except with the total disappearance of class antagonism. The Communist revolution is the most radical rupture with traditional property relations; no wonder that its development involves the most radical rupture with traditional ideas.[35]

The revolution will be accomplished in three successive stages. In the first stage, the proletariat raises itself to the position of the ruling class. Marx does not specify exactly how the take-over will happen, for this depends entirely on the social and political structure of each country. Once this take-over is achieved, a transition period—the second stage—follows, in which the proletariat exercises dictatorial powers and revolutionizes the ancient conditions of production.[36]

[35] *MEGA*, I⁶, 544; *C. M.*, p. 50.
[36] In the most advanced countries this will be accomplished by the following measures:

1. Abolition of property in land and application of all rents of land to public purposes.
2. A heavy progressive or graduated income tax.
3. Abolition of all right of inheritance.
4. Confiscation of the property of all emigrants and rebels.

As soon as the productive forces have been reappropriated by the people, the proletariat will inevitably abandon its political dictatorship, since any form of class oppression is bound to disappear when the classes themselves cease to exist. It will be replaced, in the third stage, by "an association in which the free development of each is the condition for the free development of all." [37]

The success of Communism depends entirely on the workers' awareness of its historical necessity. The major temptation of the socialist movement is to conceive of itself as a return to a preindustrial era, or as a *theoretical* reform of society according to the ideals of a social reformer. Only a *scientific* socialism which understands the social-economic development of history can advance the cause of the workers. All nonscientific forms of socialism merely offer expedients which slow down the inevitable course of history. To warn the proletariat against this waste of time and energy, Marx devotes the entire third section of the *Manifesto* to a critique of the nonscientific forms of socialism.

---

5. Centralization of credit in the hands of the State, by means of a national bank with State capital and an exclusive monopoly.

6. Centralization of the means of communication and transport in the hands of the State.

7. Extension of factories and instruments of production owned by the State; the bringing into cultivation of waste-lands, and the improvement of the soil generally in accordance with a common plan.

8. Equal liability of all to labor. Establishment of industrial armies, especially for agriculture.

9. Combination of agriculture with manufacturing industries; gradual abolition of the distinction between town and country, by a more equable distribution of the population over the country.

10. Free education for all children in public schools. Abolition of children's factory labor in its present form. Combination of education with industrial production, &c., &c.

(*MEGA,* I⁶, 545; *C. M.,* p. 50.)
[37] *MEGA,* I⁶, 546; *C. M.,* p. 51.

Marx's Critique of Nonscientific Socialism

The most reactionary of these forms is a social movement sponsored by the aristocracy and the petty bourgeoisie. After having been subdued by the industrial bourgeoisie, both classes try, as a last resort, to line up the support of the proletariat in order to recover the power which they have lost; they are only interested in their own positions and are not in the least concerned with the lot of the proletariat. They propose a return to the past on the ground that the worker's condition was better under their rule than under the bourgeoisie. But, Marx answers, their form of oppression was less severe only because it was less advanced.

> In pointing out that their mode of exploitation was different from that of the bourgeoisie, the feudalists forget that they exploited under circumstances and conditions that were quite different and that are now antiquated. In showing that, under their rule, the modern proletariat never existed, they forget that the modern bourgeoisie is the necessary offspring of their own form of society.[38]

A revival of feudalism would eventually lead merely to a new bourgeoisie and a new proletariat.

Petty bourgeois socialism shows the same lack of historical perspective: it considers the development of heavy industry as an accidental outgrowth of capitalism rather than as a historical necessity. Yet, even though its solution to the problems of modern society is utopian, petty bourgeois socialism remains significant for having brought to light (particularly in Simonde de Sismondi's work) the internal contradictions of the modern production system.

In that respect it is far superior to "German," or "true," socialism, which Marx had extensively criticized in the *Ideology*. True socialism completely ignores the social-economic facts on which an effective workers' movement should be based. It sim-

[38] *MEGA*, I⁶, 547; *C. M.*, p. 52.

ply translates French revolutionary writings into a universal
philosophy without considering the particular social-economic
situation in France which gave rise to these writings.

> The work of the German literati consisted solely in bring-
> ing the new French ideas into harmony with their ancient
> philosophical conscience, or rather, in annexing the
> French ideas without deserting their own philosophic
> point of view. . . . It is well known how the monks wrote
> silly lives of Catholic saints *over* the manuscripts on which
> the classical works of ancient heathendom had been writ-
> ten. The German literati reversed this process with the
> profane French literature. They wrote their philosophical
> nonsense beneath the French original.[39]

But Marx's main objection to true socialism is that it lacks
all historical perspective: it wants to achieve the Communist
revolution at once and skip the intermediate stages. The true
socialists imitate the French in opposing the bourgeois society
without realizing that Germany has not even reached the bourgeois era.[40]

Equally inconsistent are the attempts of some members of
the bourgeoisie to purge bourgeois capitalism of its social abuses
while preserving the system itself. "They desire the existing state
of society minus its revolutionary and disintegrating elements.
They wish for a bourgeoisie without a proletariat." [41] An example of this ambiguous attitude which tries to combine capitalism and socialism is Proudhon's *The Philosophy of Poverty*
discussed in the previous section.

But the most serious adversaries of the Communist movement are the followers of the early, utopian forms of socialism.
These systems were full of valuable insights which scientific socialism has adopted, but they were historically premature. Their
authors perceived that the social crisis has its roots in the oppo-

[39] *MEGA*, I⁶, 550; *C. M.*, p. 55.
[40] For a thorough discussion of true socialism, see A. Cornu, "German
Utopianism—True Socialism," in *A Centenary of Marxism* (ed. by Samuel
Bernstein, New York, 1948).
[41] *MEGA*, I⁶, 552; *C. M.*, p. 57.

sition of classes. Yet, because of the undeveloped state of the proletariat and the absence of the social-economic conditions necessary for its emancipation, they thought the proletariat to be incapable of any revolutionary initiative. Instead of waiting for bourgeois capitalism to develop the proper conditions for the proletarian revolution, the utopians attempted to construct a new society in an artificial way.

> Historical action is to yield to their personal inventive action, historically created conditions of emancipation to fantastic ones, and the gradual, spontaneous class organization of the proletariat to an organization of society specially contrived by these inventors. Future history resolves itself, in their eyes, into the propaganda and the practical carrying out of their social plans.[42]

Since they regarded the oppressed class as unable to help itself, the utopians tried to prove to the other classes that a new, self-created social order would be advantageous to everyone. The best-known experiments to support their theory were Robert Owen's social innovations. As director of a cotton mill in Scotland, he introduced drastic reforms in the working conditions of his laborers. He reduced the working day to ten and a half hours, placed the children in his own schools rather than using them for infant labor, paid full wages to his unemployed workers during a four-month cotton crisis, and still managed to double the value of his business in a short period of time. Owen felt that even these reforms were insufficient and that the huge profits of his company were stolen from the workers. He therefore attempted to install a Communist cooperative. The project failed, and Owen lost his money as well as his great reputation. His mistake was caused by the utopian desire to anticipate necessary social-economic developments with man-made reforms.

Marx mentions two other utopians: Henri de Saint-Simon and Charles Fourier. In an essay, *Socialism: Utopian and Scientific*—written in 1880, when Marx's views had been firmly estab-

---

[42] *MEGA*, I⁶, 554; *C. M.*, p. 58.

lished in the workers' movement—Engels gives great credit to these two early pioneers of socialism. Saint-Simon's work expressed the disenchantment of the third estate after the French Revolution, in which it had overrun the "idle" classes of nobility and clergy. Saint-Simon noticed that, in the short period of its political rule, the bourgoisie had produced more "idlers" than there were ever before. So the opposition between workers and "idlers" proved to be a social opposition which existed even *within* the third estate. The solution then was to be found in social reform rather than in a political revolution. Since the working class itself was obviously unable to achieve this, Saint-Simon called upon the scholars, manufacturers, merchants, and bankers to unite in a religious bond and to create a new production system with regulated credit. Engels comments:

> The knowledge that economic conditions are the basis of political institutions appears here only in embryo. Yet what is here already very plainly expressed is the idea of the future conversion of political rule over men into an administration of things and a direction of processes of production—that is to say, the "abolition of the State," about which there has been so much noise recently.[43]

Fourier, too, voices the nineteenth century's disappointment with the Revolution's ideal of a bourgeois society "in which reason alone would reign." For all its promises, this society turned out to be inferior to the previous one. Fourier offers no positive solution: his strength lies mainly in social satire. To the eighteenth-century idea of progress, Fourier opposes his cyclical theory of history: every civilization has a descent as well as an ascent, and the last one will close with the destruction of the human race.

Owen's Communism, Saint-Simon's economism, and Fourier's historicism all provided useful elements for the development of scientific socialism. Yet none of them grasped the importance of

[43] *Werke*, XIX, 195; *Socialism: Utopian and Scientific*, in *Selected Works*, II, 118.

the one revolutionary element of present society, the proletariat. In their appeal to the humanitarian feelings of the other classes, the utopians joined the philosophical dreamers of the eighteenth century. In Engels' words,

> Like the French philosophers, they do not claim to emancipate a particular class to begin with, but all humanity at once. Like them, they wish to bring in the kingdom of reason and eternal justice, but this kingdom, as they see it, is as far as heaven from earth, from that of the French philosophers.[44]

All the utopians were moralists, but for Marx morality itself is a superstructure of economic relations. Even when opposing the bourgeois society in the name of morality one still uses bourgeois categories. Realistic reforms can result only from a scientific study of the laws of social-economic development. Any other form of socialism can, at best, patch up some of the abuses of the capitalist order, thereby prolonging the existence of the society which gives rise to these abuses. Social utopianism in the end always becomes a reactionary movement. Social-economic developments soon overtake the reform plans of the utopians, who, rather than joining the real revolution in progress before their eyes, join the ranks of the conservatives to protect their own brain-made revolution. According to Marx,

> They hold fast by the original views of their masters, in opposition to the progressive historical development of the proletariat. They, therefore, endeavor, and that consistently, to deaden the class struggle and to reconcile the class antagonisms. They still dream of experimental realization of their social utopias . . . and to realize all these castles in the air they are compelled to appeal to the feelings and purses of the bourgeois. By degrees they sink into the category of the reactionary conservative socialists depicted above, differing from these only by more systematic pedantry, and by their fanatical and superstitious belief in the miraculous effects of their social science.[45]

44 *Werke*, XIX, 191; *Selected Works*, II, 109.
45 *MEGA*, I⁶, 555; *C. M.*, pp. 59–60.

The only efficient form of social action, says Marx, is scientific socialism. Communism is not the brainchild of a man of genius —it is the inevitable outcome of the dialectical struggle between two classes. The Communist movement will speed up this process by furthering the final requirement for the revolution, the class-consciousness of the proletariat, but it does not *create* the conditions which make the revolution a historical necessity. These conditions are brought about by an irreversible social-economic process. What is needed is not an ideological movement but a scientific study of social-economic facts. Such a study shows that the revolution is inescapable. That is why Communism today has no other task than to unite all proletarians in the consciousness of *what is*.

A Critique of The Communist Manifesto

Up to *The German Ideology,* Marx's work could be considered as basically speculative and philosophical, even though the downfall of philosophy had already been announced in his doctoral dissertation. In the *Ideology* he shows *how* philosophy must return to the praxis in which it has its roots. Historical materialism is a theory of action rather than an autonomous philosophical speculation. *The Communist Manifesto* (and *The Poverty of Philosophy* to a lesser extent because of its limited scope) is Marx's first systematic attempt to reunite thought with action. Philosophy is mentioned only in a negative, critical fashion. Even so, the *Manifesto* is much more than a revolutionary pamphlet. It is an interpretation of history which is based on social-economic data, but which develops far beyond these data into an *a priori* theory of action. The *Manifesto* contains much more than description and analysis of facts. It attempts to understand the dialectical nature of human praxis in its growth and development, and thereby to gain insight into its intrinsic teleology.

Marx's method is both empirical and *a priori*. It is empirical insofar as the *understanding* of human action must follow the action itself and must rely upon the social sciences. But by grasping the dialectical law which rules human action, historical materialism becomes able to anticipate the future course of history and to direct it to its immanent end. In evaluating the *Manifesto*, we must keep both these elements in mind. According to Marx's own principles, the dialectic of history must be discovered through a careful analysis of social-economic facts; the universal interpretation of history depends entirely upon this analysis (given the dialectical principle itself). On the other hand, it is obvious that Marx's conclusions go *beyond* the facts: they interpret them and, on the basis of this interpretation, predict future facts. Whether Marx is justified in generalizing historical conclusions is a question that we will consider later. But at least these conclusions must be solidly based on the empirical facts. If Marx's analysis does not do full justice to the facts or conflicts with them, his entire interpretation of history becomes questionable, regardless of the intrinsic value of the dialectical principle.

According to the *Manifesto*, class struggles are the determining factor of history. But one fails to see how, without a gross amount of oversimplification, all history can be reduced to social conflicts, and even more, how all social conflicts can be reduced to class struggles. The first point seems so obvious that it is hardly worth proving to a non-Marxist. For example, racial conflicts, which Marx fails to mention, cut directly across class barriers. This difference cannot be explained away by the simple assumption that one race was originally exploited by another, for the social subordination is a result rather than a cause of racial antagonism. In his essay *"Autour du Marxisme,"* Merleau-Ponty puts the objection in the following way: "It makes no sense to treat the class struggle as an *essential* fact if we are not sure that history remains faithful to its 'essence' and that the 'accidents' do not bypass it for a long time or forever." [46]

[46] Maurice Merleau-Ponty, *Sens et non-sens* (Paris, 1948), p. 213.

Even if one should grant that social conflicts can be reduced to class struggles, the whole history of civilization cannot possibly be explained in these limited terms. What can a theory of class struggle teach us about Rembrandt, Mozart, Virgil, or even Marx's own philosophy? Social-economic conditions may be responsible for the rise and acceptance of certain ideas and art forms, but this gives us no information about the creative impulse itself. To "explain" this, after the fashion of the Soviet *Encyclopedia,* is *at best* to explain something which is not relevant.

An even greater distortion of the facts is seen in Marx's polarization theory. It may be true that the number of classes has become smaller, but modern society has certainly not been reduced to two classes. The two-class opposition of the *Manifesto* is a dogma rather than a social reality. J.-Y. Calvez writes on this point:

> Looking at the social structure of France, England, the United States, Germany, Japan (to mention only States usually considered to be capitalist), we find groups which escape the dualistic classification. The middle classes, infinitely differentiated among themselves, seem to form a resistant bloc which the political events of the twentieth century do not allow us to assimilate with the bourgeoisie or the proletariat. Can one simply say that, nonetheless, the bourgeoisie uses the middle classes for its own purposes? This was certainly not the case during the Fascist era. Must we not go even further and conclude that, for instance, in France, a country with a most conservative social structure, the middle classes (in the plural) are the effectively dominating groups? [47]

Of course, Marxists will always explain the existence of these middle groups as a leftover from the past, condemned to disappear in the final stage of capitalism. Thus they remain accidental to the *essential* course of history. But these "accidents," instead of gradually disappearing, have become ever more impor-

[47] J.-Y. Calvez, *La Pensée de Karl Marx* (Paris, 1956), pp. 237–38.

tant over the past hundred years. Such an interlude, in the midst of the period which was announced for the ultimate crisis of capitalism, is too prolonged to be summarily discarded.

Marx's law of polarization seems to be based on the purely philosophical *a priori* of a Master-and-Slave dialectic, rather than on an analysis of facts. To Marx, the class struggles in France showed a (temporary) simplification of class antagonisms. But from this short-term observation, he jumps to the conclusion that all social groups everywhere will be reduced to two *classes*. Since the facts do not justify the conclusion, the entire polarization law loses its value.

With the *Manifesto* historical materialism reaches its completion. This does not mean that there is no further evolution in Marx's work. Quite the contrary, Marx himself considered his *real* work as merely begun in the *Manifesto*. The basic economic theories for which Marxism is known today (e.g., the surplus value) were hardly mentioned before 1848, and none of them received its definitive form and shape before then. (Several times we have had to refer to *Capital* for a coherent explanation of sketchy economic and sociological statements made in his early writings.) Nevertheless, at this point the synthesis of historical materialism was completed, and it did not change in the thirty-five years of active work which Marx still had ahead of him.

8

A Critique of Historical Materialism

The Nature of Marxist Dialectic

A PHILOSOPHICAL EVALUATION of historical materialism must concentrate primarily on the validity of the *dialectical method* as it is used by Marx and his followers, because for a dialectician the content of philosophy is identical with its method. In its necessary logical process, dialectical philosophy claims to capture reality's ultimate meaning. This does not necessarily lead to idealism, for the mind may discover in an empirical way the dialectical development of reality. Yet, for Hegel, it is the Spirit which constitutes this development and thus makes reality ultimately coincide with itself. In Hegel's theory, reality reaches its own perfection only when it is being *thought* in philosophy: the *ideal* is the ultimate foundation and justification of the *real*. No aspects of reality, therefore, fall beyond philosophical comprehension, not even those commonly considered purely factual, contingent, and open only to a passive, empirical understanding. For Hegel, contingency itself is a necessary moment in the Spirit's dialectical development.

Marx felt that such a comprehensive system takes away the proper character of the empirical by forcing it to be part of an aprioristic logical necessity. His early attempts in philosophy were inspired by a desire to restore the empirical to its own right, without abandoning the dialectical method. What he objected to was not Hegel's goal of understanding the real in its totality, but his aprioristic speculative-logical approach. To understand the real in itself, argued Marx, philosophy must become empirical and take its starting point in what is empirically given, rather than in such a speculative abstraction as Hegel's pure being. From Feuerbach, Marx learned that the empirical datum of human knowledge is *man* in his concrete environment. Yet, contrary to Feuerbach, Marx did not restrict this environment to the *physical* world—equally essential are the social relationships with which man interacts. Also, and most important, man's relation to nature is *dialectical,* as it was for Hegel. By maintaining this dialectical opposition to nature, Marx's philosophy avoids a deterministic interpretation of man. Yet, the dialectical character of man's relation to nature is not accepted as a speculative *a priori,* existing prior to the concrete relation itself and giving it its final foundation. The dialectic is to be *discovered empirically* in the real relation—it is a *reality,* and not an ideal relation which becomes real. The dialectical relation is an ultimate fact which requires no ulterior, ideal foundation and which cannot be reduced to a further, unifying principle (such as Hegel's self-developing Spirit).

Since the dialectic for Marx is a primary fact, one might take its philosophical formulation to be a mere generalization of empirical observations, rather than an *a priori* principle of explanation. But to do so would be to destroy the dialectic itself. For it is as a conscious and free being that man is dialectically opposed to nature; consciousness, therefore, must have as much impact upon nature as nature has upon consciousness. By making the dialectical principle into a purely empirical observation of a fact, one reduces one term of the dialectic, consciousness, to an epiphenomenon of the other term, nature. The dialectic then loses its antagonistic character and ceases to exist. Marx himself pointed this out when he rejected Feuerbach's "materialism" precisely because it did not allow any reciprocal action between man and nature.[1]

---

[1] *MEGA,* I⁵, 533; Thesis I, *Theses on Feuerbach,* in Marx and Engels, *The German Ideology* (tr. by R. Pascal, New York, 1960), p. 197, by permission of International Publishers Co., Inc. Henceforth this will be referred to as *G. I.*

In Marx's view the dialectical principle is much more than an empirical description of the relations between man and his world. It has an essentially *ideal* character, but this ideal does not exist prior to or apart from reality. It is the ideal aspect of *reality itself* and is, therefore, accessible only through empirical analysis. It is precisely this ideal, rational character which gives the dialectical principle a quality of necessity which a purely empirical description always lacks. A mere empirical study of facts can provide a hypothesis, or at most a theory, but it can never predict with the absolute confidence which gives Marxism all its power and influence. Moreover, even a hypothetical interpretation of the dialectic would infer the existence of an intelligible principle in the development of history, and at that point it would cease to be purely empirical. The mind may start its study of facts in an empirical way, but as soon as it discovers its own rationality in these facts, it takes over and becomes *a priori*.

By his acceptance of the dialectic as both a real and ideal ultimate, Marx remains faithful to the basic Hegelian thesis that the rational is real, and the real rational. He differs from Hegel in that he eliminates what he considers to be an ulterior and transcendent principle uniting the opposing terms of the dialectic—the Spirit. No superior principle is needed to unite the two terms, for their own nature is such that they imply both each other and the relation to each other. As Marx stated in the *Manuscripts,* man is nature from the very beginning, and, as he claims in arguing against Feuerbach, nature has become humanized the moment man appears in this world—it has become part of man, intimately linked to his growth and development. The unifier of the dialectical terms does not transcend the terms themselves: it is *man* who *is* both consciousness and nature and who, through his action, unites consciousness with nature. Human activity—*praxis*—replaces the self-explication of Hegel's Absolute Spirit.

Marx's dialectical theory of man overcomes the dichotomy between idealism and materialism. Hegel remains an idealist

on the side of consciousness, for the Spirit bridges the opposition between the two terms through consciousness (the ideal
term), rather than through Marx's painful and laborious synthesis by praxis. Feuerbach's materialism implies the same error
on the side of nature by its assumption that consciousness is
united with the world in a *given* physical harmony, rather than
through the strife and struggle of human action.

> Feuerbach's humanism is founded on a myth: pure nature.
> Nature and the object, for him, are "given from all eter-
> nity" in a mysterious harmony with man—a harmony
> which the philosopher alone perceives. . . . His material-
> ism is inferior to Hegel's idealism in an essential point:
> idealism started from activity; one-sidedly, yet truly, it
> tried to elucidate and elaborate this activity. Hegel saw
> that man is not "given" biologically, but that he produces
> himself in history and in his social life, that he creates
> himself in a process.[2]

But for Marx, praxis is more than a principle of consciousness: it is a prereflective unity of nature and consciousness,
which can be explicated in thought, but not initiated. As the
living unity of nature and consciousness, human activity produces both a real freedom and a free reality. The philosophical
dialectic is only the conscious explication of an initial, pre-
reflective struggle which relates consciousness to nature in such
a way that neither one is prior to the other. It is always more
than an empirical, *a posteriori* description, without ever being
a *purely* ideal principle of explanation. The practical dialectic
of human action provides the foundation for the theoretical
consciousness of the dialectic. It is in praxis, then, that Marx's
dialectical theory finds its final justification.

As a result, the dialectic remains a valid principle of interpretation only as long as it preserves a vital rapport with human
action. The moment it is stated independently of human praxis,
it becomes a purely speculative theory and degenerates either
into an idealistic principle which forces reality into a pre-exist-

ing schema of thought, or into a materialistic dogma unable to justify its own existence. The crucial problem for a dialectical theory is how a principle of action can be made into a philosophical theory while avoiding these two erroneous positions. Under no conditions can theory simply precede praxis.

In his *Critique de la raison dialectique,* Sartre shows how contemporary Marxism has gradually abandoned this basic thesis of historical materialism. It has divorced theory from initial praxis and, instead of discovering the dialectic in praxis, it dictates its own dialectical speculation to praxis. Its interpretation of history thereby becomes *"une scholastique de la totalité"* (a scholasticism of the totality) and its theory of action *"une pratique terroriste"* (a terrorist practice), liquidating whatever does not agree with its principles. To justify this dogmatic, purely *a priori* dialectical schema, contemporary Marxism falls back upon the other extreme, vulgar materialism. The dialectic of history is interpreted as one empirical fact among others, impressing itself upon the mind in the way that colors cause a photochemical reaction on the retina. Such an empiricist explanation can hardly take into account the fact that many people do not have this allegedly empirical and inescapable insight into the dialectical nature of history. But, more important, it is unable to prove what it wants to prove: the *necessity* and *universality* of the dialectical principle of interpretation. As Hume noted, no amount of purely empirical data can ever yield more than a *psychological* necessity. To be consistent with their empiricism, modern Marxists would have to reduce the dialectic of history to a psychological habit of thinking, a compulsion to see things in a dialectical way, based on a number of past experiences. In no case can such a principle have the universal necessity which dialectical materialism claims for it.

Marx's own approach is certainly more sophisticated than that. He never disconnects theory from praxis, nor does he lower the dialectic to a merely empirical principle. He certainly avoids the inconsistency of applying the dialectic in an idealistic way while justifying it in a materialistic way. For Marx the primary principle of historical materialism remains a complex dialectic of human praxis—production forces creating social relations which, in turn, create new production forces. These social-economic structures are analyzed in a purely empirical way, for only a positive study of the facts can clarify the concrete relations between man and nature, and between man and society. This positive analysis of factual material eventually leads to some general conclusions. Since these conclusions have been obtained by an empirical method, they can claim no more than the inductive universality of a scientific theory. The most general conclusion is the existence of a dialectical relation between nature and man as conscious being. While the method by which this conclusion has been reached is empirical, as in all other cases, the conclusion itself is more than empirical. Indeed, if consciousness is to be dialectically opposed to nature, it must have a certain originality, a certain *a priori*. A true dialectic requires that consciousness be free and active, as well as passive. The dialectical principle, therefore, must be more than an empirical conclusion, for this principle is precisely the formulation of the mutual *a priori* in the relation between consciousness and nature. To consider it as an empirical datum, similar to those provided by positive sciences, is to replace the dialectic by physical determinism and to take away the entire teleology of historical materialism. History is then reduced to an extension of the mechanistic laws of nature; it becomes "natural history" which is no history at all, since nature has no history.

But while the *a priori* character of the dialectical principle may provide the Marxist with the certainty that it is universally applicable, it does not give him the right to apply it indiscriminately to each new phenomenon. For the dialectic principle is *a priori* only in the sense that it formulates a basic structure underlying all history and knowledge—human praxis. But it *cannot* claim to offer a formal scheme for explaining any historical situation prior to an empirical analysis of the relevant economic and social data. To *impose* the dialectic upon history, rather than to discover it *in* history through careful analysis, is to sever the principle from actual praxis, where alone it holds true. It then becomes a purely speculative principle which is self-contradictory, since the principle itself states that no ideal value can be constituted independently of man's actual relation to nature. Applied in this formal, abstract way, it can lead only to vague generalizations which fail to bring out the specific character of the events. Historical materialism then becomes an "ideology" which lacks even the internal coherence of idealist ideologies. Marx's modern interpreters constantly vacillate between this dialectical, abstract idealism and a nondialectical, deterministic materialism.

Theory and Praxis

One may well wonder what is responsible for this strange evolution in Marxist thinking. The immediate cause of the ambiguity seems to be a confusion of human praxis with material nature. In *The German Ideology,* Marx writes:

> Our conception of history depends on our ability to expound the real process of production, starting out from the simple material production of life, and to comprehend the form of intercourse connected with this and created by this (i.e. civil society in its various stages) as the basis of all history; further, to show it in its action as State; and so, from this starting-point, to explain the whole mass of different theoretical products and forms of consciousness, religion, philosophy, ethics etc., etc., and trace their origins and growth. . . . It does not explain practice from the idea but explains the formation of ideas from material practice.[3]

In other words, there is no ideality independent of man's practical relation to nature. Most Marxists today seem to conclude

[3] *MEGA,* I[5], 27; *G. I.,* p. 28.

from this that praxis itself contains no ideal element. But this conclusion cannot be justified on the basis of Marx's own writings.

In contemporary Marxism the dialectical process is replaced by a "natural" process in which Engels' "dialectic of nature" is substituted for the dialectic of consciousness and nature. But in this new context there is no true dialectic, for there is only one univocal, homogeneous reality—nature—part of which is conscious and part of which is not. What Marx had in mind was a determination of theory by truly dialectical praxis in which the term "consciousness" cannot be reduced to the term "nature."

Yet, in the final analysis, Marx himself seems to bear the major responsibility for the inconsistencies of historical materialism. Although he never sacrifices the ideal term of praxis—consciousness—he defines praxis itself so exclusively in terms of a material life process that man's transcendence over nature becomes seriously jeopardized. Anything beyond a fulfillment of material needs is dismissed as "phantoms in the human brain," "sublimates of the material life process." [4] Man's growth and development are determined by "the material conditions determining their production." [5]

True enough, Marx insists that man himself determines the circumstances of this material process as much as they determine him.[6] But by restricting the scope of human praxis to the fulfillment of physical needs, he has made it impossible to give this active determination any content. Against Feuerbach, Marx repeatedly emphasizes the distinction between man (as conscious being) and nature,[7] but since consciousness has no independent content, he finds himself unable to make the distinction profitable. He criticizes German philosophy for having considered history, that is, the process of conscious human activity, apart from the real production of life and concludes: "With

[4] *MEGA*, I⁵, 7 (my translation).   [6] *MEGA*, I⁵, 28, 534; *G. I.*, pp. 29, 198.
[5] *MEGA*, I⁵, 11; *G. I.*, p. 7.   [7] *MEGA*, I⁵, 34; *G. I.*, p. 37.

this the relation of man to nature is excluded from history and *hence the antithesis of nature and history is created."* [8] Implied here is that man's relation to nature does not entail an antithesis between history and nature: the antithesis is a product of ideology. If Marx merely meant that nature and history must not be seen as entirely independent of each other, his criticism would be perfectly justified. But from many other passages it is obvious that Marx regards any separation between history and nature as erroneous. Describing human praxis as a material production process, he has made it impossible to distinguish nature properly from history, although his own philosophy calls for such a distinction.

If man's entire activity is directed toward the satisfaction of material needs, what makes him proceed from Marx's first stage of history—the fulfillment of immediate, natural needs—to the second stage—the creation and satisfaction of artificial needs? If human activity were restricted to a material life process, it could never pass the first stage. How could the *homo oeconomicus,* exclusively involved in a material life process, ever transcend his immediate relation to nature and produce cultural values which have no direct bearing upon his physical needs? And yet this is what man actually does; the more human he becomes, the farther he gets away from all purely physical determinations. Of course, man's cultural development takes place within his dialectical relationship to nature; man never becomes a purely spiritual being, and all his cultural achievements are deeply rooted in nature. Even at its peak, human praxis remains a dialectic with nature. Yet, man's dialectic with nature ceases to exist if human praxis is not more than a simple response to physical needs, for such a response implies no dialectical opposition to nature—it becomes part of nature itself. This kind of activity, the object of Pavlov's psychology, can, at best, be called prehuman. In *man* it never exists, for even in

[8] *MEGA,* I⁵, 28; *G. I.,* p. 30—italics ours.

his first response to natural needs, man does far more than what is just "natural," and thereby he transcends nature. He immediately starts transforming nature and imposing upon it his own conscious and (from a natural point of view) "artificial" structures.

By identifying human needs with physical needs, Marx in fact eliminates the very antithesis with nature upon which he bases the active development and humanization of man. If man as conscious being is opposed to nature at all, he must be opposed to it from the very beginning. Otherwise, the dialectic will never get off the ground. This means, paradoxical as it may sound, that although man has physical needs he never satisfies them in a purely physical way. Nature creates the needs for shelter, food, and clothing; it also provides the basic means to satisfy them. But man re-creates these needs and their fulfillment into cultural activities: he builds castles and temples, he makes his dress into a symbol of his sex, social status, and entire personality, he uses food and drink to celebrate or mourn events totally unrelated to hunger and thirst. And he does all this from the beginning. In the first satisfaction of physical needs he creates and satisfies artificial needs. His production, then, is never entirely determined by material conditions. This is not to say that it is ever independent of these conditions—man always creates in a dialogue with nature—but his creation always transcends nature.

What is lacking, then, in Marx is a careful analysis of the basic principle of historical materialism: human praxis. Marx's philosophy is essentially pragmatic; it is a theory of action, and human praxis is the ultimate fact, requiring no further justification. But such a pragmatism can be successful only when praxis itself is accurately described. Marx grossly oversimplifies it by identifying it with a fulfillment of physical needs. Fortunately, he was enough of a humanist to reject some of the conclusions which follow from his premises. More than his Communist followers, he realized the autonomy of man's cultural activity, and many passages in his work reveal a profound humanism. Yet, whenever he synthesizes his views in the theory of historical materialism, his philosophy of man lapses into shallow economism.

Marx's Materialism

It is this simplistic definition of human praxis which is ultimately responsible for Marxism's later development toward materialism. Sartre is mistaken in putting all the blame upon Marx's followers. The original fault is Marx's, even though he himself never was a materialist. If the ideal element (consciousness) in human praxis is merely "a sublimate" of a material life process, then all praxis takes place *within* nature, and there is no dialectic of consciousness *with* nature, for it is only by means of this ideal element that man can actively respond to nature and transform it. Marxism then becomes "scientific," rather than dialectical: history is created by the positive facts of nature, rather than by the response of human freedom to the challenge of nature. As Merleau-Ponty has clearly seen in *Les Aventures de la dialectique,* this sort of "scientific socialism" is constantly threatened by physical determinism. Even Sartre, who exonerates Marx of determinism, does not know what to do with the Russian review of *Capital* which Marx quotes with approval in the second edition: "Marx treats the social movement as a process of natural history, governed by laws not only independent of human will, consciousness and intelligence, but rather, on the contrary, determining that will, consciousness and intelligence." [9] For the benefit of those who might still have some doubts left about his intentions, Marx concludes: "the ideal is nothing else than the material world reflected by the human mind, and translated into forms of thought." [10]

[9] *Werke,* XXIII, 26–27; *Capital,* pp. 23, 25.
[10] Jean-Paul Sartre, *Critique de la raison dialectique* (Paris, 1960), p. 60. For a more detailed discussion of Sartre's critique of Marxism and Merleau-

Marx's economic interpretation of human praxis has an impact on his entire philosophy. The social class, for instance, is defined exclusively by a group's position in the production relations. But sociologists today agree that the class concept is not entirely determined by economic factors.[11] By identifying class relations with economic relations, Marx encloses them in the realm of economic competition and struggle. Thus the central notion of class struggle seems to follow mainly from an unduly restricted definition of class itself.

The inevitability of the proletarian revolution is based on the same economism. The revolution is inevitable only because of the autonomy which Marx ascribes to the economic development. *If* the process of economic development was really the immutable chain which Marx claims it to be, *then* the corresponding social conditions would inevitably have resulted in a revolution. In fact, however, the revolution did not come, and the conditions which at one time seemed to make it inevitable no longer exist. Marx's error is not (at least primarily) in his evaluation of the social-economic conditions of his time, but rather in his assumption that history is determined entirely by social-economic factors. This assumption excludes any possibility of a free intervention in the conditions themselves.

But human praxis is never *purely* social-economic. Undoubtedly, even the highest human activity includes a social-economic aspect, but the *total* activity is always more than that. This is true even in matters which we consider to be purely economic. A business transaction, for example, has several noneconomic aspects: the challenge which it offers, the purely social ties which it creates, or even the human satisfaction of doing something economically rewarding. Marx himself was well aware of these aspects. In the *Manuscripts* he develops them at

---

Ponty's critique of Sartre, see Wilfrid Desan, *The Marxism of Jean-Paul Sartre* (New York, 1965) .
11 J.-Y. Calvez, *La Pensée de Karl Marx* (Paris, 1956) , p. 237.

great length in discussing the creative quality of work done under the right social-economic conditions. But he fails to integrate them in his description of human praxis.

Now if nothing is purely social-economic, then a social-economic development is never inevitable. It is essentially hypothetical and could be stated in the following way: Such and such
factors will inevitably lead to this or that result, *if* left to their
own course. But man, being more than a center of physical needs
and "natural" responses to satisfy them, can almost always
change this course and thus break the chain of "inevitable"
events. Marx himself was the first to show that economic laws
are not absolute—that they are conditioned by the social structure of the capitalist system and that after this system disappears, the laws will automatically cease to exist. Yet, even though
he denied the absolute character of economic laws, Marx never
questioned the inevitability of social-economic developments.
For him the chain can be broken only by another necessity: the
proletarian revolution will take place when social-economic
conditions have made it necessary—when it becomes a matter of
physical survival for the majority of mankind. Marx rejects all
revolutionary movements based on ideas rather than on objective social-economic necessities.[12]

Of course, man is not always free to change his social-economic
situation. Sometimes only one course of action may be left open
if he is to survive at all. This is precisely the case of the proletariat in the ultimate phase of capitalism, as Marx describes it.
But such a description does not give the whole picture, for
before this final crisis was reached, several alternatives were
open, both for the workers and for the capitalists. Today's
world shows that one of those alternatives has been taken. Instead of increasing, the real proletariat, in most Western countries, has shrunk to a minority and seems to be on its way to
total disappearance.[13]

[12] This point seems to have escaped Merleau-Ponty in his earlier, Marxist
period. See his *Sens et non-sens* (Paris, 1948), p. 222.
[13] For a discussion of the changes in capitalism which were responsible for

While rejecting the absolute character of economic laws, Marx accepts a social-economic determinism which seems to leave very little room for freedom. In the decisive stages of man's historical evolution—at the beginning (the mere satisfaction of physical needs) and at the end (the final crisis of capitalism)—only the time and means of execution depend on a free choice. There certainly is no place for goals other than the ones prescribed by social-economic necessities. Freedom is an essential part of Marx's view of man, but no attempt was made to reconcile it with an equally essential social-economic determinism. As a result, there is a permanent conflict in Marx's philosophy between an authentic, pragmatic humanism and an almost materialistic economism. The economistic trend became predominant in historical materialism after Marx's death (probably under the influence of Engels). Stalin's "dialectical" materialism is hardly more than an inconsistent form of deterministic materialism and, at least on this point, there seems to be no major change in Communist thinking today.

Another essential part of Marx's philosophy which became jeopardized by this economistic view of human praxis is the social aspect of man. It would be absurd to question the social character of Marx's philosophy: for him the humanization of nature and the self-creation of man is essentially a social task. Yet, in restricting man's basic activity to a satisfaction of physical needs, Marx has in fact reduced its social character to cooperation for the obtainment of individual ends. In *The German Ideology* we read: "There exists a materialistic connection of men with one another, which is determined by their needs and their mode of production, and which is as old as men themselves." [14] Economic cooperation is essential; without it, man would not be able to survive, much less develop. Nevertheless, the fact remains that in purely economic cooperation man uses

---

his fellow man as a *means* to attain an individual end. In the discussion of the division of labor in the *Manuscripts,* Marx himself calls this a social form of individualism. To make human cooperation truly social, Marx should have described the original praxis in terms of *social needs* as well as individual ones, and this cannot be done on a purely physical basis.

This weakness in the foundation of Marx's social philosophy already shows in his *Critique of Hegel's Philosophy of the State,* in which he criticizes the modern State for separating the social sphere from man's *real* life, that is, his life in the economic society. Marx proposes that the social sphere be reinstated in the reality of the economic society. But by restricting the social to the economic sphere Marx makes it subordinate to limited interests. The truly social goes much deeper: it is not subordinate to anything, but rather is that which makes the individual into a person. Marx's position on the social condition of man comes dangerously close to the eighteenth-century natural right theory, according to which man is by nature an individual being—he comes to live in society only to remedy the accidental limitations of his individuality. Of course, Marx would have rejected such an individualistic theory: in discussing man's social relations, he takes the social as a *primary* fact. Yet, his economism prevents him from integrating these views into his total theory of man.

Marx's narrow definition of human praxis may well be the result of a basic ambiguity in his theory of alienation.[15] In Hegel's *Phenomenology* the alienation consisted in the objectivation of consciousness. Marx could not accept such an ideal definition, for, in his opinion, it identified man with consciousness and considered as alienation that which constitutes the very being of *man*—his objective relation to nature. Consciousness, for Marx, is not autonomous; it is part of *man* and determined by man's dialectical relation to his environment. Marx retained the alienation in man's relation to nature, but with two essential differences: (1) It is *man* who is alienated, not conscious-

---

[15] Calvez first attracted attention to this ambiguity.

ness. (2) Man's alienation does not coincide with his objectivation: it is only a particular form of it—a particular economic
system in which man becomes estranged from his *authentic*
relation to nature. Dialectical materialism, then, shows how this
economic system of alienation will inevitably be overcome.

This interpretation leads to major difficulties, however. Indeed, if the Communist society overcomes man's alienation, the
dialectic itself is bound to disappear, for without alienation
there can be no dialectic. And if man's relation to nature is no
longer oppositional, he must, ultimately, become *part* of nature.
Historical materialism, then, in its final stage turns into pure
naturalism, not basically different from ordinary materialism.

The alternative to this solution would be to accept two dialectical processes, independent of each other: man's relation to
nature—his objectivation; and man's inauthentic relation to
nature—his alienation. The elimination of man's alienation in
the Communist society would leave the dialectic of objectivation
intact. Even in the Communist society man would still be dialectically related to nature. Yet, even this interpretation raises
two grave problems: First, Marxism still has to prove the possibility of a dialectic without alienation. The idea itself seems
almost contradictory, for how can an oppositional, dynamic relation exist unless the first term of the dialectic is *estranged*
from itself?

Second, if alienation is not identical with man's essential relation to nature, how does it ever start? To see it as a fortuitous
event would destroy the most basic principle of historical materialism that the development of history is always determined by
necessary factors. To state that capitalism is a necessary stage in
man's dialectical relation to nature does not help the argument
unless one can point out *how* and *why* it necessarily enters that
relation. Marx seems to be unable to do this, for nothing in
man's essential relation to nature, as he describes it, makes the
economic "alienation" of capitalism into a necessity.

A Marxist might say that the expansion of production relations necessarily leads to a division of labor, which, in turn, gives

rise to the capitalist separation of labor from the means of production. But this still does not explain why some people had to be deprived of their means of production. Nothing in the development of the productive forces makes this deprivation *necessary*. J.-Y. Calvez shows that the expropriation of capitalism is an act of violence which, unlike the final reappropriation of the proletariat, does not follow from the expansion of production relations. In fact, the division of labor on which capitalism is partly based presupposes a *socialization* of productive forces, a pooling of resources which calls for increased cooperation among the producing individuals.

> Capitalism does not result from individualized productive forces which presuppose private ownership of the means of production, but from social productive forces or from productive forces on their way to socialization (technically speaking). But, according to historical materialism, productive forces which become social do not require private production relations—quite the contrary, as we may learn from Marx when he writes on the decline of capitalism. Why not say then, that the new productive forces which appeared in Europe at the end of the Middle Ages should normally have led to *cooperation* and not to a private ownership of the means of production? [16]

The expropriation, then, cannot be explained through the necessary development of the productive forces at the dawn of the capitalist era, since this development was made possible by increasing socialization. Far from being a social-economic necessity, this expropriation seems to be a purely accidental fact, a left-over from feudalism, for which there is no place in the dialectic of historical materialism.

By identifying the alienation with a particular social-economic system for which he is unable to show the dialectical necessity, Marx has undermined the necessary character of his entire dialectic. Historical materialism thereby becomes a social-economic theory with no more than an empirical, factual basis. Its pre-

[16] Calvez, p. 610.

dictions of the future depend entirely on the value of its empirical analysis—and the facts have proved that this analysis is incomplete. But even more unfortunate, from a philosophical point of view, is Marx's reduction of man's alienation to a social-economic level. This lowers the entire dialectic of human praxis, for the alienation is the hinge on which the dialectic turns. If man alienates himself in a particular social-economic system, then his *entire* activity must be social-economic in Marx's sense of the word.

It is not surprising that a dialectic based on such a limited view of human praxis lacks the necessity which is the trade-mark of a true dialectic. Since human activity is never merely social-economic, to look for a dialectical necessity in man's social-economic development is to seek the impossible. Other factors, equally basic to the praxis, can always deflect the social-economic process from its original course. At best the dialectic of historical materialism could provide a working hypothesis helpful in discovering facts, but more often than not the facts will conflict with the hypothesis and make it a useless preconception.

One cannot but regret this trend toward economism in a philosophy which contained such a profound and original theory of action. The subject of Marx's philosophy is *man* as a self-creating, dynamic, and historical being who shapes his destiny in a real (not a purely ideal) relation to the world. Its starting point is the pre-reflective and wholly given reality of the *praxis* by which man, in communion with his fellow man, appropriates nature. Its end is a messianic salvation of man so total that all need for a transcendent redemption ceases to exist. Yet, its economistic limitation has converted this humanism into a rigid system of oversimplifications, which as a rule of action leads to terror and constitutes a dangerous threat to human dignity.

Index

231